JUST PLAIN FILTHY

JUST PLAIN FILTHY

The Story Behind Book Banning's Trial of the Century

Anthony Aycock

BLOOMSBURY LIBRARIES UNLIMITED
NEW YORK • LONDON • OXFORD • NEW DELHI • SYDNEY

BLOOMSBURY LIBRARIES UNLIMITED
Bloomsbury Publishing Inc, 1359 Broadway, New York, NY 10018, USA
Bloomsbury Publishing Plc, 50 Bedford Square, London, WC1B 3DP, UK
Bloomsbury Publishing Ireland, 29 Earlsfort Terrace, Dublin 2, D02 AY28, Ireland

BLOOMSBURY, BLOOMSBURY LIBRARIES UNLIMITED and the Diana logo are
trademarks of Bloomsbury Publishing Plc

First published in the United States of America 2026

It is important for readers to understand that the definitions, information, and lesson ideas
presented in this text are only applicable to United States copyright law. Readers must
conduct their own due diligence to be sure that the lessons within this book and the
resources on the accompanying website are applicable to their locale.

Cover design: Chloe Batch
Cover image © iStock.com/THEERADECH SANIN

Library of Congress Control Number: 2026930640

ISBN: HB: 979-8-216-19647-1
         ePDF: 979-8-216-19649-5
         eBook: 979-8-216-19648-8

Typeset by Integra Software Services Pvt. Ltd.
Printed and bound in the United States of America

For product safety-related questions, contact productsafety@bloomsbury.com

To find out more about our authors and books, visit www.bloomsbury.com
and sign up for our newsletters.

To Maria, Edge, and Cary:

What a mess this book, and life, would be without you.

The books that the world calls immoral are books that show the world its own shame.

—OSCAR WILDE

[T]he truth is, that when a Library expels a book of mine and leaves an unexpurgated Bible lying around where unprotected youth and age can get hold of it, the deep unconscious irony of it delights me and doesn't anger me.

—MARK TWAIN

CONTENTS

Introduction **Bible Drill Meets** *Penthouse* **Forum**

I did not learn about sex in school. I did not learn about it on TV. I did not learn about it from Larry Flynt, Marvin Gaye, or Revenge of the Nerds. Aviaries and apiaries played no part in my intimate education.[1]

I did not learn about sex from my friends, who were confused and awkward like me. Or an older sibling, which I don't have. Or my parents, a Southern Baptist pastor and his wife. I doubt they were embarrassed or found the subject sinful. They probably assumed I had other sources of information. The Bible, for instance. Song of Solomon, chapter 7, offers the Hebrew equivalent of "back that thang up":

> [1] How beautiful are thy feet with shoes, O prince's daughter! the joints of thy thighs are like jewels, the work of the hands of a cunning workman.
> [2] Thy navel is like a round goblet, which wanteth not liquor: thy belly is like an heap of wheat set about with lilies.
> [3] Thy two breasts are like two young roes that are twins.

Game of Thrones, alas, was not yet available.[2]

Where did I learn about sex? Books. At first, it was romance novels. I was twelve or thirteen when I found a bag of them in a closet at my grandmother's house and, purely by chance, opened one right to a steamy scene. My curiosity growing, I tried it with another book. Then another. Soon I was trying it in bookstores, drugstores, Walmart. I got to where I could find the sex scenes in minutes. It was a bona fide skill. Bible drill meets *Penthouse* Forum.

After a while, I grew restless with the genre. The books, with their idyllic settings and one-note characters and euphemisms for genitalia, didn't seem realistic. In search of something better, I found Susan Isaacs. In her second novel, *Close Relations*, Marcia reminisces about how she lost her virginity: "'I'll be careful,' he whispered, finding his place again quite quickly. I writhed a little, trying to displace him, but he moved with me. 'God, oh, God, it's so hot inside there,' he said […] I did not bleed. We wrapped the condom in Kleenex."[3] This was competent narration, but the language is a bit reserved. I had a difficult time picturing what was going on.

That was less of a problem with *Modern Women*, Ruth Harris's biting portrayal of 1960s New York publishing, as well as her homage to that era's sexual revolution. Harris was more direct, with a grittiness that Isaacs lacked:

> Not only was [Owen's penis] the size of a Louisville Slugger but, even more miraculously, Jane learned that Owen knew exactly how to use it. He knew how and when to put it in, when to move it around, and when to pull it back a bit. He knew when to go fast and when to go slow, when to put it in inch by inch, and when to go full throttle forward and jam it in all the way.[4]

Finally, I worked my way up to Jackie Collins, who makes Isaacs and Harris sound like Elizabeth Barrett Browning, as in this hell-for-leather passage from *Chances*:

"Gino–no!"

"A c'mon, Susie. Let me just put it there, just next to you. I won't put it in–I swear I won't!"

"But, Gino … "

"There I told you. Doesn't that feel good?"

"Mmmm … I guess … But don't move, *promise* you won't move."

"Course not. I just want to be next to you, that's all." Gently he eased his prick inside her.

"What are you doing?" she squealed.

"Just gettin' comfortable," he replied, easing his hand down between her legs–feeling for the magic button.

Susie gave a little sigh. He had found it.

"Feel nice?" he enquired solicitously.

"Oh yes, Gino, oh yes."

All set. No problem. Keeping his fingers on target he started to screw her properly […] Susie was becoming agitated, wriggling and gasping alarmingly. He increased his stroke.

God but he loved the feel of pussy.[5]

(You won't find *that* in Song of Solomon.)

***

Children of the future may not have access to scenes like these. Efforts to censor library materials are fueling fights all over the country. The American Library Association reported more than seven hundred book challenges in 2021, the most in two decades.[6] In 2022, that number nearly doubled, and it surged again in 2023 to 4,240 unique titles.[7] PEN America, one of the nation's leading networks of writers, recorded more than *ten thousand* instances of book bans in 2023–2024, more than tripling the previous year's number. Of the most commonly banned titles, 57 percent included sex or sex-related topics and content; 44 percent and 39 percent, respectively, featured characters of color and LGBTQ characters.[8]

Florida led the nation in bans (4,561), with Iowa (3,671) not far behind. Other leading states include Texas (538), Wisconsin (408), Virginia (121), and Kentucky (100). The driver of these bans is often new state legislation. For instance, Florida's House Bill 1069, which took effect in July 2023, created a statutory process for book banning.[9] Iowa's Senate Bill 496, which took effect in July 2023, prohibited materials from having any description or depiction of a "sex act." It also outlawed classroom discussions of LGBTQ+ identities.[10] In Montana, when passages from a book under consideration for banning were read aloud in the state Senate, one legislator replied, "It looks like there needs to be some book burning."[11] The Missouri legislature went so far as to criminalize the actions of anyone, including librarians, who provides access to a book deemed "sexually explicit."[12] Similarly, an Oklahoma law singled out employees of schools and public libraries as eligible for criminal prosecution for exposing students to indecent material.[13]

History being cyclical, uncanny connections exist between the 2020s and an earlier decade: the 1970s. Both saw a bungled military retreat (Saigon then, Kabul now), civil rights protests, and spikes in the cost of goods. One saw a former president pardoned; the other, convicted. Vinyl is back, with more than forty-four million albums sold in 2022. ABBA released new music in 2021, the Rolling Stones in 2023. Flare jeans, wrap dresses, and bucket hats have been revived. *Star Wars* is still a thing. So is *Rocky*. *Willy Wonka* has a prequel, *Halloween* and *The Exorcist* have sequels, and *Fantasy Island* has been remade.

Censorship is another parallel. It exists in every era, of course, though the 1970s, like now, saw an upswing. It has many opponents. It also has defenders who are, if not as legion, just as vociferous. Ultimately, censorship is a question about what people should and should not know. Who has the right to opine? To report? To decide whether a thing is true or false? Righteous or wretched? Information or ignominy? Myron Pitts, columnist for the *Fayetteville Observer*, refers to censors not as book banners but book killers. "A book," he writes, "is just pages and a cover, or characters and images on a screen. Book bans are about killing ideas, and for preventing other people from discovering those ideas."[14]

Over the years many cases have involved book bans. One of the most crucial began in 1975 in Nassau County, New York: *Board of Education, Island Trees Union Free School District No. 26 v. Pico*, which stemmed from a school board's desire to ban eleven books in its district:

- Oliver LaFarge's *Laughing Boy*;
- Richard Wright's *Black Boy*;
- Bernard Malamud's *The Fixer*;
- zoologist Desmond Morris's *The Naked Ape*;
- *Down These Mean Streets* by the Afro-Puerto Rican poet Piro Thomas;
- Eldridge Cleaver's *Soul on Ice*, which he wrote as an inmate at California's Folsom State Prison;
- Kurt Vonnegut's *Slaughterhouse-Five*;
- *Best Short Stories of Negro Writers*, edited by Langston Hughes;
- the anonymous drug memoir *Go Ask Alice*;
- Alice Childress's *A Hero Ain't Nothin' but a Sandwich*; and
- *A Reader for Writers*, edited by Jerome W. Archer and Joseph Schwartz.

No one had complained about these books. There had been no challenges, no letters to the editor, no public shouting matches. Unlike other bans this book will discuss, the Island Trees board was not reacting to worried parents, well-meaning quidnuncs, or even, in the words of Woody Allen, "one of those guys with saliva dribbling out of his mouth who wanders into a cafeteria with a shopping bag screaming about socialism."

The board simply acted. Like a sleeper cell.

In the process, it gave us the first—and so far, only—library book ban case to be decided by the United States Supreme Court. Immensely important, but with a complicated history, it was book banning's trial of the century. Covered by *The New York Times*, *The Washington Post*, and other major newspapers, it was highly contentious, generating seven separate Supreme Court opinions—a steep number. The case has been featured in journal articles, reprinted in law textbooks, highlighted in leading constitutional law treatises, and cited by hundreds of subsequent judicial decisions. Pico vs Island Trees was an indie rock band in the early 2000s. In "Read It and Weep," an episode of TV's *Family Ties*, Alex P. Keaton quotes from the case ("Local school boards may not remove books from school library shelves simply because they dislike the ideas contained in those books, and seek by their removal to prescribe what shall be orthodox in politics, nationalism, religion or other matters of opinion") when he learns that Jennifer can't do her book report on *Huckleberry Finn* because the school has banned it.[15] I wrote an essay for *The Missouri Review* about the case ("Desperately Seeking Sources") because it was so intriguing. That essay is the basis for this book.

Island Trees v. Pico deserves a place alongside the Supreme Court's most famous disputes: *Marbury v. Madison*, *Plessy v. Ferguson*, *Brown v. Board of Education*, *Roe v. Wade*. Yet, in 2026, it is largely forgotten outside academe.

Now, I'm afraid, is the perfect time for a refresher.

Notes

1 Anthony Aycock, "Desperately Seeking Sources," *Missouri Review*, October 20, 2023, https://missourireview.com/desperately-seeking-sources-by-anthony-aycock/.

2 Ibid.

3 Susan Isaacs, *Close Relations*, repr. ed. (Harper Perennial, 2009), 120.

4 Ruth Harris, *Modern Women* (St. Martins, 1989), 113–14.

5 Jackie Collins, *Chances* (Warner Books, 2000), 26–27.

6 "State of America's Libraries Report," American Library Association, https://www.ala.org/news/state-americas-libraries-report-2022.

7 "American Library Association Reports Record Number of Unique Book Titles Challenged in 2023," American Library Association, https://www.ala.org/news/2024/03/american-library-association-reports-record-number-unique-book-titles.

8 "Banned in the USA: Beyond the Shelves," PEN America, November 1, 2024, https://pen.org/report/beyond-the-shelves/.

9 Ibid.

10 Ibid.

11 Blair Miller, "Opponents Ask Committee to Kill Montana 'Obscenity' Bill as Backer Calls for Book Burning," *Daily Montanan*, April 10, 2023, https://dailymontanan.com/2023/04/10/opponents-ask-committee-to-kill-montana-obscenity-bill-as-backer-calls-for-book-burning/.

12 Mo. Rev. Stat. § 573.550.

13 Okla. Stat. tit. 70, § 11-202.

14 Myron B. Pitts, "Here Is the Full List of 'Reviewed' Books—Cumberland Schools Must Halt Book-Killers," *Fayetteville Observer*, February 17, 2023, https://www.fayobserver.com/story/opinion/2023/02/17/pitts-cumberland-schools-should-stop-the-book-killers-in-their-tracks/69911886007/.

15 Nat Hentoff, "Michael J. Fox for the First Amendment," *Washington Post*, March 4, 1998, https://www.washingtonpost.com/archive/opinions/1988/03/05/michael-j-fox-for-the-first-amendment/35286f3f-9eb2-421b-8bcf-0bec9815d27f/.

1 Faithful Watchdogs

We all know what a five-alarm fire the 1960s were. Vietnam. Riots. Bombings. Bay of Pigs. Cuban Missile Crisis. The "Day the Music Died." JFK, RFK, MLK: all killed. So were Malcolm X and Medgar Evers. Bikinis, bell-bottoms, and beehives. *The Feminine Mystique*. The Milgram experiments. Ken Kesey and the Merry Pranksters. Woodstock. Sexual revolutions. "Turn on, tune in, drop out." The space race. ARPANET, which became the internet. Charles Manson. The Beatles.[1]

Everything couldn't fit into that one decade, so the 1970s got the overflow: Watergate. Stagflation. Gas rations. Bloody Sunday. Lucy (i.e., *Australopithecus afarensis*). Sony Walkman, Apple, and Pong. MKUltra. Patty Hearst. Jim Jones. Ted Bundy and John Wayne Gacy, Son of Sam and Hillside Strangler. *The Texas Chainsaw Massacre*. Significant social progress was followed by pushback from old-guard conservatives, who worried that such reforms would rot us into Third World status. Political violence sought to make noise but not much else. "There were many, many bombings," said Rachel Kleinfeld, a senior fellow at the Carnegie Endowment for International Peace, "but usually at night, or after called-in warnings. The goal was not to kill people; it was to affect decisions."[2]

And there was censorship.

***

Efforts to ban books had always been there, of course. And in the 1970s, those efforts exploded. According to education researcher Michael Sturm, the number of censorship initiatives increased more than 300 percent from 1966 to 1975.[3] In the early 1970s, the American Library Association's Office for Intellectual Freedom averaged one hundred book challenges or so a year. By decade's end, there were *ten times more*.[4] Would-be censors condemned all sorts of literary portraits:

unorthodox families, radical politics, race, unflattering portraits of American authority, any mention of Christ, any mention of sex.[5]

Some of the attacks were sobering, as when, on an overcast day in December 1977, the Warsaw, Indiana, Senior Citizens Club built a bonfire and chucked in forty copies of the self-help treatise *Values Clarification: A Handbook for Practical Strategies for Teachers and Students*.[6] Others offered a bit of high camp, such as the campaign of Tom Williams, a Baptist minister in Abingdon, Virginia. Characterizing his local library as a "dispenser of hard-core pornography at public expense" for circulating such titles as Philip Roth's *Goodbye, Columbus*, Harold Robbins's *The Lonely Lady*, and Sidney Sheldon's *Bloodline*, Williams accused the head librarian of "feloniously corrupting the minds of children." The librarian, in turn, accused the preacher of book theft. When Williams tried to get excerpts from these raunchfests published in the local newspaper, the editor in chief refused, calling Williams a "nipplehead."[7]

And there was the school board in Anchorage, Alaska, that voted in 1976 to ban the *American Heritage Dictionary* after the ultraconservative People for Better Education assembled a list of scurrilous entries, such as "bed" (meaning "to have sexual intercourse with") and "ball" (a slang term for "testicle"). The next day, the Anchorage Assembly sent a disappointed letter to the school board, worrying about "preservation of individual and academic freedoms" and warning that the board's actions could "stimulate further censorship pressures." Assembly chairman Dave Rose described the ban as "absolutely ludicrous." Another member, Lidia Selkregg, declared, "I'm shocked at the board's action. A dictionary is a most sacred document." A third member, Fred Chiei, said, "Now I suppose they'd like to go for the Bible. Lots of good words with dirty meanings there."[8] Though the ban was never formally lifted, everyone eventually forgot about it, making it fodder for those internet lists of weirdest laws in America.

Yet another controversy in Ridgefield, Connecticut, a town of about twenty-five thousand situated in the foothills of the Berkshire Mountains, could be seen as a *Pico* precursor. In April 1970, a group called Concerned Parents of Ridgefield denounced the Ridgefield Board of Education's plans for a federally funded junior program called Project TELL. The program would provide health instruction, including sex education, at the town's junior high school. Norman Little, the head of Concerned Parents, said, "We consider any such activity as part of the school's curriculum or programs an unacceptable and unjustifiable incursion on the right of privacy of both children and their parents."[9] Five months later, Little latched onto *Playing It Cool*, a 1964 anthology that included such oft-censored writers as Langston Hughes, Martin Luther King Jr., and Claude Brown, author of *Manchild in the Promised Land*.

Perhaps cowed by Concerned Parents' aggression, the board voted in 1972 to remove from classrooms Mike Royko's book *Boss*, an exposé of Chicago Mayor

Richard Daley. Defending the decision, board member Leo Carroll, a former police officer, said, "The first time I opened the book, I came across a section that said the police had burglarized some establishments belonging to peace groups. Now tell me, do you think a policeman would do something like that?"[10]

The banning made national news, with stories appearing from *The New York Times* to the *Los Angeles Times*. One political cartoon compared the board to Nazi book burners. The Authors League of America, now the Authors Guild, called the board's action an "example of fear of the printed word, intolerance and a shocking disregard for the Constitutional principles of free speech."[11] But Carroll was just getting started. After *Boss*, he pivoted to Eldridge Cleaver's *Soul on Ice* (sound familiar?) and *Police, Courts and the Ghetto*, a sociological study by Marjorie Kilbane and Patricia Claire, saying there was "nothing of redeeming social or educational value in the books."[12] Teachers threatened to strike, but the board dug in.

Tensions might have risen higher if not for a poodle. A poodle hanging from a tree.

The dangling dog belonged to Elfrieda Travostino, president of the Ridgefield Teachers Association, who also told police that an anonymous caller told her she or her children might be next.[13] Fido was fine, if a little bewildered, and in February 1973, the board lifted its book bans. It also, as recompense, eliminated the social studies classes in which the books had been assigned. No lawsuits were filed; no arrests were made. Eventually, the imbroglio faded away.

***

Not so with *Island Trees v. Pico*, which is only one of the disputes that made Long Island, New York, something of a civil rights flash point in the latter half of the twentieth century. In 1964, for instance, abortion-rights activist Bill Baird opened one of the nation's first clinics in Hempstead, a town in the southwest part of the county. This was six years before abortion became legal in New York state and nine years before *Roe v. Wade*. A former medical student, Baird became an abortion advocate when he saw a woman die in a Manhattan hospital after trying the procedure on herself—with a coat hanger. Called a "blasphemer" and "Dr. Death" by his opponents, Baird operated several clinics that, at their peak, served ten thousand women a year.[14]

A decade later, in 1974, a jury of eight men and four women needed only fifty-five minutes to acquit Dr. Vincent Montemarano in the death of Eugene Bauer, a terminally ill cancer patient at the Nassau County Medical Center. It was only the second "mercy killing" prosecution of a physician in United States history—a charge that would later land the Michigan pathologist Jack Kevorkian in prison, forever lodging him in the public consciousness.[15]

Another hospital, this one at the State University of New York at Stony Brook, became the site of a struggle over Baby Jane Doe, an infant born on October 11,

1983, with spina bifida, hydrocephaly, and microcephaly. Without surgery to reduce the fluid in her skull, she would die within weeks; with surgery, she might live a number of years, but her disabilities would be severe. Her parents decided to forgo surgery—a decision that prompted a lawsuit seeking to force it. Trial judge Melvyn Tanenbaum ordered the surgery, but *one day later*, an appeals court overruled him. President Ronald Reagan's Department of Health and Human Services then got involved, suing the hospital for violating the Rehabilitation Act of 1973, but lost.[16]

Book banning's trial of the century began in 1975 in the Island Trees Union Free School District, one of fifty-seven districts in Nassau County, which, with Kings and Queens Counties, covers the western third of Long Island. It was one of the county's smaller districts, with a budget of around $11 million in the mid-1970s.[17] Created in 1902 as a common school district (this meant it could operate only a K–8 school; it became a union free district in 1951 so that a junior high, and later a high school, could be added), Island Trees encompassed parts of four towns: Seaford, Plainedge, Bethpage, and Levittown.[18]

Most of the county was farmland until after World War II, when people began arriving from New York City thanks to an acute housing shortage. What they found was a mass of planned communities with pretty, affordable houses. Levittown was one such community. Real estate developer and Seabee William Levitt came home from the war and saw an opportunity: others like him would be returning, and they would need places to live. So, he and his brother, Alfred, started buying land and building houses, which they sold for $7,990 with a 5 percent down payment (0 down for veterans).[19] The project was wildly successful, and similar communities began popping up everywhere, earning Levitt the epithet "father of modern America suburbia."[20]

(Not everyone was a fan, of course. "The community has an almost antiseptic air," said one *Time* magazine profile.[21] Sociologist Lewis Mumford described Levittown as a "uniform environment from which escape is impossible."[22] For Levitt, these were features, not bugs. Anticipating the ideological warfare that would engulf his town decades later, he said, "No one who owns his own house and lot can be a Communist. He has too much to do."[23])

Meanwhile, Nassau County grew and grew. From 1950 to 1960, the population swelled from 672,765 to 1.3 million—a 93 percent increase. By 1970, it had jumped to 1.4 million.[24] The county was extraordinarily homogenous, with white people making up nearly 98 percent of the population.[25] George Vescey, writing for *The New York Times*, reported that, among forty-three hundred students in the Island Trees district, not one was Black.[26]

Such racial congruity leads to a certain amount of political and social sameness. "For much of the 20th century," wrote one *Times* reporter, "the Nassau Republicans were thought of as the suburban counterpart to the Daley machine in Chicago and, earlier, New York City's Tammany Hall"[27]—in other words, unbeatable. Vescey quotes Colleen Mulvihill, an Island Trees student, as saying that "most of the people in this district are Irish and Italian who think a certain way, and they want everybody else to think that way."[28] The district has "civil servants from all over—the Nassau Highway Department, the New York City Sanitation and Fire Departments and the New York and Nassau Police Departments,"[29] said one resident in 1976. This has created a community "more involved psychologically with the ills of [New York City]"—that is, afraid of *turning into* the city.[30] "[A] lot are barely holding on here ... they want to look back to the 'good old days' and they value traditionalism."[31] Music executive Russell Rieger, who grew up in Island Trees and was one of the plaintiffs alongside Steven Pico, said it best when he told me that many of his friends and neighbors there were "as Archie Bunker as you can imagine."[32]

Two of those Daley-esque Republicans were Frank Martin—NYPD sergeant, former president of the Island Trees Taxpayers Association, and vice-chair of the Island Trees school board—and board chair Richard Ahrens, a "boyishly good-looking" diesel mechanic at LaGuardia Airport.[33] (To me, he resembled a young Carl Sagan.) Along with a third board member, Patrick Hughes, Ahrens and Martin paid $25 each to attend an educational conference September 19–21, 1975, in Watkins Glen. Also attending, according to Ahrens, were a Heritage Foundation attorney; George Archibald, a legislative assistant to US Representative John Conlon; and "other speakers with reputations in education circles who spoke about ... litigation involving the control of textbooks and library books in the school." This included "a Mr. Fike from Kanawa [*sic*] County, West Virginia which had undergone such litigation."[34] (More about Kanawha County in Chapter 4.)

The keynote speaker at Watkins Glen was Genevieve Klein, an educator, former member of the New York State Board of Regents, and outspoken conservative. "If you are a parent who believes that reading, writing, spelling and arithmetic are basic tools necessary for developing into a contributing member of society," she told the group, "then you know that parental control is an immediate necessity. If there is to be any hope for saving another generation from becoming functional idiots, the time to act is now."[35]

The conference was sponsored by Parents of New York United, or PONY-U, a conservative group headed by right-wing activist Janet Mellon, who had formed the group twenty years earlier when she was "appalled" that her oldest daughter was taking a course that "taught boys how to sew and girls how to shave."[36] The group had spent years organizing opposition to sex and "human relations" education in schools, as well as to student busing in upstate New York. Two months before Watkins Glen, it had hosted a talk titled "Book Censorship in Our Schools" at the Central Fire Station in Ithaca, New York.[37]

Mellon was an enemy of many types of books. At the conference, she circulated "crudely typed and reproduced" lists of thirty-two titles "considered objectionable by some persons together with excerpts from them containing the more objectionable material."[38] The lists included, for example, *Soul on Ice*, which bore the all-caps comments "SEDITIOUS AND DISLOYAL" and "FULL OF ANTI-AMERICAN MATERIAL AND HATE FOR WHITE WOMEN. WHY WOULD TEACHERS WANT HIGH SCHOOL STUDENTS TO READ THIS????"[39] About *Go Ask Alice*, the list maker warned, "Parents, do not be fooled by the movie version of this book. It reads a lot different. If teachers cannot find a better book than this to illustrate drugs are bad then what are we paying them for."[40] A third book, Helen Colton's *Our Sexual Evolution*, was decried because it "has chapters on Group Marriage, Communes, Abortion, Contraceptives etc. It also promotes women's lib." Worst of all, it "costs $5.95 of our tax dollars."[41]

Ahrens and Martin brought copies of these lists home but didn't act on them until November 7, 1975: Winter School Night at the high school. Under cover of awkward teen dancing, the pair slipped into the library; riffled through the card catalog; and discovered, in addition to *Soul on Ice*, eight other volumes in PONY-U perdition. A tenth book, *A Reader for Writers*, turned up at the junior high school. Finally, book eleven, Bernard Malamud's *The Fixer*, was found lurking on a twelfth-grade syllabus.

The matter simmered until February 24, 1976, when the board, after one of its regular meetings, asked Irving Carroll and Ernest Valenze, the principals of Island Trees' two high schools, to remove the books from the library shelves. Three days later, Superintendent Richard Morrow sent Ahrens a memo questioning this action. "We don't know," he wrote, "who developed the list, nor the criteria they used."[42] He reminded Ahrens of the existing policy for book challenges (Board Policy 6163.1), which called for Morrow to appoint a committee to study the issue and make recommendations. Morrow was sympathetic to the board's feelings, pointing out that they weren't that different from the parents' and predicting that any study committee would agree to the books' unsuitability. A unilateral ban, on the other hand, "would surely create a furious uproar—not only in the staff, but across the community, Long Island and the state. I don't believe you want such an uproar, and I certainly don't."[43]

Ahrens agreed to the study committee. Yet he thought the board should read the books first, so instead of buying additional copies for that purpose, he persisted in taking the libraries' copies. As Morrow predicted, "The matter became public knowledge and was seized with relish by a highly antagonistic press. All hell broke loose."[44] Ahrens responded with a March 19 press release that is worth quoting in full:

The Board of Education finds it necessary to call this press conference because of distortions, misinformation, and the obvious attempt by the New York Daily News in a cartoon published this morning, to characterize two members of the Board as a pair of shady hoods who surreptitiously sneak into school buildings under cover of darkness to snatch library books.

It comes as no surprise to this Board of Education that it is once again the subject of attack by Teacher Union leaders, headed by Walter Compare. With the election of school board candidates just two months away, the Teachers'

Union is once again attempting to discredit the Board and win the seats for two union-backed lackeys.

And now for the truth. In September 1975, Board members Ahrens, Hughes, and Martin attended a conference at Watkins Glen, New York, sponsored by Parents' of New York, United. The purpose of the conference was to discuss education in general, and the parents role in education in particular.

While at the conference, we learned of books found in schools throughout the country which were anti-American, anti-Christian, anti-Semitic,[45] and just plain filthy. Upon their return, Ahrens and Martin in early November went to the Senior High School to check the card catalog to see if any of these objectionable books were in our library. We discovered nine such books. We neither removed books, nor cards from the card file.

At the next meeting of the Board, the entire Board discussed how to handle this situation, realizing that to make the titles of the books public might cause a sudden run on the library by the students. The Board decided that the Principals of the Senior and Junior High Schools would be called in and be directed to gather up the books in question and bring them to the entire Board, for review. This order was carried out earlier this month. The Board is presently reviewing the contents of the books.

To date, what we have found is that the books do, in fact, contain material which is offensive to Christians, Jews, Blacks, and Americans in general. In addition, these books contain obscenities, blasphemies, brutality, and perversion beyond description.

This Board of Education wants to make it clear that we in no way are BOOK BANNERS or BOOK BURNERS. While most of us agree that these books have a place on the shelves of the public library, we all agree that these books simply DO NOT belong in school libraries, where they are so easily accessible to children whose minds are still in the formulative stage, and where their presence actually entices children to read and savor them. As US Commissioner of Education, T. H. Bell, has said, "Parents have a right to expect that the schools, in their teaching approaches and their selection of instructional materials, will support the values and standards that their children are taught at home. And if the schools cannot support those values, they must at least avoid deliberate destruction of them."

We who are elected by the community, are the eyes and ears of the parents. It is our duty, our moral obligation, to protect the children in our schools from this moral danger as surely as from physical and medical dangers.

We have some books which have been reviewed, marked, and underlined. However, if they are read in front of a television camera, the FCC would never permit it to be aired. This stuff is too strong for adult viewers, but some of our educators feel it is appropriate for child consumption.

We are sure that when most of our teachers are given the opportunity to review the material, they will side with the Board, and against the Executive Committee of their own union. When most of the parents review these books, we are confident they will back us to the hilt, grateful that we have done our job and remained as they elected us … their faithful Watchdogs.

Finally, we have the books here for your inspection. We will gladly make copies of individual pages to the UN believers.[46]

At a March 30 public meeting of the school board, Morrow reiterated his concerns. "There is no question," he said, "that under [state] law a local board of education has the ultimate responsibility to approve or disapprove reading material which will be used in the schools."[47] Yet the board, in his view, had done four things wrong:

1 they removed the books without considering the views of the community;
2 they evaluated the books by reading only excerpts;
3 they relied on a third-party list; and
4 they bypassed the district's official review procedures.[48]

His recommendations were as follows:

1 appoint a review committee immediately;
2 instruct the committee to review all eleven books and make recommendations on this by May 7; and
3 return the books to the libraries in the interim, "with the understanding that every parent has the right and the responsibility to supervise the materials his child reads."[49]

Morrow also urged everyone—press, parents, and the board—"to refrain from further charges and recriminations, and to give this procedure time to function as it was intended."[50]

Ahrens declined to return the books to the shelves, but he did agree to the review committee. "We want to get different views," Ahrens said, and his next words were ominous: "But in the end we will make the decision. We do not have to abide by the committee's recommendation."[51]

The committee was appointed on April 6, three days before the announcement that Morrow was leaving Island Trees to head the Massena, New York, school system (at a $4,500 pay cut).[52] Charged with evaluating the books on the basis of "educational suitability," "good taste," "relevance," and "appropriateness to age and grade level," it consisted of four community members:

1 Donald Ferris, former Board of Education member;

2 Thomas Lane, a 1972 Island Trees High School graduate and a student at Farmingdale Community College;

3 George O'Donnell, a postal employee and district resident for two years; and

4 Carol Sachs, parent and president of the Island Trees PTA Council.[53]

It also included four Island Trees staff members:

1 Robert Amato, high-school social studies teacher;

2 Irving Carroll, high-school principal;

3 Charles Lipp, high-school English teacher; and

4 Richard Segerdahl, elementary-school principal.[54]

(No library staff was included, perhaps because at least some people blamed the contretemps on the Island Trees librarian for having the books in the first place. "In recent months," wrote *Village Voice* columnist—and free speech enthusiast— Nat Hentoff, "Irene Turin has been frequently and deliberately harassed." This included "various invidious comments made to her, such as the charge that she is assuming the role of a 'Fagin,' leading astray the students of Island Trees as the Dickens' character did the urchins of London.")[55]

The committee met several times over the next two months. On April 29, it voted 6–2 to restore *The Fixer* to the Modern Literature curriculum.[56] As for the rest of the books, the voting went as follows:

Meeting	Book Title	Vote
May 12	*Laughing Boy*	8 keep, 0 remove
May 12	*Slaughterhouse-Five*	4 keep, 4 remove
May 26	*Black Boy*	8 keep, 0 remove
May 26	*Go Ask Alice*	7 keep, 1 remove
May 26	*A Hero Ain't Nothin' but a Sandwich*	4 keep, 4 remove
June 16	*The Naked Ape*	2 keep, 6 remove
June 16	*Down These Mean Streets*	3 keep, 5 remove
June 16	*Soul on Ice*	4 keep, 4 remove

A second vote was held on *Slaughterhouse-Five* on whether to place it on a restricted shelf. That vote was 5 yes, 3 no. The last two books, *A Reader for Writers* and *The Best Short Stories by Negro Writers*, could not be evaluated before the June 28 meeting at which the board decided each book's fate. Didn't matter. All but two—*Laughing Boy* and *Black Boy*—were kept in exile.[57]

In response, letters to the editor of *Newsday*, the Nassau County newspaper, poured in. Many writers reacted with outrage, disgust, or sarcasm. One wag recommended further bannings: *The Scarlet Letter*, because a minister seduces a young woman; *Romeo and Juliet*, for the nurse's "filthy tongue"; and the Book of Genesis, because Lot is a horny old drunk.[58] In contrast, Frank Martin defended the ban, claiming that "letters are coming into the school district at the rate of four to one in our favor."[59] He invoked Communism, saying that it "undermines the moral fiber of a nation" before asking rhetorically, "[w]hat better way to corrupt our youngsters than by subjecting them to decadent and deviant literature in the schools?"[60] Finally, he encouraged *Newsday* to "keep the pot boiling…. You are inadvertently waking up hundreds of sleeping parents who thought all was well with their schools. And when the giant awakens, his roar of anger will be deafening, and the counter-reformation in education will have begun."[61]

As for the banned authors, they didn't take it lying down. In an August 11 speech at Hofstra University, Kurt Vonnegut said that the Island Trees board members "are in the wrong society. If these people find this society uncongenial, then let 'em go to another country, one where the government worries about people putting ideas into their children's heads."[62] Later, he wrote in *The New York Times*: "Such lunks [the board members] are often the backbone of volunteer fire departments and the United States Infantry and cake sales and so on, and they have been thanked often enough for that. But they have no business supervising the educations of children in a free society. They are just too bloody stupid."[63] Bernard Malamud also chided the "self-appointed censors" who "reveal their intellectual and emotional meagreness,"[64] but this was a billet-doux compared to Desmond Morris, who decried the Island Trees board as "hatchet-faced ladies with hard eyes and cowrie-shelled lips hovering with ill-concealed rage just around the corner."[65]

Lunks. Emotional meagreness. Hatchet-faced. You take a towering risk when you piss off wordsmiths.

To Ahrens, none of this was the board's problem. "This is all politics," he complained. "If you want to tell your child about this wonderful book, you can take her to the public library. I would not dream of trying to take that book out of the public library. That would be censorship—and we are not censors."[66]

Perhaps he thought that would settle the matter. Maybe he thought most people wouldn't care. No doubt he counted on all those Archie Bunkers in the community to stick together and support him. He certainly didn't expect seven years later to be standing before nine black-robed jurists, struggling to explain why he felt threatened by some F-bombs, a little raciness, and Kurt Vonnegut's screwball plots.

Richard Ahrens had not reckoned on Steven Pico.

Notes

1   Anthony Aycock, "Desperately Seeking Sources," *Missouri Review*, October 20, 2023, https://missourireview.com/desperately-seeking-sources-by-anthony-aycock/.

2   Ned Parker and Peter Eisler, "Political Violence in Polarized U.S. at Its Worst since 1970s," *Reuters*, August 9, 2023, https://www.reuters.com/investigates/special-report/usa-politics-violence/.

3   Michael Sturm, "Censorship: Where Do We Stand?," *American Secondary Education* 12, no. 3 (1983): 5–8.

4   Colin Campbell, "Book Banning in America," *New York Times Book Review*, December 20, 1981, 1, 16.

5   Aycock, "Desperately Seeking Sources."

6   Ibid.

7   Blaine Harden, "'Shocked' Va. Preacher Trying to Ban 'Hard-Core Porn' from Town's Library," *Washington Post*, December 14, 1980, https://www.washingtonpost.com/archive/local/1980/12/15/shocked-va-preacher-trying-to-ban-hard-core-porn-from-towns-library/7febc78f-6e87-424a-a84e-d7fb3400444a/.

8   David Reamer, "Was a Dictionary Really Banned in Anchorage?," *Anchorage Daily News*, September 25, 2022, https://www.adn.com/alaska-life/2022/09/25/was-a-dictionary-really-banned-in-anchorage-heres-the-real-story-of-how-the-book-was-outlawed-in-schools/.

9   Jordan Nathaniel Fenster, "How Banning Books in One CT Town Caught National Attention and Changed a Community," *CT Insider*, April 29, 2023, https://www.ctinsider.com/connecticut/article/book-ban-ridgefield-connecticut-17922192.php.

10 Ibid.

11 Ibid.

12 Ibid.

13 Ibid.

14 Rhoda Amon, "A Long-Running Morality Play," *Newsday* (Nassau ed.), June 21, 1998, H13.

15 Ibid.

16 Ibid.

17 Michael Alexander and Robert E. Kessler, "Island Trees Returns 'Book-Banners,'" *Newsday* (Nassau ed.), May 27, 1976, 3.

18 Island Trees School District, "History of Island Trees," https://islandtrees.org/apps/pages/index.jsp?uREC_ID=415303&type=d.

19 Colin Marshall, "Levittown, the Prototypical American Suburb–A History of Cities in 50 Buildings, Day 25," *The Guardian*, April 28, 2015, https://www.theguardian.com/cities/2015/apr/28/levittown-america-prototypical-suburb-history-cities.

20 Ibid.

21 Ibid.

22 Ibid.

23 Ibid.

24 John Farley, "Book Censorship in the Senior High School Libraries of Nassau County, New York," (PhD dissertation, New York University, 1964, 65.

25 Michele Ingrassia, "Banned Books and Battles over School," *Newsday* (Nassau ed.), December 13, 1976, 5A.

26 George Vescey, "Giving Books an F," *New York Times*, March 28, 1976, 16.

27 Nicholas Fandos, "In the Land of George Santos, Machine Politics Fuels a GOP Revival," *New York Times*, February 12, 2024, https://www.nytimes.com/2024/02/12/nyregion/republicans-nassau-pilip-santos.html.

28 Vescey, "Giving Books an F," 16.

29 Ingrassia, "Banned Books," 5A.

30 Ibid.

31 Ibid.

32 Aycock, "Desperately Seeking Sources."

33 Alexander and Kessler, "Island Trees Returns 'Book-Banners,'" 3.

34 *Pico v. Island Trees*, 638 F. 2d 404, 407 (2d Cir. 1980).

35 Laura Pappano, "A Brief History of the Grand Old Tradition of Banning Books," *Literary Hub*, January 30, 2024, https://lithub.com/a-brief-history-of-the-grand-old-american-tradition-of-banning-books/.

36 Michele Ingrassia, "Island Trees Ban Has Upstate Root," *Newsday* (Nassau ed.), March 22, 1976, 1.

37 Pappano, "A Brief History."

38 638 F. 2d, 407.

39 Ibid.

40 Ibid., 408.

41 Ibid, 409.

42 Ibid.

43 Ibid.

44 Transcript of Examination before Trial of Richard Ahrens, February 17, 1978.

45 Some sources write this as "anti-Sem[i]tic," as though the press release misspelled the word. Other sources don't suggest a misspelling. I have written the word as it appears in the Supreme Court Joint Appendix, the official collection of case-related documents.

46 Island Trees Board of Education Press Release, March 19, 1976.

47 Statement concerning the Book Issue by Richard Morrow, superintendent, March 30, 1976.

48 Ibid.

49 Ibid.

50 Ibid.

51 "Island Trees: Rebuttal Time," *New York Times*, April 4, 1976, 4.

52 Michele Ingrassia, "School Chief Quitting in Island Trees," *Newsday* (Nassau ed.), April 9, 1976, 19.

53 Letter from Richard Morrow, superintendent, April 8, 1976.

54 Ibid.

55 Nat Hentoff, "Learning about the First Amendment," *Newsday* (Nassau ed.), June 8, 1977, 57.

56 Report of the Island Trees Book Review Committee, July 1, 1976.

57 Ibid.

58 "Citizens React to the Banning of Books," *Newsday* (Nassau ed.), August 5, 1976, 77.

59 Frank Martin, "Defending the Book Ban," *Newsday* (Nassau ed.), August 16, 1976, 45.

60 Ibid.

61 Ibid.

62 Ed Lowe, "'Nothing but a Writer,'" *Newsday* (Nassau ed.), August 12, 1976, 11.

63 Kurt Vonnegut, Bernard Malamud, and Desmond Morris, "Banned Authors Answer Back," *New York Times*, March 28, 1976, 16.

64 Ibid.

65 Ibid.

66 Vescey, "Giving Books an F," 16.

2 The Sounds of Silencing

was born in 1973 in Hillsborough, North Carolina, about forty miles northwest of Raleigh, the state capital. My father was a Southern Baptist pastor. A moderate Southern Baptist, if you can believe that. He never embraced, for instance, the inerrancy of the Bible. To him, certain accounts—the Garden of Eden, Noah and the Ark, Jonah and the Great Fish—are important for their spiritual truth, not their historical veracity. This makes them not unlike Jesus' parables.

Politically, too, my father is a rara avis. He voted for Hillary Clinton, accepts evolution and women deacons, and supports marriage equality. I became a librarian and carried over his worldview to the question of censorship, which I used to say I abhorred in all situations. I am more centrist these days. Censoring, like lying, is justifiable in some instances.

Island Trees school district, circa 1976, was not such an instance.

Nor was it for Steven Pico, a soft-spoken artist and the lead plaintiff in book banning's trial of the century. "I was about eight," he told me in his unmistakable Long Island accent, when Martin Luther King Jr. was shot—his first political memory. He is in his sixties now and no longer resembles a young Kirk Cameron. Kent State, the moon landing, *Tinker v. Des Moines*—these were not backdrops of Steven's adolescence; they were theater-in-the-round.[1]

By the time of Nixon, Reagan, and the rise of anti-intellectualism in politics, the die was cast on his personal convictions: bullies needed people to stand up to them, and he wasn't going to shy away.

Steven's first chance came in the fall of 1976, three months after the Island Trees board voted to cleanse the library of nine naughty books. It was the start of his senior year, and he had been named editor of the *Bulldog*, Island Trees High's student newspaper. The school board, in what could be called a September surprise, voted to merge the paper with its own monthly newsletter, effectively abolishing the *Bulldog*.

The official reason, according to Superintendent Walf Oglesby, was that Phil Cooper, the teacher who had served as the paper's faculty adviser, was not continuing in that role. No one had volunteered to replace him, and district rules prevented student publications from operating without an adviser. Did Cooper retire? Fall ill? Win the lottery? No. He was asked to step down because the paper a year earlier had published a photograph of another teacher, Lee Spallone, holding his nose above the caption, "What I think of the Football Team?"[2]

The board denied this assertion, claiming that it merely offered to print the newspaper because the latter had no faculty adviser (forgetting, I suppose, that it was likely the reason for this vacancy). Frank Martin insisted that it was not an act of suppression. "The paper is being made so it can slip into the newsletter," he said. "If [students] want 1,000 copies to sell in the school, as they have done in the past, that will be done…. There won't be any integration as far as the newsletter and student articles are concerned."[3]

Richard Ahrens likewise said he never intended to abrogate the paper, though he conceded that, under the auspices of the newsletter, stuff like the Spallone photo wouldn't be allowed. Oglesby was the sharpest critic: "We want news reporting, not editorializing. If you have any school pride you wouldn't allow the publication of a statement saying the team 'stinks.'"[4] It wasn't his first content crackdown. Librarian Irene Turin claimed that Oglesby didn't allow Island Trees libraries to have books on the Panama Canal or the metric system, which he considered a "communist plot." He also forbade Richard and Daniel Gatti's *Encyclopedic Dictionary of School Law* on the grounds that it could be "used against us."[5]

There was outrage, of course, with students and faculty assailing the board and defending Cooper. Steven Pico said, "The book scandal isn't resolved yet; now they're adding to the controversy."[6] Finally, on October 27, the board revived the *Bulldog* with social studies teacher Alice Korman as adviser. "My function," she said, "is to tell what I think, and [the students] then can do what they want to do," adding that she would not have disallowed the Spallone photo.[7] The best part? Korman didn't think the board was aware that her brother was Jules Feiffer: counter culturalist, satirist, and winner of the Pulitzer Prize for Editorial Cartooning.

Pico 1, bureaucracy 0.

Steven's second chance was the book removals. As student council president, he attended school board meetings and knew the members well. They were the bankers and farmers and store owners of Levittown and the surrounding areas. He didn't want to fight them, but book banning ran counter to everything he had been taught about democracy. Some of the writers—Richard Wright, Langston Hughes—were dead and couldn't defend themselves, and it seemed natural to him to assume that role.

"Simply put," he told me, "I had to do everything in my power to make sure these voices were not silenced."[8]

***

Such silencing is as old as civilization itself.

Plato's *Republic* describes a system of censorship reflecting the belief that law shaped opinions and that men could be penalized for statements that offended public sensibilities, undermined common morality, or otherwise threatened the community's stability. Indeed, history's most famous philosopher, Socrates, was tried, convicted, and executed for, among other things, failing to acknowledge the deities that other Athenians worshipped. Centuries later, Jesus of Nazareth was put to death for similarly inflammatory speech.

With the invention of the printing press in the fifteenth century, people were given new opportunities to become exposed to ideas. Authorities, meanwhile, earned another method for controlling that exposure. The Roman Catholic Church, for instance, knew that if everyone could read religious texts, it would lose its monopoly on the meaning of those texts. It thus began compiling lists of off-limits books, culminating in the 1559 *Index Librorum Prohibitorum*, which existed until 1966(!) and at one point included works by Gustave Flaubert (*Madame Bovary*), Edward Gibbon (*The History of the Decline and Fall of the Roman Empire*), Galileo, and Casanova.[9]

Governments made similar efforts at ideological constraint. In England, Henry VIII required all books to be examined and licensed by the Privy Council. Elizabeth I continued that policy during her reign, enlisting the Stationers' Company—the printers' professional guild—to license and track all publications. In April 1638, political agitator John Lilburne was arrested for importing subversive books, fined £500, and publicly flogged.[10] This display, plus Parliament's 1643 Ordinance for the Regulating of Printing, which formalized the licensing requirement, spurred the poet John Milton to pen *Areopagitica*, a monument of free speech defense. "Let [Truth] and Falsehood grapple," wrote Milton; "who ever knew Truth put to the worse in a free and open encounter?" It is an argument, basically, for a marketplace of ideas, one in which he imagined truth always prevailing.

Milton also recognized that censorship is a slippery slope. Again, *Areopagitica*: "[W]ho kills a man kills a reasonable creature, God's image; but he who destroys a good book, kills reason itself, kills the image of God, as it were, in the eye." Even Shakespeare was sterilized. When his play *Richard II* first came up for licensing in 1595, Edmund Tilney, the Master of the Revels, cut out the scene of Richard's deposition. It would not be restored in full until the 1623 publication of the First Folio.[11]

In the United States, censorship got its start only a few years after the founding of Plymouth Colony. In 1637, the English lawyer Thomas Morton published *New English Canaan*, a description of the New World inspired by his own disastrous visit in the 1620s. The book criticized the Puritans' harsh treatment of Native Americans, for which the former outlawed the book.[12] A decade or so later, on October 16, 1650, William Pynchon, called by Daniel Crown the "forgotten founding father of colonial New England,"[13] saw his book *The Meritorious Price of*

Our Redemption* burned by officials in Boston. Other one-off book bans followed, such as the case of publisher Peter Holmes, who in 1821 was convicted of the crime of printing a "lewd and obscene novel." That novel was *Memoirs of a Woman of Pleasure*, or *Fanny Hill*, which would become one of history's most-banned books.

Yet it was not until the Comstock Act of 1873 that a national appetite for literary restriction surfaced. Named for Anthony Comstock, a Connecticut-born merchant who founded the New York Society for the Suppression of Vice, opposed everything from prostitution to medical patents, and wore mutton chops that nearly touched his shirt collar, the Act made it illegal to send "obscene, lewd or lascivious," "immoral," or "indecent" publications through the mail, as well as to sell, give away, or even possess such material.[14] Comstock was made a special agent of the US Postal Service to enforce the law, and enforce it he did. Paul Buchanan estimates that Comstock destroyed fifteen tons of books, 284,000 pounds of plates for printing "objectionable" books, and nearly four million pictures.[15]

Comstock died in 1915, but censorship didn't perish with him. The National Legion of Decency, founded in 1934, and its sister group, the National Organization for Decent Literature (1938), were Catholic cabals that inveighed against immorality in books, movies, magazines, even comic books. Comics have their own history of embattlement courtesy of German-born psychiatrist Fredric Wertham. In his 1954 book *Seduction of the Innocent*—and later in testimony before the US Senate Subcommittee to Investigate Juvenile Delinquency—Wertham claimed that Batman and Robin were gay, Wonder Woman was a lesbian, Superman was a fascist, and "Hitler was a beginner compared to the comic-book industry."[16]

Groups on the prowl for "subversive" books included the American Legion and the Daughters of the American Revolution (DAR), whose mission was to keep America's public schools "fundamentally Anglo-Saxon."[17] Anne Rogers Minor, DAR president from 1920 to 1923, said, "We want no teachers who say there are two sides to every question."[18] Textbooks containing critiques of capitalism, economic equality, or the health of American democracy were withdrawn from the classroom throughout the 1950s. In 1953, one of America's most prolific prohibitors, Senator Joseph McCarthy, led an effort to remove books from the US Department of State's Overseas Libraries, a network of American libraries in other countries whose purpose was diplomacy and information sharing.

---

*   The pamphlet's complete, mouthfully title was: *The meritorious price of our redemption, iustification, &c. Cleering it from some common errors; and proving, Part I. 1. That Christ did not suffer for us those unutterable torments of Gods wrath, that commonly are called hell-torments, to redeem our soules from them. 2. That Christ did not bear our sins by Gods imputation, and therefore he did not bear the curse of the law for them. Part II. 3. That Christ hath redeemed us from the curse of the law (not by suffering the said curse for us, but) by a satisfactory price of attonement; viz. by paying or performing unto his father that invaluable precious thing of his mediatoriall obedience, wherof his mediatoriall sacrifice of attonement was the master-piece. 4. A sinners righteousnesse or justification is explained, and cleered from some common errors.*

The most powerful censorship regime of the first half of the twentieth century was the Boston-based New England Watch and Ward Society, whose work gave rise to the chilling coinage "Banned in Boston." Founded in 1879 as the New England Society for the Suppression of Vice, it fought to stamp out social ills such as liquor, drugs, dance halls, gambling, and prostitution. There was also a focus on "impure literature"—mostly crime stories in pulp magazines, though occasionally there was bigger game.

In October 1882, for example, the Boston publisher James Osgood released a new edition of Walt Whitman's *Leaves of Grass*. Whitman originally self-published the book in 1855, and several new versions had appeared since then, though most were commercial failures. Osgood's is considered the definitive edition.[19] It had sold fifteen hundred copies when Osgood was informed that the book "has been officially classified by [District Attorney Oliver Stevens] as obscene literature."[20] Of course, such charges had dogged *Leaves of Grass* from the beginning, and Whitman was in no mood to be conciliatory. He agreed to a few textual changes, but when Stevens wanted more, including total excision of the poems "A Woman Waits for Me" and "To a Common Prostitute," the writer balked. He and Osgood parted ways, with Whitman "taking the plates, 325 copies in sheets, and $100 in cash."[21]

The person behind Stevens's tactics? Reverend Frederick Baylies Allen, founder and secretary of the Watch and Ward Society.[22]

The situation left ill feelings all around. Whitman's friend William Douglas O'Connor wrote, "Osgood … the infernal idiot should have defied the District Attorney, published his official warning as an advertisement, stood a suit, won it, and sold a million copies of Walt's book on the strength of it. The jackass."[23] Yet Whitman got the last laugh. He found another publisher, Rees Welsh & Company of Philadelphia, whose edition sold out in a day. Welsh was thrilled. He tried to get the book banned in Philadelphia, noting that "the Boston fools have already made for me more than $2,000."[24] Whitman, age sixty-five, used his share of the money to buy the house in Camden, New Jersey, where he would spend the rest of his life—the first and last house he ever owned.[25]

By the early 1900s, the Watch and Ward Society had become Boston's leading light. Belle epoque America was reform minded. Politicians worked to make the country a better and safer place to live. They passed regulations, cleaned up city governments, improved working conditions in factories and living conditions in slums, and even began an environmental movement. In 1913, the Seventeenth Amendment allowed direct election of United States senators. Between 1886 and 1923, Andrew Carnegie donated funds for more than sixteen hundred public library buildings in the United States, which became known as Carnegie Libraries.

Many people these days think of censorship as a mossbacked endeavor, but to Bostonians, it was of a piece with progressive emphases on social welfare. Thus, one observer called the Watch and Ward Society "a kind of enlightened civic conscience."[26] To another, it was "a sort of Moral Board of Health."[27] In 1911, former Harvard University President Charles William Eliot praised the Society for investigating social evils and combatting them "by drying up the sources of immorality and crime."[28]

By the 1920s, America was experiencing major changes. The "Roaring Twenties" ushered in a more fast-paced, consumerist lifestyle that embraced new technologies such as cars, radio, and film. The Eighteenth Amendment kicked off America's decade-long experiment with Prohibition; the Nineteenth Amendment gave women the right to vote. Censorship also became a more cohesive movement. Boston, with its heavy Irish Catholic influence, was an early cynosure. The Boston Booksellers Committee, founded in 1915, became the main agent of censorship organizing. Comprising three Watch and Ward officials and three pliable store owners, the group evaluated new publications and told the city's booksellers which titles should not be stocked. Though it had no formal power, the Committee became hugely influential. One word from J. Franklin Chase, the Watch and Ward Society's leader and a Committee organizer, "and the targeted book or books disappeared from all Boston bookshelves."[29] The Committee even asked the district attorney for informal opinions about which books to ban. It was a sort of censorship CIA.[30]

The system worked for years, a bridge over troubled water, until the 1920s, when gadfly journalist H. L. Mencken published a series of articles in his *American Mercury* magazine lampooning the Watch and Ward Society. In 1926, Mencken published "Hatrack," Herbert Asbury's essay about a "Scarlet Woman" from his hometown. Asbury described her as "a scrawny creature called variously Fanny Fewclothes and Hatrack ... the latter in deference to her figure."[31]

Outraged, Chase banned the magazine. Looking to force the issue, Mencken proposed selling Chase a copy in public: specifically, Boston's "Brimstone Corner," a curve of cobblestone in front of Park Street Church where the Puritans had reportedly spread hot ashes in a sort of Hell diorama. Chase would then order Mencken's arrest, enabling him to test the ban in court. This they did, surrounded by a hooting crowd, on April 5, 1926.[32]

One day later(!), the trial began, with Judge James Parmenter presiding. A confident Mencken testified that "Hatrack" was not obscene, that he never printed anything obscene, and that the Watch and Ward Society deserved his attacks on it due to its censorious regime. Asbury chimed in that he and Mencken had done nothing wrong because "Hatrack" was, in fact, true. Judge Parmenter, in Mencken's words, "sat listening in silence—an old man with a scrubby gray mustache, wrapped in a much wrinkled black gown ... wearing an expression of profound judicial calm."[33] Parmenter read "Hatrack" and dismissed the charges the next day, saying, "I cannot imagine any one reading the article in question and finding himself or herself attracted towards vice."[34]

Mencken, as you might imagine, was smug in victory. A year later, he was still crowing about it. To the *Baltimore Sun*, he remarked,

It is possible for anyone to have a book suppressed in Boston merely by advancing the idea. I wager that I could suppress four books in as many minutes if I should go to Boston and make the effort. Boston presents a most marvelous picture of allowing fanatics undisputed power. Among the civilized element all resistance has been suppressed.[35]

The society, however, was just getting started. Over the next two years, it would ban more than sixty books.[36] In April of 1927, the new district attorney, William Foley, revoked the hands-off arrangement with the Booksellers Committee, catching the latter unawares.[37] This was a problem: an unrestrained DA would do no one any good. Not to mention, New York publishers were starting to pull books from Boston shops. A spokesperson for the Massachusetts Library Club commented glumly: "It has now come to pass ... that the most conscientious librarian or the most conscientious bookseller is in danger of fine and imprisonment, that literature is shackled, that responsible adult citizens are no longer free to decide for themselves what they shall read and think."[38]

Perhaps another lawsuit would be just what the doctor ordered.

The test case for that suit was Theodore Dreiser's elephantine novel *An American Tragedy*. An Indiana-born journalist who interviewed such celebrities as Andrew Carnegie, Marshall Field, and Thomas Edison and who was talked out of returning from a European vacation aboard the Titanic,[39] Dreiser was no stranger to censorship. His novel *The Genius*, first published in 1915, was "deemed so shocking that its sale was immediately prohibited by the New York Society for the Suppression of Vice."[40] In 1916, *Sister Carrie*, which Donald L. Miller called "the greatest of all American urban novels,"[41] was attacked by censors for its immorality, and the book was banned in New York City and Cincinnati. [42]

An American Tragedy was based on the 1906 murder of Grace Brown, who was pregnant, and the trial of her lover, Chester Gillette, who was found guilty and sentenced to death. It was banned in Boston for "obscene language." On April 16, 1927, Donald Friede, vice president of Boni & Liveright, Dreiser's publisher, traveled to police headquarters and persuaded Lieutenant Daniel Hines to buy a copy of *An American Tragedy*.[43] (In fact, Friede was more than a vice president— he owned half the company, buying into it with his father's money. Though he missed out on Thomas Wolfe's *Look Homeward, Angel* and James Joyce's *Ulysses*, Friede discovered Dreiser, bought the American rights to Radclyffe Hall's *The Well of Loneliness*, and married M. F. K. Fisher. Not bad for a guy who was kicked out of Harvard, Yale, and Princeton.)[44]

Hines bought the book and immediately asked a judge to issue a summons for Friede. A week later, Friede appeared in municipal court, defended by ACLU cofounder Arthur Garfield Hays. Hays had a résumé ripped from the law school textbooks, having represented H. L. Mencken in the "Hatrack" business plus having been part of the defense teams for Tennessee schoolteacher John T. Scopes (the

"Monkey Trial") and Italian anarchists Nicola Sacco and Bartolomeo Vanzetti.[45] He thought it unfair to condemn an entire work on the basis of one passage. Hays also took issue with the statutory standard for obscenity: "manifestly tending to corrupt the morals of youth." He called Lieutenant Hines to the stand and asked if the book had corrupted his morals. Hines said no.[46]

Judge James Devlin, however, *had* found the book obscene and fined Friede $100. Hays appealed to the state superior court, insisting that the book's value "should not be judged by its effect on moronic minds."[47] That trial began two years later, on April 16, 1929. This time, Hays showed up with Dreiser, who testified to his novel's non-obscenity. Hays also called as a witness the legendary defense lawyer Clarence Darrow, who read aloud passages of *An American Tragedy*—a spectacle, but it worked. The jury "leaned forward to catch his words as he read of a girl's appearance before a doctor as related in the book. A tenderness crept into his voice as he read the girl's impassioned plea to the physician."[48] Afterward, Hays told the jury that more than four hundred passages in the Bible showed a greater "frankness of expression" than anything in *An American Tragedy*. "What book of the ages," he asked rhetorically, "which has stood as literature would stand up under the tests which have been applied to Dreiser?"[49]

That night, hundreds gathered at Ford Hall Forum for an anticensorship rally. People carried placards that read "Verboten" and "Taboo." There were skits and speeches. Birth control pioneer Margaret Sanger sat on stage, gagged. A letter from Upton Sinclair was read aloud in which he said, "I would rather be banned in Boston than read anywhere else" because "when you are banned in Boston you are read everywhere else."[50] Next day, the door was slammed on further merriment when the jury found Friede guilty. An appeal to the Massachusetts Supreme Judicial Court also failed, resulting in Friede's fine climbing to $300,[51] which is more than $5,000 in today's money.

Just in time for the Great Depression.

***

Though Hays's holistic argument—that a book should not be reduced to its most controversial content—did not result in his client's acquittal, it did inject the idea into judicial deliberations. That injection led to a different result in a more famous case: *United States v. One Book Called Ulysses*.[52]

Written by Dublin, Ireland, native James Joyce and published in Paris by American expatriate Sylvia Beach on February 2, 1922—Joyce's fortieth birthday—*Ulysses* is one of the world's most important novels, a masterpiece of modernist thought and linguistic virtuosity. A reimagining of Homer's *Odyssey*, the book takes place on a single day, June 16, 1904, and tells the story of three characters: Stephen Dedalus, Leopold Bloom, and Bloom's wife, Molly. *Ulysses* brims with wordplay, symbolism, and historical and literary allusions. It is also bawdy, raunchy, and occasionally disgusting.

Prior to 1922, Joyce published excerpts of the book in a Chicago-based magazine called *The Little Review*, run by Jane Heap and Margaret Anderson. An April 1920 excerpt, the so-called Nausicaa section, describes Leopold Bloom masturbating on a beach as a young woman, Gerty MacDowell, flashes him a bit of thigh while watching fireworks with her friends. Actually, "describes" might be an overstatement. Look at Joyce's rendition of the, uh, climactic moment:

[Gerty] would fain have cried to him chokingly, held out her snowy slender arms to him to come, to feel his lips laid on her white brow, the cry of a young girl's love, a little strangled cry, wrung from her, that cry that has rung through the ages. And then a rocket sprang and bang shot blind blank and O! then the Roman candle burst and it was like a sigh of O! and everyone cried O! O! in raptures and it gushed out of it a stream of rain gold hair threads and they shed and ah! they were all greeny dewy stars falling with golden, O so lovely! O, so soft, sweet, soft![53]

Not exactly the Marquis de Sade, is it? Yet some subscribers complained, and the US Postal Service began seizing and destroying issues of the magazine. In September 1920, John Sumner, secretary of the New York Society for the Suppression of Vice, filed a complaint. A month later, Heap and Anderson were arrested and charged under the Comstock Act.

The pair was tried in February 1921 before a panel of three judges. Defending them was John Quinn, a friend and patron of Joyce. Quinn was a huge supporter of Irish artists. He arranged William Butler Yeats's first North American tour in 1903–1904, put on an exhibition of the painter George Russell, and provided copyright—and literary—advice to the playwright John Millington Synge.[54] In the summer of 1916, on the recommendation of their mutual friend Ezra Pound, Quinn began sending Joyce money. Later, he bought the manuscript of Joyce's play *Exiles*.[55]

Yet Quinn was not the best choice of lawyer. For one thing, he wanted to produce a bound volume of *Ulysses* and thus was keen to end its serialization. He also didn't like his clients, writing in an October 16, 1920, letter: "I have no interest at all in defending people who are stupidly and brazenly and Sapphoistically and pederastically and urinally, and menstrually violat[ing] the law, and think they are courageous."[56] This might explain his quixotic argument, which was that *Ulysses* was too inscrutable to be considered obscene. And if someone *did* get what was going on, they were likely to feel enraged, not engorged. "That's what *Ulysses* does," Quinn told the judges. "It makes people angry. They want to break something. They want somebody to be convicted. They feel like prosecuting everybody connected with it, even if they don't know how to pronounce the name 'Ulysses.' But it doesn't drive them into the arms of some siren. And, after all, it isn't a crime to make someone angry."[57]

After such advocacy, how could the judges *not* rule against Anderson and Heap? The two were fined $100 and ordered to stop releasing excerpts of *Ulysses*. A dejected Anderson quit the magazine not long after, ceding control to Heap. By 1929, it had ceased publication altogether.

For the next ten years, the book remained unavailable in the United States. Then, in 1932, Bennett Cerf had an idea. With partner Donald Klopfer, Cerf had founded the publisher Random House five years earlier, and he needed a best seller, which he thought *Ulysses* could become.[58] There had been a few editions since Sylvia Beach's, only one of which was produced in America: a 1929 pirated version by the king of counterfeits, Samuel Roth, over which Joyce had sued, claiming a violation of his "right of publicity."[59] Cerf was eager to put out an authorized edition. How, though, could he circumvent the Comstock Act?

Enter Morris Ernst.

Ernst was the general counsel of the American Civil Liberties Union and a Joyce fanboy who was delighted to accept Cerf's case. His strategy was to bring a copy of *Ulysses* into the country and have it seized by US Customs agents as a violation of the Tariff Act of 1930, also called the Smoot-Hawley Tariff, which prohibited the import of materials having to do with abortion, treason, threats of harm, or a lottery. It also criminalized "obscene matter."[60]

The seizure took a couple of tries, as customs agents ignored the book at first: according to one official, "Everybody brings that in. We don't pay any attention to it."[61] Yet it ultimately ended up in the hands of Assistant US Attorney Samuel Coleman, who considered it a masterpiece. Coleman was reluctant to bring charges, though charges ultimately were filed, and the case was tried not by a jury but, like *Pico v. Island Trees** decades later, by a single judge.

That judge was John Munro Woolsey of the Southern District of New York. Woolsey was no stranger to obscenity cases. In 1931, he had overseen two others: *United States v. One Obscene Book Entitled "Married Love"* and *United States v. One Book, Entitled "Contraception."* Both books were by Marie Stopes, a Scottish-born paleobotanist and birth control advocate. Woolsey found neither book obscene. Of *Married Love*, he wrote that it

emphasizes the woman's side of sex questions. It makes also some apparently justified criticisms of the inopportune exercise by the man in the marriage relation of what are often referred to as his conjugal or marital rights, and it pleads with seriousness, and not without some eloquence, for a better understanding by husbands of the physical and emotional side of the sex life of their wives.[62]

---

*   A word about case names. When the original lawsuit was filed, it was called *Pico v. Island Trees* because Steven Pico, the plaintiff, initiated it. That name remained until the US Supreme Court, when it was changed to the now-familiar *Island Trees v. Pico* because the Island Trees school board was the party who initiated that appeal.

He noted that *Contraception* was a "scientific" book and the first "dealing fully with its subject-matter—the theory, history, and practice of birth control." Rather than inciting lust,

> the emotions aroused by the book are merely feelings of sympathy and pity, evoked by the many cases instanced in it of the sufferings of married women due to ignorance of its teachings. This, I believe, will be the inevitable effect of reading it on all persons of sensibility unless by their prejudices the information it contains is tabooed.[63]

For *Ulysses*, the government's argument was threefold:

1. it contained too much sex and "unparlorlike" language;
2. it was blasphemous; and
3. it provoked coarse thoughts and desires.

The argument was based on *Regina v. Hicklin* (1868), a British case in which Sir Alexander James Edmund Cockburn, 10th Baronet, defined "obscenity" as "the tendency ... to deprave and corrupt those whose minds are open to such influences, and into whose hands a publication of this sort may fall."[64] It was, in 1933, the leading case on the subject.

The argument against *Ulysses* wasn't without merit, especially with passages such as this from the "Penelope" episode, in which Molly Bloom lies in bed beside her husband and reminisces about when the two first had sex:

> he must have come 3 or 4 times with that tremendous big red brute of a thing he has I thought the vein or whatever the dickens they call it was going to burst ... better for him to put it into me from behind the way Mrs Mastiansky told me her husband made her like the dogs do it and stick her tongue as far as ever she could ... I'll tighten my bottom well and let out a few smutty words smellrump or lick my shit or the first thing that comes into my head.[65]

Ernst, however, emphasized the book's literary excellence and cultural significance. He submitted copies of positive reviews by F. Scott Fitzgerald and Theodore Dreiser and noted that T. S. Eliot intended to teach the book in his course at Harvard.[66] As for its obscenity, he echoed John Quinn in arguing that *Ulysses* "is far too tedious and labyrinthine and bewildering for the untutored and impressionable who might conceivably be affected by it. Such people would not get beyond the first dozen pages."[67] Admitting that the book "contain[s] occasional episodes of doubtful taste," he said those passages represent a minor percentage of the text and made what would turn out to be a game-changing argument: *Ulysses* must not "be judged on the basis of isolated passages."[68]

Woolsey was sympathetic. He said he found the book moving and that it "bothered, stirred, and troubled" him. Parts of it, he confessed, "almost drove me frantic."[69] Yes, there were sexual passages, but he saw them as integral to Joyce's milieu—turn-of-the-century working-class Dublin. Moreover, they were necessary for getting into the minds of the characters. In a now-famous line, Woolsey asserted that *Ulysses* contained "no dirt for dirt's sake."[70]

Rejecting the "most susceptible reader" test of *Regina v. Hicklin*, Woolsey wrote that "[w]hether a particular book would tend to excite [lustful and impure] impulses and thoughts must be tested by the court's opinion as to its effect on a person with average sex instincts," likening it to the "reasonable man" in the law of torts.[71] He also agreed with Ernst that "reading 'Ulysses' in its entirety, *as a book must be read on such a test as this*, did not tend to excite sexual impulses or lustful thoughts, but that its net effect on them was only that of a somewhat tragic and very powerful commentary on the inner lives of men and women" (italics added).[72]

Bottom line: *Ulysses* "may, therefore, be admitted into the United States."[73]

Woolsey handed down his decision on December 6, 1933. Immediately, Random House's typesetters got to work. A print run of ten thousand copies was issued on January 25, 1934, and it was a hit.[74] Woolsey's opinion appeared at the front of the book, and Joyce supplied a publication history. Yet there was one last hurdle: an appeal to the Court of Appeals for the Second Circuit.

That appeal was heard by a panel of three judges: Billings Learned Hand, one of America's greatest jurists; his cousin, Augustus Noble Hand; and the prosaically named Martin Manton. The government argued that Judge Woolsey had erred in not following *Regina v. Hicklin*, meaning that *Ulysses* should have been deemed obscene on the basis of its undeniably sex-drenched passages.[75] Again, Ernst argued that the book should be considered as a whole.[76]

It was not the first time Ernst had faced off with the Second Circuit over this issue. Four years earlier, he and a couple of colleagues had argued *United States v. Dennett*, which in many ways presaged the *Ulysses* case. Mary Ware Dennett was a writer, suffragette, and reproductive rights activist, as well as a foil of Margaret Sanger, with whom she disagreed on almost everything. (About Sanger, Dennett wrote, "She was a charming vision in a reddish gown.... But oh, her English, and her facts that aren't facts, and her logic that isn't logic, and her amazing faculty for being the whole 'moomunt!'" Sanger replied crisply, "I am inclined to believe that a sanitarium is the proper place for her.")[77]

In 1915, Dennett wrote a pamphlet titled *The Sex Side of Life: An Explanation for Young People*. It describes male and female sexual anatomy (with illustrations), and although it hints at their functions, it does not narrate the act of intercourse. The pamphlet was progressive in some ways ("Don't ever let any one drag you into nasty talk or thought about sex. It is *not* a nasty subject. It should mean everything that is highest and best and happiest in human life") and, in others, a product of its time ("[N]o man is ever proud of his connection with a prostitute and no prostitute is ever proud of her business").[78]

The pamphlet was reprinted in February 1918 as an article in the journal *Medical Review of Reviews*. Dennett also distributed copies privately, usually through the mail. This naturally put her in conflict with the Comstock Act. Hubert Work, the US Postmaster General, declared *The Sex Side of Life* "unmailable" and "indecent," and in 1929, he got her indicted. The trial made national news. Assistant US Attorney James E. Wilkinson called *The Sex Side of Life* "pure and simple smut" and said it would "lead our children not only into the gutter, but below the gutter and into the sewer."[79] It took the jury only forty-five minutes to find her guilty.

On January 15, 1930, Dennett, with the help of Morris Ernst, appealed to the Second Circuit, which reversed her conviction. Augustus Hand delivered the opinion two months later. Acknowledging that "any article dealing with the sex side of life and explaining the functions of the sex organs is capable in some circumstances of arousing lust," he rejected the idea that "the risk of imparting instruction outweighs the disadvantages of leaving [adolescents] to grope about in mystery and morbid curiosity."[80] The Comstock Act, he wrote, "was never thought to bar from the mails everything which *might* stimulate sex impulses. If so, much chaste poetry and fiction, as well as many useful medical works would be under the ban."[81] Therefore, he reasoned, "[a]ny incidental tendency to arouse sex impulses which such a pamphlet may perhaps have is apart from and subordinate to its main effect."[82]

For the *Ulysses* case, Augustus Hand delivered the court's opinion on August 7, 1934. Learned Hand joined it, while Judge Manton dissented. In echoes of his opinion in *Dennett*, Augustus acknowledged that some passages in *Ulysses* "are of a vulgarity that is extreme," but he insisted that others "are of beauty and undoubted distinction," while "the book as a whole has a realism characteristic of the present age."[83] Then he lowered the boom on the prosecution:

It is settled, at least so far as this court is concerned, that works of physiology, medicine, science, and sex instruction are not within the [Tariff Act], though to some extent and among some persons they may tend to promote lustful thoughts.... We think the same immunity should apply to literature as to science, where the presentation, when viewed objectively, is sincere, and the erotic matter is not introduced to promote lust and does not furnish the dominant note of the publication. *The question in each case is whether a publication taken as a whole has a libidinous effect.* The book before us has such portentous length, is written with such evident truthfulness in its depiction of certain types of humanity, and is so little erotic in its result, that it does not fall within the forbidden class (emphasis added).[84]

The *Hicklin* test, in other words, was no more. Books could not be banned on the basis of a dick joke here or there but must be evaluated in their entirety.

Judgment affirmed.

***

The fate of *Ulysses* led to more belletristic battles. One was *Roth v. United States*. Samuel Roth was a publisher and bookseller who had already spent a year in jail for producing pirated works. In the 1950s, he was convicted again, this time on four counts of "the mailing of books, periodicals, and photographs (and circulars advertising some of them) alleged to be 'obscene, lewd, lascivious, filthy and of an indecent character.'"

The Second Circuit Court of Appeals upheld the conviction, as did the United States Supreme Court on June 24, 1957. Writing for the majority, Justice William Brennan, who would write the plurality opinion in *Island Trees v. Pico* twenty-five years later, held that obscenity was not "within the area of constitutionally protected speech or press" and that the First Amendment was not intended to protect every utterance or form of expression, such as materials that were "utterly without redeeming social importance."[85] Rejecting the *Hicklin* test and narrowing Augustus Hand's definition of obscenity, Brennan wrote that the correct test was "whether, to the average person, *applying contemporary community standards*, the dominant theme of the material, taken as a whole, appeals to prurient interest" (emphasis added).[86]

The decision satisfied no one. Conservatives thought it too tolerant of sexual imagery, whereas liberals felt it infringed on the rights of consenting adults.[87] Moreover, unlike the *Ulysses* case, there was no need to consider literary merit. Roth was "widely reviled" for producing magazines such as *American Aphrodite*, the "finest in literary smut," which included

> things like mild erotic line drawings, some piece of long-out-of-print British literature (the "scandalous" seventeenth-century plays of Aphra Behn appear in many issues), a "bawdy" new translation from Chaucer, and something truly shocking, like nude photos of ten-year-old girls taken in Victorian brothels.[88]

Literariness *was* a concern in *People of California v. Lawrence Ferlinghetti*, a California state case decided only four months later. Ferlinghetti was a poet and cofounder of San Francisco's City Lights Bookstore, which became the epicenter of the Beat Movement. City Lights was also a publisher, and on November 1, 1956, it released Allen Ginsberg's *Howl and Other Poems*, a bellwether of American verse.

Ferlinghetti was arrested and charged for his decision to "willfully and lewdly print, publish and sell obscene and indecent writings, papers and books, to wit: 'Howl and Other Poems.'"[89] Ginsberg was no prude: his poems are full of references to illicit drug use as well as heterosexual and homosexual activity. Yet the book was not titillation; it was a cri de coeur. When Ferlinghetti first heard Ginsberg read "Howl," he "knew the world had been waiting for this poem, for this apocalyptic message to be articulated…. The repressive, conformist, racist, homophobic world of the 1950s cried out for it."[90]

There was no jury trial in the case. Rather, the decision fell to municipal court judge Clayton W. Horn, who, using Justice Brennan's language from *Roth*, wrote that "Howl" was not "without redeeming social importance." He noted that the poem "presents a picture of a nightmare world"; that it is "an indictment of those elements in modern society destructive of the best qualities of human nature"; and that it "presents a picture of an individual who is a specific representation of what the author conceives as a general condition."[91] Acknowledging that "[t] here are a number of words used in 'Howl' that are presently considered coarse and vulgar in some circles of the community" and that the prosecutors "state that it is not necessary to use such words and that others would be more palatable to good taste,"[92] he said this doesn't matter. In fact, it would be grievous to enforce conformity. "Would there be any freedom of press or speech," he wrote, "if one must reduce his vocabulary to vapid innocuous euphemism? An author should be real in treating his subject and be allowed to express his thoughts and ideas in his own words."[93]

And, with that, he found Ferlinghetti not guilty.

Horn's ruling led to another high-profile case involving Grove Press, a publisher that specialized in the avant-garde. Grove had accepted Samuel Beckett's *Waiting for Godot* when no other publisher would touch it and had also published early work by Ginsberg, Jack Kerouac, William Burroughs, and other Beats.

In 1959, Grove's owner, Barney Rosset, brought out the first-ever American edition of British writer D. H. Lawrence's 1928 novel *Lady Chatterley's Lover*, which was sure to outrage censors. After the postmaster general declared the book obscene, Rosset sued. His lawyer, Charles Rembar, looked at Justice Brennan's opinion in *Roth v. United States*, which grouped literature into two categories— works with redeeming social importance and works without—and posited a third track: works that are redeeming *and* obscene.[94] It was the conclusion Augustus Hand had reached nearly three decades earlier in the *Ulysses* case.

Would the argument work again?

It would. On July 21, 1959, District Court Judge Frederick Bryan ruled in favor of Grove. Explaining that, in *Roth*, Justice Brennan "did not attempt to apply [obscenity] standards to a specific set of facts" but "merely circumscribed and limited the excluded area in general terms," Bryan set out to fill the void: "[i]t is no less the duty of this court in the case at bar to scrutinize [*Lady Chatterley's Lover*] with great care and to determine for itself whether it is within the constitutional protections afforded by the First Amendment."[95]

After noting all the book's positive reviews, and that it sported a preface by Pulitzer Prize winner and former Librarian of Congress Archibald MacLeish,

Bryan observed that the book "is replete with fine writing and with descriptive passages of rare beauty. There is no doubt of its literary merit."[96] Yes, it included bawdy passages, but even if those passages could "arouse shameful, morbid and lustful sexual desires in the average reader, they are an integral, and to the author a necessary part of the development of theme, plot and character."[97] Quoting Judge Woolsey, Bryan ruled that the book is not "dirt for dirt's sake" and may therefore not be restricted. A year later, the Second Circuit agreed.

Lady Chatterley's Lover was also the subject of a six-day jury trial in the United Kingdom, which ended in an even more sensational exoneration for its British publisher, Penguin Books. Nowadays, the un-banning is seen as "a crucial step in liberalising the country's cultural landscape, encouraging frank public discussion of sexual behaviour that meant sex was no longer a taboo in art and entertainment. It also shifted views on major human rights issues including the legalisation of homosexuality and abortion, the abolition of the death penalty and divorce reform."[98] (Quite a legacy for a book that F. R. Leavis, who was otherwise Lawrence's most enthusiastic literary champion, called "repellent," "insufferable," and "a bad novel.")[99]

And the cases kept pouring in. After his victory vis-à-vis *Lady Chatterley's Lover*, Barney Rosset tried again, this time with Henry Miller's autobiographical novel *Tropic of Cancer*, which US Customs had banned in 1934. Some of it will make readers tug at their collars, such as this meditation by the narrator (also called "Henry Miller"):

O Tania, where now is that warm cunt of yours, those fat, heavy garters, those soft, bulging thighs? There is a bone in my prick six inches long. I will ream out every wrinkle in your cunt, Tania, big with seed. I will send you home to your Sylvester with an ache in your belly and your womb turned inside out. Your Sylvester! Yes, he knows how to build a fire, but I know how to inflame a cunt. I shoot hot bolts into you, Tania, I make your ovaries incandescent.[100]

Rosset's 1961 edition was an immediate best seller and a target for lawsuits. By the time the Supreme Court heard an appeal from a Florida district court, the book was involved in more than one hundred cases. *Grove Press, Inc. v. Gerstein* was decided the same day, June 22, 1964, as another case, *Jacobellis v. Ohio*, which involved a theater manager, Nico Jacobellis, showing the 1958 French film *The Lovers* about a dinner party that turns sexual. In both, the court found that the works in question were not obscene.

Jacobellis is the fuller opinion. In it, the court expands its obscenity definition from *Roth*, emphasizing that a work may not be banned unless it is "*utterly* without redeeming social importance" (emphasis added).[101] This means that if a work has any amount of literary or artistic value, then it must be allowed. (*Jacobellis* is also the more famous opinion—one of the most famous, in fact, due to Justice Potter Stewart's obscenity definition in his concurrence: "I know it when I see it.")[102]

Two years later, the justices fiddled with the definition again. In *Memoirs v. Massachusetts* (1966), a case in which that old offensive standby, *Fanny Hill*, was again at issue, the court set up a three-part obscenity test: "(a) the dominant theme of the material taken as a whole appeals to a prurient interest in sex; (b) the material is patently offensive because it affronts contemporary community standards relating to the description or representation of sexual matters, and (c) the material is utterly without redeeming social value."[103]

Finally, in *Miller v. California* (1973), an appeal of the conviction of another so-called smut peddler, Marvin Miller (no relation to Henry), Chief Justice Warren Burger articulated what is pretty much still the law today:

> The basic guidelines for the trier of fact must be: (a) whether 'the average person, applying contemporary community standards' would find that the work, taken as a whole, appeals to the prurient interest [as in *Roth*], (b) whether the work depicts or describes, in a patently offensive way, sexual conduct specifically defined by the applicable state law, and (c) whether the work, taken as a whole, lacks serious literary, artistic, political, or scientific value.[104]

Burger also invalidated the "utterly without redeeming social value" language as part of any constitutional analysis. It was a 5–4 decision, indicating a significant rift among the justices.

Island Trees v. Pico would turn that rift into a gorge.

***

These rulings created an opening for writers to indulge, in the words of Kirk Curnutt, "in unprecedented spurts of naughty words and metaphorical flights of fleshy fancy."[105] Soon, sex was everywhere. In 1969, Philip Roth (no relation to Samuel) gave the world *Portnoy's Complaint*, which the *New Yorker* called "one of the dirtiest books ever published."[106] A year later appeared Judy Blume's *Are You There God? It's Me, Margaret*, which, for its attention to sex, periods, and other teenage fixations, isn't just a young adult classic: it helped create the genre. TV writer Gail Parent's novel *Sheila Levine Is Dead and Living in New York* (1972) was an American precursor to *Bridget Jones's Diary*, a genre perfected by Erica Jong in her debut novel, *Fear of Flying* (1973), which critic Jane Kamensky called "a book so sexually frank that you may have found it hidden in your mother's underwear drawer."[107]

Even narratives that weren't about sex had sexually charged passages. Peter Benchley's *Jaws* (1974), for instance, has an entire subplot that is absent from the movie: an affair between boy-next-door Matt Hooper and Sheriff Brody's wife, Ellen. And that doesn't take into account nonfiction explorations such as

The Sensuous Woman (1969), *Everything You Always Wanted to Know about Sex** (**But Were Afraid to Ask*) (1969), *Our Bodies, Ourselves* (1970), *The Sensuous Man* (1971), *The Joy of Sex* (1972), the collaborations of William Masters and Virginia Johnson, and Gay Talese's *Thy Neighbor's Wife* (1981), a journalistic deep dive into America's sexual revolution.

The backlash came in the form of the so-called New Right, a movement that celebrated the free market and lamented the decline of traditional social values and roles. Tired of hippies and protests, plus a government that, in their view, overindulged poor people and minorities, these neoconservatives elected Richard Nixon in 1968 and were delighted when his administration began undoing the progress of the previous decade. Taxes, speed limits, environmental regulations, affirmative action, school desegregation—seemingly every government action was derided as "overreach." In 1979, political conservatism and Christianity, which had long formed parallel tracks across America, merged when Jerry Falwell and Paul Weyrich founded the Moral Majority.

Progress or retreat. Enlightenment or eschewal. *Star Trek* or *Little House on the Prairie*. Will the real United States please stand up?

The Supreme Court, too, suffered from this identity crisis. None of the aforementioned cases—*Roth, Jacobellis, Memoirs v. Massachusetts, Miller v. California*—was unanimous or anywhere close. In fact, some were decided not by the majority of justices but by a plurality, a kind of judicial Cold War that results in less-enforceable verdicts (*Island Trees v. Pico* would be decided this way). Dissenting justices wrote more, and sharper, opinions, questioning what they saw as a developing anything-goes jurisprudence.

And there were cases where censorship still won—cases such as *Ginzburg v. New York* (1968). Ralph Ginzburg (no relation to Allen Ginsberg) was convicted in Philadelphia of mailing three obscene publications: *Eros*, a hardcover magazine of expensive format; *Liaison*, a biweekly newsletter; and *The Housewife's Handbook on Selective Promiscuity*. The Third Circuit Court of Appeals affirmed the conviction, as did the Supreme Court. Writing again for the majority, Justice Brennan ruled that the publications were suffused with the "leer of the sensualist" because they discussed sexual concerns "without restraint" and engaged in "pandering," which he defined as "the business of purveying textual or graphic matter openly advertised to appeal to the erotic interest of their customers."[108] In other words, it wasn't just the publications themselves but Ginzburg's intent—his "deliberate representation of [the] publications as erotically arousing"—that could be used as evidence to establish illegal obscenity.[109]

Such turmoil set the stage for book banning's trial of the century.

Notes

1 Anthony Aycock, "Desperately Seeking Sources," *Missouri Review*, October 20, 2023, https://missourireview.com/desperately-seeking-sources-by-anthony-aycock/.

2 Michele Ingrassia, "Board Chief Denies Abolishing Paper," *Newsday* (Nassau ed.), October 1, 1976, 17.

3 Ibid.

4 Robert E. Kessler, "Island Trees Kills Student Newspaper," *Newsday* (Nassau ed.), September 30, 1976, 3.

5 "Book Banning Remains a Threat," *Unscrewed* 14, no. 2 (1983): 3.

6 Ingrassia, "Board Chief Denies Abolishing Paper," 17.

7 Robert E. Kessler, "Island Trees Lifts Its Ban on Paper," *Newsday* (Nassau ed.), October 28, 1976, 19.

8 Aycock, "Desperately Seeking Sources."

9 Robert Sarwak, "The Catholic Index of Forbidden Books: A Brief History," *Intellectual Freedom Blog*, February 21, 2018, https://www.oif.ala.org/catholic-index-forbidden-books-brief-history/.

10 Patrick Chinnery, "John Lilburne," *First Amendment Encyclopedia*, July 2, 2024, https://firstamendment.mtsu.edu/article/john-lilburne/.

11 Janet Clare, "The Censorship of the Deposition Scene in *Richard II*," *Review of English Studies* 41, no. 161 (1990): 89–94.

12 Colleen Connolly, "How America's First Banned Book Survived and Became an Anti-Authoritarian Icon," *Smithsonian Magazine*, October 2, 2023, https://www.smithsonianmag.com/history/how-americas-first-banned-book-survived-and-became-an-anti-authoritarian-icon-180982971/.

13 Daniel Crown, "The Price of Suffering: William Pynchon and The Meritorious Price of Our Redemption," *Berfrois*, December 10, 2015, https://www.berfrois.com/2015/12/the-price-of-suffering-william-pynchon-and-the-meritorious-price-of-our-redemption/.

14 An Act for the Suppression of Trade in, and Circulation of, obscene Literature and Articles of immoral Use, 17 Stat. 598 (1873).

15 Paul D. Buchanan, *The American Women's Rights Movement: A Chronology of Events and of Opportunities from 1600 to 2008* (Branden Books, 2009).

16 David Hadju, *The Ten-Cent Plague: The Great Comic-Book Scare and How It Changed America* (Picador, 2009), 264.

17 Adam Laats, "Moms for Liberty Is Riding High. It Should Beware What Comes Next," *Slate*, August 29, 2023, https://slate.com/human-interest/2023/08/moms-for-liberty-parental-rights.html.

18 Ibid.

19 Lisa Hix, "Walt Whitman—Patriotic Poet, Gay Iconoclast, or Shrewd Marketing Ploy?," *Collectors Weekly*, May 3, 2016, https://www.collectorsweekly.com/articles/walt-whitman/.

20 Frederick P. Hebb Jr., "When Boston Censored Walt Whitman," *New York Times Magazine*, June 19, 1927, 19.

21 Ibid.

22 Paul S. Boyer, "Book Censorship in the Twenties," *American Quarterly* 15, no. 1 (1963): 3–24.

23 Hebb, "When Boston Censored Walt Whitman," 19.

24 Ibid.

25 Justin Kaplan, *Walt Whitman: A Life* (Simon & Schuster, 1980).

26 Boyer, "Book Censorship in the Twenties," 5.

27 Ibid.

28 Ibid., 6.

29 Paul Boytinck, "'Hatrack': A Chronology and Narrative History of This Celebrated Legal Case," *Menckeniana* 222 (2018): 1–19.

30 Anthony Aycock, "Not Just the Dog-Eared Pages," *History News Network*, June 3, 2025, https://www.hnn.us/article/the-literary-opinion-of-the-court.

31 Herbert Asbury, "Hatrack," *American Mercury*, April 1926, 571.

32 Boytnick, "'Hatrack,'" 5.

33 Ibid.

34 Ibid., 6.

35 "Mencken Assails Boston's Book Ban," *Baltimore Sun*, March 13, 1927, 20.

36 F. Lauriston Bullard, "Boston's Book Ban Likely to Live Long," *New York Times*, April 28, 1929, 7.

37 "Boston Book Ban Tightens," *Los Angeles Times*, April 15, 1927, 5.

38 Bullard, "Boston's Book Ban," 7.

39 Greg Daugherty, "Seven Famous People Who Missed the Titanic," *Smithsonian Magazine*, March 1, 2012, https://www.smithsonianmag.com/history/seven-famous-people-who-missed-the-titanic-101902418/.

40 "The Genius," University of Illinois Press, https://www.press.uillinois.edu/books/?id=c031007.

41 Donald L. Miller, *City of the Century* (Simon & Schuster, 1996), 263.

42 Jolie Sheffer, "Theodore Dreiser's Sister Carrie and the Urbanization of Chicago," *Digital Public Library of America*, https://dp.la/primary-source-sets/theodore-dreiser-s-sister-carrie-and-the-urbanization-of-chicago.

43 "Publishers Test Boston Book Ban," *New York Times*, April 17, 1927, 23.

44 Donald Friede, *The Mechanical Angel* (Knopf, 1948).

45 Aycock, "Not Just the Dog-Eared Pages."

46 "Dreiser Novel Sale Costs $100 Fine," *New York Herald Tribune*, April 23, 1927, 5.

47 "Publisher Loses Boston Test Case," *New York Times*, April 23, 1927, 14.

48 "Darrow Reads to Jury Part of Dreiser's Work," *New York Times*, April 18, 1929, 2.

49 Ibid.

50 Paul Kemeny, *The New England Watch and Ward Society* (Oxford University Press, 2018), 271.

51 Ibid.

52 Aycock, "Not Just the Dog-Eared Pages."

53 James Joyce, *Ulysses* (Shakespeare and Company, 1922), 349.

54 Richard and Janis Londraville, "The Mighty John Quinn, Defender of *Ulysses*," *Irish America*, June 15, 2017, https://www.irishamerica.com/2017/06/the-mighty-john-quinn-defender-of-ulysses/.

55 Ibid.

56 Holly Baggett, "The Trials of Margaret Anderson and Jane Heap," in *A Living of Words: American Women in Print Culture*, ed. Susan Albertine (University of Tennessee Press, 1995), 169–88.

57 Londraville, "The Mighty John Quinn."

58 Douglas O. Linder, "The Ulysses Trials: An Account," https://www.famous-trials.com/ulysses/2664-the-ulysses-trials-an-account.

59 Ibid.

60 Tariff Act of 1930, 46 Stat. 590 (1930).

61 Linder, "The Ulysses Trials."

62 *United States v. One Obscene Book Entitled "Married Love,"* 48 F. 2d 821 (S.D.N.Y. 1931).

63 *United States v. One Book, Entitled "Contraception,"* 51 F. 2d 525 (S.D.N.Y. 1931).

64 *Regina v. Hicklin*, 11 Cox C.C. 19 (1868).

65 Joyce, *Ulysses*, 729.

66 Linder, "The Ulysses Trials."

67 Ibid.

68   Ibid.

69   Ibid.

70   *United States v. One Book Called "Ulysses,"* 5 F. Supp. 182, 184 (S.D.N.Y. 1933).

71   Ibid.

72   Ibid., 185.

73   Ibid.

74   Linder, "The Ulysses Trials."

75   Ibid.

76   Ibid.

77   Peter C. Engelman, "The Rivalry between Margaret Sanger and Mary Ware Dennett," *ProQuest History Vault*, https://www.sc.pages04.net/lp/43888/562698/Sanger_Dennett%20essay_1.pdf.

78   Mary Dennett, "The Sex Side of Life: An Explanation for Young People," *Internet Archive*, https://archive.org/stream/thesexsideoflife31732gut/31732-8.txt.

79   Sharon Spaulding, "The Sex Education Pamphlet That Sparked a Landmark Censorship Case," *Smithsonian Magazine*, September 30, 2021, https://www.smithsonianmag.com/history/the-sex-education-pamphlet-that-sparked-a-landmark-censorship-case-180978754/.

80   *United States v. Dennett*, 39 F. 2d 564, 568 (2d Cir. 1930).

81   Ibid., 596.

82   Ibid.

83   *United States v. One Book Entitled "Ulysses,"* 72 F. 2d 705, 706 (2d Cir. 1934).

84   Ibid., 707.

85   354 U.S. 476, 484 (1957).

86   Ibid., 489.

87   Richard Pacelle Jr., "Roth v. United States (1957)," *First Amendment Encyclopedia*, January 13, 2025, https://firstamendment.mtsu.edu/article/roth-v-united-states/.

88   Dan Piepenbring, "Smuthound," *The Paris Review*, June 24, 2014, https://www.theparisreview.org/blog/2014/06/24/smuthound/.

89   "People of the State of California v. Lawrence Ferlinghetti," *FIRE*, https://www.thefire.org/research-learn/people-state-california-v-lawrence-ferlinghetti.

90   Lawrence Ferlinghetti, "'Howl' at the Frontiers," in *Howl on Trial: The Battle for Free Expression*, ed. Bill Morgan and Nancy Peters (City Lights, 2006), 1.

91   "People of the State of California v. Lawrence Ferlinghetti."

92   Ibid.

93   Ibid.

94   Maureen Corrigan, *Banned Books, Burned Books: Forbidden Literary Works: Guidebook* (Wondrium, 2023), 21.

95   *Grove Press, Inc. v. Christenberry*, 175 F. Supp. 488, 494 (S.D.N.Y. 1959).

96   Ibid., 500.

97   Ibid.

98   Catherine Baksi, "Lady Chatterley's Legal Case: How the Book Changed the Meaning of Obscene," *The Guardian*, August 1, 2019, https://www.theguardian.com/law/2019/aug/01/lady-chatterleys-legal-case-how-the-book-changed-the-meaning-of-obscene.

99   David Ellis, "F. R. Leavis," in *D. H. Lawrence in Context*, ed. Andrew Harrison (Cambridge University Press, 2018), 291.

100   Henry Miller, *Tropic of Cancer* (Grove Press, 1961), 5.

101   *Jacobellis v. Ohio*, 378 U.S. 184, 191 (1964).

102   Ibid.

103   *Memoirs v. Massachusetts*, 383 U.S. 413 (1966).

104   *Miller v. California*, 413 U.S. 15, 24 (1973).

105 Kurt Curnutt, "Introduction," in *American Literature in Transition: 1970–1980*, ed. Kurt Curnutt (Cambridge University Press, 2018), 12.

106 Chris Cox, "Portnoy's Complaint—Still Shocking at 40," *The Guardian*, September 7, 2009, https://www.theguardian.com/books/booksblog/2009/sep/07/portnoys-complaint-shocking-49.

107 Jane Kamensky, "'Fear of Flying' Is 50. What Happened to Its Dream of Freedom through Sex?," *New York Times*, November 9, 2023, https://www.nytimes.com/2023/11/09/books/review/erica-jong-fear-of-flying.html.

108 *Ginzburg v. United States*, 383 U.S. 463 (1966).

109 Ibid., 470.

3 The Dirty Dozen (Minus One)

n the fall of 1976, Steven Pico stood at a crossroads. He was a senior. Student body president. Editor of the *Bulldog*. He was well-liked and had a good relationship with the school board. Now, that relationship was in danger of fraying. He knew that a lot of people in the district sided with the board—70 percent, according to one poll.[1] "My parents heard from anonymous callers who said I would not receive scholarships for college if I pursued the case," he recalled in a 2013 interview.[2] One board member even hinted that Pico could be sued personally. No one would have blamed him if he had thought, *Screw this. Let someone else handle it. It's not my fight.*

Except it was. It's everyone's fight, he told himself, or it should be. So, fight he did, starting with the American Library Association (ALA).

You might assume that the ALA was a wellspring of anticensorship activity from the moment of its founding in 1876. In fact, it was not. "A review of library literature reveals relatively few articles on intellectual freedom prior to the 1930s," wrote Judith Krug, former director of the ALA Office of Intellectual Freedom, "and many of the articles that did appear supported censorship and only quibbled over the degree and nature of it."[3]

Things changed in 1938, when a Des Moines, Iowa, public library adopted a "Bill of Rights for the Free Public Library" written by its director, Forrest Spaulding, in response to growing concerns about the worldwide rise of suppression of free speech.[4] The following year, John Steinbeck's novel *The Grapes of Wrath* was banned—and burned—in a number of places, including Kern County, California, the endpoint of the Joad family's migration. Some Kern County residents were angry at Steinbeck's portrayal of them as unsupportive rednecks. In August 1939, by a vote of 4 to 1, the county board of supervisors approved a resolution banning *The Grapes of Wrath* from county libraries and schools.[5] In a failed effort to overturn the ban, librarian Gretchen Knief wrote a letter to the board, arguing that "banning books is so utterly hopeless and futile. Ideas don't die because a book is forbidden reading."[6]

Under increasing pressure to take a stand, the ALA adapted the Des Moines statement into its first-ever Library's Bill of Rights. The document doesn't mention censorship outright, urging instead that "[a]s far as available material permits, all sides of questions on which differences of opinion exist should be represented fairly and adequately in the books and other reading matter purchased for public use."[7] A 1944 revision made a less ambiguous but still unsatisfying correction before a bona fide prohibition appeared in 1948: "Censorship of books, urged or practiced by volunteer arbiters of morals or political opinion or by organizations that would establish a coercive concept of Americanism, must be challenged by libraries in maintenance of their responsibility to provide public information and enlightenment through the printed word."[8]

In 1953, the ALA created another seminal document, the Freedom to Read Statement. Claiming that "parts of the country are working to remove books from sale, to censor textbooks, to label 'controversial' books, to distribute lists of 'objectionable' books or authors, and to purge libraries," it exhorted librarians to circulate "the widest diversity of views and expressions, including those that are unorthodox, unpopular, or considered dangerous by the majority."[9] A decade later, in 1967, the association's metamorphosis from censorship spectator to free speech champion was complete with the creation of the Office of Intellectual Freedom.

***

If your idea of Steven Pico is one who was looking to rush into a fray, any fray, think again. In fact, he was a reluctant paladin. He knew that he lacked the backing of a large part of the Island Trees community. Yet he feared—no, he *knew*—the school board was mollycoddling students.

He talked to the American Library Association and was told that it didn't have the resources for what could be a long legal fight. Then he tried the American Civil Liberties Union (ACLU). Finally, he ended up at the New York Civil Liberties Union, whose lawyers asked him to find a few more students to join him as plaintiffs. These ended up being fellow high schoolers Russell Rieger, Jacqueline Gold, and Glenn Yarris, whose parents, Richard and Edna, were leaders of the Right to Read Association.

The fifth and final plaintiff, eighth grader Paul Sochinski, was a strategic recruitment by Steven. Because Paul wouldn't finish high school for five more years, he would likely still be in school if and when the case made it to the Supreme Court, thereby nullifying the issue of mootness. (A case becomes "moot," or no longer a case, when the issue behind it stops being "live," which would happen when Steven and his friends were no longer Island Trees students and therefore, unencumbered by the district's policies.)[10]

The five students filed their complaint (i.e., the document that begins a lawsuit) on January 4, 1977, announcing it at a press conference attended by their attorneys, NYCLU dignitaries, and Kurt Vonnegut himself. Jacqueline Gold articulated the stakes of the case: "Some people learn from the books. Levittown is a community where we don't see much of what is in those books…. And there are no blacks in Levittown. The board wants to shelter us."[11] Vonnegut, a veteran of book bans, was more taciturn: "I'm distressed that this should happen in my country."[12] Board president Richard Ahrens took a pugnacious tack: "We intend to go the whole route, as far as we have to go…. The issue here is not just the books, but who decides what's best for Island Trees: the parents or the NYCLU. We believe that every district in the country has a stake in this."[13]

Following the press conference, most of the plaintiffs settled back into being students, leaving the legal work to the lawyers. Not Steven Pico. After high school, he enrolled at Haverford, a Quaker college three miles west of Philadelphia, graduating in 1981 with degrees in political science and English literature while also remaining integral to the case. He spoke to reporters. Did PBS interviews. Appeared on *Donahue* and the *Today* show. Took part in a PEN America-sponsored event called "Forbidden Books," in which famous authors—Toni Morrison, John Irving, Erica Jong, E. L. Doctorow—read passages from challenged books.[14] One was L. Frank Baum's *The Wonderful Wizard of Oz*, which, along with its sequels, had endured a fifteen-year ban from the Detroit Public Library "because they give the wrong approach to life."[15] Its excerpts were read by Margaret Hamilton, the movie's Wicked Witch of the West.

One thing Steven doesn't discuss a lot is himself. It makes him uncomfortable. Every time I asked about his family, his job, or his personal life, he politely demurred. He said he has been offered book deals and movie offers, all of which he turned down. What matters to him, what has always mattered, is those eleven banished texts. They are what he wants to talk about.

Fine. Let's talk about them.

Oliver La Farge, *Laughing Boy* (1929)

Born in 1901 to affluent parents in New York City, La Farge could easily have become the next Henry James. As a boy, he attended the prestigious Groton School in Massachusetts, followed by Harvard University. His grandfather, the artist John La Farge, was a friend of James's.[16] When Oliver became a writer, however, he eschewed drawing room novels about well-heeled white Britons and Americans.

Instead, he wrote about Indians.

In 1924, while still a student at Harvard, La Farge went on the second of two archaeological trips to the Lukachukai Mountains in northeast Arizona. The mountains are located in the Navajo Nation, and La Farge spent many hours talking to Navajo people. When the expedition was over, La Farge and two friends stayed behind, intending to ride horses, *City Slickers*-style, from Lukachukai to the Grand Canyon.

From these experiences, he forged his first novel, *Laughing Boy*, whose titular character, a young Navajo man, falls for Slim Girl, who had been raised by white Americans. The two marry, but the tribe doesn't approve of Slim Girl's worldliness. Moreover, she is hiding something: a double life as an "escort" for white men. When Laughing Boy catches her with a client, she explains that, years ago, a white man pretended to love her in exchange for sex. He abandoned her when she got pregnant, and when she lost the baby, her only solace came from local prostitutes. Eventually, she joined their coterie.

Laughing Boy won the Pulitzer Prize in 1930, beating out other seemingly more deserving—certainly more famous—novels: Thomas Wolfe's *Look Homeward, Angel*, Ernest Hemingway's *A Farewell to Arms*, and William Faulkner's *The Sound and the Fury*. It was praised for its rich and layered portrayal of Native people. "Reviews were uniformly friendly and encouraging,"[17] wrote D'Arcy McNickle in *Indian Man: A Life of Oliver La Farge*, who thought the key to the book's success was its blending of the exotic, little-known world of the Navajos with an exciting story. "The blending was done so skillfully," wrote McNickle, "that the socialite sitting in her townhouse and the urban literary critic could read the narrative and have a sense of participation."[18]

One era's rich and layered, however, can be a later era's banal and patronizing. The Laguna Pueblo writer Leslie Marmon Silko writes that La Farge, though he clearly cared about the Navajo, nevertheless got them wrong: "As an expression of anything Navajo, especially with relation to Navajo emotions and behavior, the novel was a failure. And for the non-Navajo or non-Indian, it is worse than a failure: it is a lie."[19]

In an appendix to his dissenting opinion in the *Island Trees v. Pico* ruling, Supreme Court Justice Lewis F. Powell Jr. included a list of "excerpts which led the Board to look into the educational suitability of the books in question." What were those excerpts from *Laughing Boy*? There were only two, both of which discuss Slim Girl in the most anodyne terms:

- "I'll tell you, she is all bad; for two bits she will do the worst thing."
- "I was frightened when he wanted me to lie with him, but he made me feel all right. He knew all about how to make women forget themselves, that man."[20]

Excerpts from the other books are a bit more startling, as we shall see.

Richard Wright, *Black Boy* (1945)

Wright's autobiography of growing up poor in the South and then moving to Chicago, where he became a writer as well as a member of the Communist Party, is a classic, an instant best seller that became a Book-of-the-Month Club selection and is still in print nearly eighty years later.

It has also had a target on its spine since day one. In 1945, US Senator Theodore Bilbo, a Mississippian who admitted to membership in the Ku Klux Klan and once sponsored a bill aiming to deport twelve million Black Americans to Liberia, called *Black Boy* "the dirtiest, filthiest, lousiest, most obscene piece of writing that I have ever seen in print" before observing that "it comes from a Negro, and you cannot expect any better from a person of his type."[21]

Over the years, *Black Boy* has been banned or challenged many times, including in Texas, Michigan, Florida, Louisiana, Tennessee—and, of course, New York. Justice Powell's list includes Wright's childhood taunting of the Jewish owners of a neighborhood grocery store:

We black children—seven, eight, and nine years of age—used to run to the Jew's store and shout:

Jew, Jew, Jew
What do you chew?

Or we would form a long line and weave back and forth in front of the door, singing:

Jew, Jew
Two for five
That's what keeps
Jew alive.

Or we would chant:

Bloody Christ killers
Never trust a Jew
Bloody Christ killers
What won't a Jew do?

To one of the red headed Jewish boys we sang:

Red head
Jewish bread
Five cents
A Jewish head.

To the fat Jewish woman we sneered:

Red, white, and blue
Your pa was a Jew
Your ma a dirty Dago
What the hell is you?[22]

Wright experienced this sort of racism himself, of course. His lifelong battle with it is part of what makes his memoir compelling. In one of the most famous instances, Wright was living in Memphis, Tennessee, in the mid-1920s. He arrived at work one day to hear his white coworkers denouncing an article by H. L. Mencken in the local paper. "I wondered what on earth this Mencken had done to call down upon him the scorn of the South," Wright mused.[23] The Baltimore-born journalist had published numerous books by then, including his classic *The American Language*. Wright wanted to read some of it, and the library downtown seemed like the perfect place.

Except Blacks were not welcome within its walls.

Despairing that none of his coworkers will help him, Wright remembered Mr. Falk, a man "whose attitude did not fit into an anti-Negro category, for I had heard the white men refer to him as a 'Pope lover.' He was an Irish Catholic and was hated by the white southerners."[24] Falk lent Wright his library card, but there was a demeaning stipulation: Wright must pretend he was picking up books for Falk, as his servant. It was the only way Wright could access the library.

The scheme worked, and Wright read book after book, awakening to a world that was threatening to pass him by:

I now knew what being a Negro meant. I could endure the hunger and I had learned to live with hate. But to feel that there were feelings denied me, that the very breath of life itself was beyond my reach, that more than anything else hurt, wounded me. I had a new hunger. In buoying me up, reading also cast me down, made me see what was possible, what I had missed.[25]

Bernard Malamud, *The Fixer* (1966)

Russia, 1911. A Christian boy's mutilated corpse is found in a cave near Kyiv in modern-day Ukraine. Menahem Mendel Beilis, a Jewish factory worker, is falsely arrested by the Czarist secret police and accused of ritually murdering a Christian boy to use his blood in baking matzo for Passover. Despite two years of imprisonment and torture, Beilis refuses to implicate himself or other Jews.

Or:

Russia, 1911. Yakov Bok, a Jewish handyman whose marriage has ended, decides to leave his shtetl and seek his fortune in the wider world. He goes to Kyiv in modern-day Ukraine and tries to help people, but his kind gestures backfire. He offers a ride to an old woman, and his cart breaks down. He helps an older Jewish man, and observers turn against him, falsely accusing him of murdering a Christian boy. Eventually, Bok is arrested and held for two years, awaiting trial at the hands of Russian officials bent on the destruction of Jews. When the trial comes, Bok is friendless and broken, at a loss to understand his role in a cruel universe.

One of the above stories is true. The other is the plot of *The Fixer*, which won the National Book Award and the Pulitzer Prize and is considered one of America's finest books by one of America's finest authors. Can you guess which is which?

Go on, guess. I'll wait …

Ready? *The Fixer* is story number two, most of which takes place after Bok's arrest and focuses on the case against him, the deterioration of his mental state, and how both connect to wider social ills.

Malamud is part of the pantheon of Jewish-American writers that includes Philip Roth, Joseph Heller, Norman Mailer, and Saul Bellow. An earlier novel, *The Magic Barrel*, also won the National Book Award; and *The Natural*, his first book, became the classic film starring Glenn Close and Robert Redford.

The Fixer includes a generous helping of the F-word, which was likely one reason the Island Trees board banned it. Justice Powell's list also mentions two other lines, no doubt chosen for their blasphemous overtones:

- "No more noise out of you or I'll shoot your Jew cock off."
- "Also, there's a lot of fucking in the Old Testament, so how is that religious?"[26]

As for Mendel Beilis, he was acquitted following a 1913 trial. The story was imperial Russia's Dreyfus affair, a staggering expression of anti-Semitism and one catalyst of the public outrage that led to the Bolshevik Revolution. Beilis himself became an international celebrity, moving to the United States in 1921 and publishing a memoir called *The Story of My Sufferings*. He died in Saratoga Springs, New York, in 1934.

After *The Fixer* came out, Beilis's son David Beilis wrote to Malamud, accusing him of plagiarizing Beilis's memoir and complaining that Malamud had debased the memory of his father by depicting Yakov Bok as "an angry, foul-mouthed, cuckolded, friendless, childless blasphemer."[27] Malamud wrote back, assuring David Beilis that he saw the latter's parents and the Boks as nothing alike, though history has obscured this separation. These days, the two stories, one fact, the other fiction, are, in the words of historian Albert Lindermann, "inextricably fused (and confused)."[28]

Piri Thomas, *Down These Mean Streets* (1967)

In his classic 1945 essay "The Simple Art of Murder," Raymond Chandler, author of *The Big Sleep*, *The Long Good-bye*, and other detective classics, wrote, "Down these mean streets a man must go who is not himself mean, who is neither tarnished nor afraid."[29] Twenty-two years later, Piri Thomas borrowed the first four words of this line for his autobiography.

The son of a Puerto Rican mother and a Black Cuban father, Thomas chronicled his childhood in Spanish Harlem, his family's move to Long Island, his use of heroin (or "horse"), his stint in the merchant marine, and his seven-year prison stay for armed robbery and assaulting a police officer. Racism, poverty, and violence formed its triple helix theme. The book was a best seller, joining works such as Claude Brown's *Manchild in the Promised Land* and *The Autobiography of Malcolm X* in awakening white America to the squalor and danger of minority life in big cities.

The book has earned decades of praise from writers. Novelist Daniel Stern called it "another stanza in the passionate poem of color and color-hatred being written today."[30] Poet Martin Espada said, "Because he became a writer, many of us became writers. Before 'Down These Mean Streets,' we could not find a book by a Puerto Rican writer in the English language about the experience of that community, in that voice, with that tone and subject matter."[31]

Curiously, Justice Powell included no excerpts from *Down These Mean Streets* in his appendix. Yet it had to be Thomas's tone—raw, anguished, hostile to boundaries—plus his references to violence, not to mention homosexual encounters, that landed the book on Island Trees' banned list.

Nor were Ahrens and his colleagues the first to feel this way. On March 31, 1971, four years prior to Island Trees, the board of Community School District 25 in New York voted 5–3 to remove all the copies from its junior high libraries, not because it offers a gritty view of life in New York's Puerto Rican community but "because the portrayal includes vulgarities and descriptions of sexual acts."[32]

The resulting lawsuit was dismissed by Chief District Court Judge Jacob Mishler. On appeal, the Second Circuit Court, in a departure from its *Ulysses* decision, called *Down These Mean Streets* "depressing, ugly and violent," observing that "[a]cts of criminal violence, sex, normal and perverse, as well as episodes of drug shooting are graphically described."[33] It then upheld the ban, reasoning that

> Since we are dealing not with the collection of a public book store but with the library of a public junior high school, evidently some authorized person or body has to make a determination as to what the library collection will

be. It is predictable that no matter what choice of books may be made by whatever segment of academe, some other person or group may well dissent. The ensuing shouts of book burning, witch hunting and violation of academic freedom hardly elevate this intramural strife to first amendment constitutional proportions.[34]

Besides, the court argued, no real harm was done. Yes, a book was yanked from a library, "but the librarian has not been penalized, and the teacher is still free to discuss the Barrio and its problems in the classroom."[35]

Desmond Morris, *The Naked Ape* (1967)

Remember that 2006 essay "What Shamu Taught Me about a Happy Marriage"? It caused a stir when it was published, becoming "one of the most emailed New York Times articles ever," according to the *Times*, and earning its author, Amy Sutherland, a book deal.[36] The essay describes how Sutherland used animal training techniques to erase her husband's irksome habits. For instance, using the technique of "approximations"—rewarding the small steps toward learning a whole new behavior—she got her husband to stop leaving dirty socks on the floor.[37] The concept of "incompatible behavior" ended his practice of crowding her while she cooked: she assigned him to chop vegetables, the theory being that he couldn't do that *and* hover.[38] Most helpful was "least reinforcing syndrome," which is when the trainer makes no reaction to an animal's bad behavior.[39] (Guess who started finding his own wallet and keys when Sutherland pulled that one?)

Four decades earlier, another writer compared humans to animals, though not for laughs. "There are one hundred and ninety-three living species of monkeys and apes," began Desmond Morris in his now-notorious study. "One hundred and ninety-two of them are covered with hair. The exception is a naked ape self-named *Homo sapiens*."[40] An Oxford-trained zoologist and ethnologist—as well as, oddly, a surrealist painter—Morris believed that, despite our cultural and scientific achievements, humans were actually just apes. Our behavior, therefore, could be better understood by comparing it to that of other apes.

Specifically, Morris paid a lot of attention to humans' sexual behavior, arguing that it serves a far greater purpose than mere reproduction. For example, face-to-face mating, though all but unknown in the animal kingdom, was for Morris a key method that couples use to maintain loyalty. His descriptions of sex acts are about as bawdy as Fermat's theorem: "This broadening of the penis results in the female's external genitals being subjected to much more pulling and pushing during the performance of pelvic thrusts. With each inward thrust of the penis, the clitoral region is pulled downwards and then with each withdrawal, it moves up again."[41]

Yet, according to Justice Powell's list, such passages formed the basis of the Island Trees ban.

So, most likely, did the entire premise of *The Naked Ape*. Despite having nearly one hundred years to get used to it, by the 1970s, many Americans were still troubled by the idea of evolution. "Fierce anti-evolutionary rhetoric," wrote University of Florida zoologist Ronald Edwards in 2016, "although practically devoid of content or even relevance, became infused with the force of anti-communism and patriotism, as well as real money from televangelism and church-centered community organizing and was now feared and courted as a genuine political force."[42] Such rhetoric must have reached Morris, who addressed it in 1983 in his preface to a new edition of *The Naked Ape*. And he didn't stint on the snark:

> I knew that some people resented being called animals, as though this was in some way disgusting—an insult to human dignity.... Of course, I guessed that I might shock some of the more starry-eyed escapists—people who were still gullible enough to believe the old fairy-tales designed to keep superstitious medieval peasants in their place—and I also suspected that the deliberate frankness of some of my statements might prove distasteful to the more sheltered puritans. But I was in no mood to compromise or to soften my message.[43]

Eldridge Cleaver, *Soul on Ice* (1968)

Born on August 31, 1935, in the minuscule town of Wabbaseka, Arkansas, Eldridge Cleaver grew up surrounded by violence, both at home—his father, Leroy, a waiter and nightclub entertainer, beat his mother, Thelma, who was a schoolteacher—and on the streets of Los Angeles, where his family moved in 1946. The young Cleaver racked up arrests for petty theft and marijuana possession, ending up in Soledad State Prison in 1954. Released a couple of years later, he was arrested again in 1957, this time for sexual assault. He went to San Quentin and then Folsom State Prison, where he stayed until December 1966, missing by thirteen months Johnny Cash's legendary performance at the prison on January 13, 1968.[44]

While at Folsom, Cleaver did a couple of things that would alter the course of his life. One was to join the Nation of Islam. This got him thinking about larger political issues, such as "Black power," a precursor to the modern Black Lives Matter movement.[45] *Black Power* was the title of Richard Wright's account of his 1953 trip to Africa's Gold Coast, four years before it became the independent nation of Ghana. Subtitled "A Record of Reactions in a Land of Pathos," the book is a meditation on many things: colonialism, activism, history, promise.

Wright didn't use the term in a political sense, but it acquired that meaning a decade later, when Stokely Carmichael, later known as Kwame Ture, in a speech in Greenwood, Mississippi, following the murder of civil rights activist James Meredith, said, "This is the twenty-seventh time I have been arrested and I ain't going to jail no more! The only way we gonna stop them white men from whuppin' us is to take over. What we gonna start sayin' now is Black Power!"[46] Carmichael elaborated on the term in his 1967 book *Black Power: The Politics of Liberation*, which he wrote with Charles V. Hamilton: "It is a call for black people in this country to unite, to recognize their heritage, to build a sense of community. It is a call for black people to define their own goals, to lead their own organizations."[47]

Another expression of the movement was Bobby Seale and Huey P. Newton's Oakland-based Black Panther Party, which Cleaver joined after his release from Folsom. Cleaver quickly rose to prominence, becoming the party's minister of information and, with his wife, Kathleen, leading the "Free Huey" movement after Newton was arrested in 1967 for the fatal shooting of Oakland police officer John Frey.[48]

In 1968, Cleaver himself was wounded in a police shootout. He ran for president as a member of the Peace and Freedom Party until his parole was revoked, forcing him to flee the country. He lived in Algeria and then Paris until 1975, when he returned to spend a final eight months in prison, after which he tried to start his own religion—Chrislam, a mishmash of Christianity and Islam—before becoming a Christian, joining the Republican Party, and endorsing Ronald Reagan.[49]

The other crucial thing Cleaver did at Folsom was write the essays that would later be published as *Soul on Ice*. The book divides them into four sections: "Letters from Prison," which tell the story of Cleaver's crimes and arrests; "Blood of the Beast," in which he discusses race relations and promotes Black power; "Prelude to Love—Three Letters," which are missives he exchanged with famed civil rights attorney Beverly Axelrod; and "White Woman, Black Man," Cleaver's ruminations on masculinity and sexuality.

For the most part, he writes movingly on topics such as religion, race riots, the Vietnam War, the murders of Malcolm X and Emmett Till, US foreign policy, and influential Black people such as Martin Luther King Jr. and Muhammad Ali. There are, however, a number of iffy passages, such as this one from Justice Powell's list:

There are white men who will pay you to fuck their wives. They approach you and say, "How would you like to fuck a white woman?" "What is this?" you ask. "On the up-and-up," he assures you. "It's all right. She's my wife. She needs black rod, is all. She has to have it. It's like a medicine or drug to her. She has to have it. I'll pay you. It's all on the level, no trick involved. Interested?"[50]

And:

Rape was an insurrectionary act. It delighted me that I was defying and rampling upon the white man's law, upon his system of values, and that I was defiling his women—and this point, I believe, was the most satisfying to me because I was very resentful over the historical fact of how the white man has used the black woman. I felt I was getting revenge. From the site of the act of rape, consternation spreads outwardly in concentric circles. I wanted to send waves of consternation throughout the white race.[51]

On occasion, it is just possible to empathize with the Island Trees board's desire to yank books from impressionable young hands. This is one of those occasions.

Langston Hughes, editor, *Best Short Stories of Negro Writers* (1969)

In his well-known poem "Theme for English B," which served as a kind of prologue to the Black Power movement, Langston Hughes acknowledged the differences between Black and white people but suggested that those differences should not make them enemies. In fact, Hughes saw a naturalness, an inevitability, and perhaps a beauty in that shorter-than-it-seems distance between the two races.

It was an optimism not shared by many white people Hughes encountered.

Born in Joplin, Missouri, in 1901, Hughes was one of the most prolific American writers of the twentieth century, producing eleven books of fiction, twelve plays, nineteen poetry collections, and more. A leading light of the Harlem Renaissance, he became political early on, aligning himself with the Communist Party USA, an organization that was pro-labor, antiracist, and an advocate for justice. One of its most high-profile moves was helping with the defense of the Scottsboro Boys, nine Black teenagers accused in Alabama of raping two white women in 1931.[52]

Hughes also traveled extensively in the Soviet Union and in 1937 reported on the Spanish Civil War, praising the Republican forces resisting General Francisco Franco's coup attempt.[53] Such leftist views made him a target of the House Un-American Activities Committee, created in 1938 to investigate people and organizations suspected of having Communist ties. (Other Black artists who were investigated were Paul Robeson, W. E. B. Du Bois, Charlotta Bass, Canada Lee, Dorothy Dandridge, Sidney Poitier, Lena Horne, Richard Wright, Hazel Scott, Harry Belafonte, Ferdinand Smith, and Alphaeus Hunton.)[54]

In 1953, Hughes testified before Joseph McCarthy's Senate Permanent Subcommittee on Investigations. The poet was obliging, telling McCarthy and Roy Cohn, who was McCarthy's—and later Donald Trump's—lawyer, that he no longer admired the Soviet Union, never joined the Community Party, and didn't believe in its ideology, even, possibly, when it appeared in his own works.[55]

At one point, Cohn quoted from Hughes's collection *Scottsboro Limited*: "Rise, workers and fight, audience, fight, fight, fight, fight, the curtain is a great red flag rising to the strains of the Internationale."[56] Then he asked whether that statement was contrary to Hughes's beliefs.

"Sir," Hughes replied, "I don't think you can get a yes or no answer entirely to any literary question."[57]

Cohn then quoted Hughes's poem "Ballads of Lenin": "On guard with the workers forever—The world is our room!"[58]

Hughes responded, "That is a poem. One cannot state one believes every word of a poem."[59]

And so it went.

The Island Trees Board may not have known about Hughes's twenty-year-old charges of Communism, but they still found plenty to object to in *Best Short Stories of Negro Writers*. Justice Powell listed many phrases:

- "like bat's shit and camel piss"
- "That no-count bitch of a daughter of yours is up there up North making a whore of herself."
- "You need some pussy. Come on, let's go up to the whore house on the hill."
- "Oh, these bastards, these bastards, this God damned Army and the bastards in it. The sons of bitches!"
- "But she had straight firm legs and her breasts were small and upright. No doubt if she'd had children her breasts would be hanging like little empty purses."
- "In profile, his penis hung like a stout tassle. She could even tell that he was circumcised."[60]

(Bat's shit? Camel piss? I'll say one thing for the board: they had an eye for the outré.)

Kurt Vonnegut, *Slaughterhouse-Five* (1969)

When Kurt Vonnegut's sixth novel appeared four months before the Apollo 11 crew became the first humans to walk on the moon, his publisher, Dell, had no idea that it was making history. How could it? Since 1921, the company founded by George T. Delacorte had mainly published comic books, pulp magazines, and paperback mysteries, with a little science fiction thrown in.[61]

That last category likely accounts for *Slaughterhouse-Five*, the story of Billy Pilgrim, a World War II veteran who, like Vonnegut himself, had survived the bombing of Dresden. Billy develops an unusual problem: he becomes "unstuck in time" and starts shifting from one event to the next, reliving his life out of order. Oh, and he gets abducted by Tralfamadorians, aliens who first showed up in Vonnegut's second novel, *Sirens of Titans*, and are "two feet high, and green, and shaped like plumber's friends."

Slaughterhouse-Five was Vonnegut's first best seller, staying on *The New York Times* list for sixteen weeks and peaking at number four.[62] It was nominated for Nebula and Hugo Awards, losing both to Ursula K. Le Guin's *The Left Hand of Darkness*. It also appeared on *Time* magazine's 2005 list of 100 Greatest English Language Novels since 1923[63] and has never been out of print, with nearly three hundred editions and translations into more than twenty languages.[64]

It is also no stranger to suppression. "Since it was published," wrote Betsy Morais in *The Atlantic*, "*Slaughterhouse-Five* has been banned or challenged on at least 18 occasions."[65] One of those occurred in 1972 in the Oakland County, Michigan, school system, prompting a judge to call the book "depraved, immoral, psychotic, vulgar, and anti-Christian."[66]

A year later, Charles McCarthy (of course, his name would be "McCarthy"), chairman of the Drake Public School Board in North Dakota, arranged for thirty-two copies of the book to be laid inside the high school's coal burner and *set on fire*. This outraged Vonnegut. On November 16, 1973, he sent McCarthy a letter, explaining, as only Vonnegut could, that he is not among the "sort of ratlike people who enjoy making money from poisoning the minds of young people" that censors imagine writers to be.[67] Rather, in his view, "books are sacred to free men for very good reasons […]. If you are an American, you must allow all ideas to circulate freely in your community, not merely your own."[68] (Kurt Vonnegut was a lot of things. One thing he was not was diffident.)

Island Trees had some of the same objections to *Slaughterhouse-Five*: profanity, coarseness, sexual content. The board also found the book blasphemous. In one scene, Billy's friend, Eliot Rosewater, who had also appeared in an earlier Vonnegut book, *God Bless You, Mr. Rosewater*, tells Billy about a (fictional) sci-fi writer named Kilgore Trout. In one of Trout's novels, *The Gospel from Outer Space*, an alien presents to Earth a new book of the Bible, one in which Jesus was a "nobody" and "a pain in the neck to a lot of people." To amuse themselves, the people crucified Jesus. "And then," quoted Justice Powell's list, "just before the nobody died … The voice of God came crashing down. He told the people that he was adopting the bum as his son … God said this: 'From this moment on, He will punish horribly anybody who torments a bum who has no connections.'"[69]

Go Ask Alice (1971)

Q: What do Daniel Defoe, Davy Crockett, and Friedrich Nietzsche have in common?

A: An unfortunate connection to falsity.

Defoe wrote what is often called the first-ever novel in the English language. Its full title was *The Life and Strange Surprizing Adventures of Robinson Crusoe, of York, Mariner: Who lived Eight and Twenty Years, all alone in an un-inhabited Island on the Coast of America, near the Mouth of the Great River of Oroonoque; Having been cast on Shore by Shipwreck, wherein all the Men perished but himself. With An Account how he was at last as strangely deliver'd by Pyrates. Written by Himself.*

Most people just call it *Robinson Crusoe.*

Novels are works of fiction, yet when the book appeared in 1719, many thought it was the actual writings of a shipwreck survivor.[70] After all, it's there in the title: *Written by Himself.* A century later, printers T. K. and P. G. Collins released *Col. Crockett's exploits and adventures in Texas: wherein is contained a full account of his journey from Tennessee to the Red River and Natchitoches, and thence across Texas to San Antonio; including many hair-breadth escapes; together with a topographical, historical, and political view of Texas*, with that same amazing attribution: *Written by Himself.* In fact, the author was not the Alamo hero but, most likely, the playwright Richard Penn Smith.[71]

As for Nietzsche, he supposedly wrote *My Sister and I*, a memoir detailing his incestuous relationship with his sister Elisabeth, as well as an affair with the wife of the composer Richard Wagner. The book was published in 1951 by Boar's Head Books and distributed by Seven Sirens Press. Right away, Nietzsche scholars questioned the book's authenticity, and almost no one now believes it is authentic. The answer should have been obvious even to nonspecialists. Who owned Seven Sirens Press? That old fabulist, Samuel Roth.[72]

Q2: What does any of this have to do with *Go Ask Alice*?

A2: Everything, man.

Written by "Anonymous," the book purports to be the recovered diary of a fifteen-year-old loner who ran away from home, sought refuge in drugs and sex, and pulled herself together in the end, though not for long. It concludes with an epilogue claiming that the diarist died of an overdose. Was it suicide? An accident? That isn't important, according to the "editor." What *is* important is that "she was only one of thousands of drug deaths that year."[73]

Go Ask Alice was, in fact, a hoax. Its true author was Beatrice Sparks, a Mormon youth counselor who turned the book's success into a cottage industry. Her other titles include *Jay's Journal*, which deals with Satanism; *It Happened to Nancy: By an Anonymous Teenager* (AIDS); *Kim: Empty Inside: The Diary of an Anonymous Teenager* (eating disorders); and *Annie's Baby: The Diary of Anonymous, A Pregnant Teenager* (self-explanatory).[74]

The Island Trees board found a lot to object to in *Go Ask Alice*. Here are some of the passages from Justice Powell's list:

- "I wonder if sex without acid could be so exciting, so wonderful, so indescribable. I always thought it just took a minute, or that it would be like dogs mating."
- "Doris was ten and had humped with who knows how many men in between. And when Doris had just turned eleven her current stepfather started having sex with her but good … she put up with the sonofabitch balling her till she was twelve."
- "now when I face a girl it's like facing a boy. I get all excited and turned on. I want to screw with the girl, you know, and then I get all tensed-up and scared."
- "I'd rather screw with a guy … sometimes I want one of the girls to kiss me. I want her to touch me, to have her sleep under me."
- "Another day, another blow job … If I don't give Big Ass a blow he'll cut off my supply … Big Ass makes me do it before he gives me the load. Everybody is just lying around here like they're dead and Little Jacon is yelling, 'Mama, Daddy can't come now. He's humping Carla.'"
- "Then he said that all I needed was a good fuck."
- "It might be great because I'm practically a virgin in the sense that I've never had sex except when I've been stoned."
- "I hope you have a nice orgasm with your dog tonight."[75]

That last line was one Steven Pico mentioned in our conversation. Quoted it from memory, word for word. You never forget some things, even after fifty years.

A Reader for Writers (1971)

Remember Parents of New York United? The cabal whose list of objectionable books became the impetus for the book removals by the Island Trees board? *A Reader for Writers* was on that list. Edited by Jerome Archer and Joseph Schwartz, the book was an anthology of works by Eudora Welty, Joan Didion, Joseph Conrad, Nathaniel Hawthorne, and other literary greats, organized by theme and intended as teaching tools. What troubled the Parents group was "Malcolm X: Mission and Meaning," an essay by Robert Penn Warren originally published in *The Yale Review* in 1967. According to the group, the essay "equates Malcolm X, considered by many to be a traitor to this country, with the founding fathers of our country."[76]

This is a dubious claim. The passage they were likely referring to is: "Malcolm X was of that breed of Americans, autodidacts and homemade successes, that has included Benjamin Franklin, Abraham Lincoln, P. T. Barnum, Charles A. Edison, Booker T. Washington, Mark Twain, Henry Ford, and the Wright Brothers."[77] Of these compeers, only Benjamin Franklin would be considered a "founding father." Some of the others make for impressive company. But Henry Ford, the antisemite? P. T. Barnum, who "began his career in show business by going into debt to buy a superannuated female slave"?[78] These analogues don't dignify Malcolm X, much less deify him. Elsewhere, Warren compares him to Joseph Smith, founder of Mormonism, further suggesting that his judgment was nothing to get worked up over.

Warren's essay appears in the third edition, not the second, which was the edition in the Island Trees library.* Thus, the Island Trees students did not have access to it (in their library, anyway). Why, then, did the board ban this book? Because of a different entry: *A Modest Proposal For preventing the Children of Poor People From being a Burthen to Their Parents or Country, and For making them Beneficial to the Publick*, now called simply *A Modest Proposal*.

Written by Jonathan Swift, the Anglo-Irish author of *Gulliver's Travels*, the essay describes the plight of starving beggars in Ireland before recommending a solution: cooking and eating children. It is an ironic suggestion, a fact that becomes apparent when Swift goes on to discuss what the solution should not be (which is, of course, what he thinks it *should* be):

> Therefore let no man talk to me of other expedients: Of taxing our absentees at five shillings a pound: Of using neither clothes, nor household furniture, except what is of our own growth and manufacture: Of utterly rejecting the materials and instruments that promote foreign luxury: Of curing the expensiveness of pride, vanity, idleness, and gaming in our women: Of introducing a vein of parsimony, prudence and temperance: Of learning to love our country, wherein we differ even from Laplanders, and the inhabitants of Topinamboo: Of quitting our animosities and factions, nor acting any longer like the Jews, who were murdering one another at the very moment their city was taken: Of being a little cautious not to sell our country and consciences for nothing: Of teaching landlords to have at least one degree of mercy towards their tenants. Lastly, of putting a spirit of honesty, industry, and skill into our shop-keepers, who, if a resolution could now be taken to buy only our native goods, would immediately unite to cheat and exact upon us in the price, the measure, and the goodness, nor could ever yet be brought to make one fair proposal of just dealing, though

---

* George Lipp, attorney for the Island Trees board, clarifies this during oral arguments at the US Supreme Court.

often and earnestly invited to it. Therefore I repeat, let no man talk to me of these and the like expedients, 'till he hath at least some glympse of hope, that there will ever be some hearty and sincere attempt to put them into practice.[79]

There is no profanity in *A Modest Proposal*. No sex. No drugs. No anti-Americanism. Why ban it then? Richard Ahrens called the essay "irrelevant to the curriculum,"[80] which is one of the lamest pretexts ever.

And it may have helped Steven Pico win at the Supreme Court.

Alice Childress, *A Hero Ain't Nothin' but a Sandwich* (1973)

Benjie Johnson, the thirteen-year-old protagonist of Alice Childress's novel *A Hero Ain't Nothin' but a Sandwich*, lives in a rundown tenement building in Harlem with his mother, grandmother, and stepfather, Butler, the only one of the four who works. Benjie's life is hard because, in his words, "My block ain't no place to be a chile in peace. Somebody gonna cop your money and might knock you down … you on your own and [adults] got they thing to do, like workin, or goin' to court, or seein' after they gas and letrit bills."[81] As an escape, he experiments with heroin and becomes addicted. Soon, Benjie is going to school high, stealing from his family, and alienating his stepfather, who makes the desperate but unwise decision to move out of the house. Eventually, Benjie gets clean, and Butler returns, but there is a lot of work to do before the family can be whole.

Born in Charleston, South Carolina, Childress moved in with her grandmother in Harlem at the age of nine. Her grandmother was the daughter of a slave, and she encouraged Childress to follow her dreams. In 1939, she studied drama at the American Negro Theatre, and in 1949, she directed and starred in her own one-act play, *Florence*. She would go on to write thirteen more plays plus five novels, including *A Hero Ain't Nothin' but a Sandwich*, whose portrait of heroin abuse was an all-oo-common one in the 1970s.

Heroin is derived from opium, as is morphine, which was first synthesized by German chemist Friedrich Sertürner in 1803.[82] Called "God's own medicine,"[83] opiates were popular in the United States throughout the nineteenth century. Drugstores stocked tonics steeped in the stuff, and doctors prescribed them for upper- and middle-class women suffering from neurasthenia, now called chronic fatigue syndrome, and other conditions. Though hypodermic needles had existed for centuries—English astronomer and physicist Christopher Wren gave dogs intravenous injections in 1656[84]—they were perfected in the mid-1800s. Shots of morphine were a popular pain reliever, and mainspring of addiction, during and after the Civil War.[85]

Heroin was a response to this. It was created in 1895 by another German, Heinrich Dreser, head of Bayer's pharmacological laboratory. (Bayer was the inventor of aspirin, meaning Dreser "was responsible for the launch of two drugs that have shaped the way we live.")[86] Soon, what was once a cure for addiction became a scourge itself. Heroin was at the center of the Harlem jazz scene in the 1930s and 1940s and, later, the Beatnik lifestyle. Between 1965 and 1970, the number of addicts in the United States reached an estimated 750,000.[87] In his 1969 Special Message to the Congress on Control of Narcotics and Dangerous Drugs, President Nixon, commenting on the "serious national threat" of drug abuse, wrote that "New York City alone has records of some 40,000 heroin addicts, and the number rises between 7,000 and 9,000 a year."[88] In an echo of the Civil War–era morphine problem, one congressional investigation revealed that 10–15 percent of Vietnam servicemen in 1971 had a heroin addiction.[89]

Despite being central to the plot of *A Hero Ain't Nothin' but a Sandwich*, heroin didn't feature in the three passages on Justice Powell's list. The star of those was the F-word:

- "Hell, no! Fuck the society."
- "The hell with the junkie, the wino, the capitalist, the welfare checks, the world … yeah, and fuck you too!"
- "They can have back the spread and curtains, I'm too old for them fuckin' bunnies anyway."[90]

However, Steven Pico has suggested that the book was banned for reasons besides vulgarity. One was that grammatically slipshod "ain't" in the title. The other was more political. Nigeria Greene is one of Benjie's teachers who tries to save the boy from himself. At one point, Greene offers the following speech:

Only two picture on my wall when I came here … George Washington and Abraham Lincoln […] George was a slaveholder, and he had it put in his will to free all his slaves *after* his death. But he owned a slave woman whose cookin was so fine that he freed her while he was livin. She musta really known how to barbecue![91]

This, according to Steven, was the "anti-American" in Richard Ahrens's "anti-American, anti-Christian, anti-Semitic, and just plain filthy" formulation.

Maybe Ahrens preferred the cherry tree story.

Notes

1   Ari L. Goldman, "After 14 Months, a Vote on 'the Books,'" *New York Times*, May 22, 1977, 17.

2   Debra Lau Whelan, "NCAC Talks to the Man Behind Pico v. Board of Ed," National Coalition against Censorship, July 9, 2013, https://ncac.org/news/blog/ncac-talks-to-the-man-behind-pico-v-board-of-ed.

3   Judith F. Krug, "Intellectual Freedom and the American Library Association (ALA): Historical Overview," in *Encyclopedia of Library and Information Sciences*, 3rd ed. (Taylor & Francis, 2010), 2821.

4   Matthew T. Bolen, "The American Library Association, US Government, and the Fight for Intellectual Freedom, 1939–1953" (master's thesis, University of North Carolina Chapel Hill, 2006).

5   Lynn Neary, "'Grapes of Wrath' and the Politics of Book Burning," NPR, September 30, 2008, https://www.npr.org/2008/09/30/95190615/grapes-of-wrath-and-the-politics-of-book-burning.

6   Ibid.

7   "The Library's Bill of Rights" (pamphlet, American Library Association, 1939).

8   "Library Bill of Rights" (pamphlet, American Library Association, 1948).

9   "The Freedom to Read" (pamphlet, American Library Association and American Book Publishers Council, 1953).

10 Anthony Aycock, "Desperately Seeking Sources," *Missouri Review*, October 20, 2023, https://missourireview.com/desperately-seeking-sources-by-anthony-aycock/.

11 Michele Ingrassia, "Suit Filed to Stop School's Book Ban," *Newsday* (Nassau ed.), January 5, 1977, 19.

12 Ibid.

13 Ibid.

14 Timothy Moore, "Night of the Banned," *Washington Post*, April 5, 1982, https://www.washingtonpost.com/archive/lifestyle/1982/04/06/night-of-the-banned/65abe048-f8f4-49c6-9926-80d1001e2554/.

15 Chelsea Rose, "Detroit Public Library Once Banned the Wizard of Oz for 15 Years," WKFR 103.3, April 10, 2023, https://wkfr.com/detroit-wizard-of-oz-ban/.

16 Paul Kleinpoppen, "Some Notes on Oliver La Farge," *Studies in American Indian Literatures* 10, no. 1 (1986): 69–120.

17 D'Arcy McNickle, *Indian Man: A Life of Oliver La Farge* (Indiana University Press, 1971), 57.

18 Ibid., 55.

19 Debbie Reese, "Oliver La Farge's LAUGHING BOY," *American Indians in Children's Literature*, March 21, 2009, https://americanindiansinchildrensliterature.blogspot.com/2009/03/oliver-la-farges-laughing-boy.html.

20 *Island Trees v. Pico*, 457 U.S. 853, 902–3 (1982).

21 Hazel Rowley, *Richard Wright: The Life and Times* (Henry Holt, 2001), 319.

22 *Island Trees v. Pico*, 457 U.S. 853, 902 (1982).

23 David A. King, "The Library Card Episode in Richard Wright's 'Black Boy,'" *Georgia Review*, March 19, 2021, https://georgiabulletin.org/commentary/2021/03/the-library-card-episode-in-richard-wrights-black-boy/.

24 Ibid.

25 Richard Wright, *Black Boy*, Forum Books ed. (World Publishing, 1947), 219–20.

26 *Island Trees v. Pico*, 457 U.S. 853, 898 (1982).

27 Jay Beilis, Jeremy Simcha Garber, and Mark S. Stein, eds., *Blood Libel: The Life and Memory of Mendel Beilis*, (Beilis Publishing, 2011), 229.

28 Albert S. Lindemann, "Beilis Case," in *Antisemitism: A Historical Encyclopedia of Prejudice and Persecution*, ed. Richard S. Levy (ABC-CLIO, 2005), 63.

29 Raymond Chandler, "The Simple Art of Murder," *Atlantic Monthly*, December 1944, https://www.theatlantic.com/magazine/archive/1944/12/the-simple-art-of-murder/656179/.

30 Joseph Berger, "Piri Thomas, Spanish Harlem Author, Dies at 83," *New York Times*, October 19, 2011, https://www.nytimes.com/2011/10/20/books/piri-thomas-author-of-down-these-mean-streets-dies.html.

31 Ibid.

32 Gene I. Maeroff, "Book Ban Splits a Queens School District," *New York Times*, May 9, 1971, 71.

33 *President's Council v. Community School Board, No. 25*, 457 F. 2d 289, 291 (2nd Cir., 1971).

34 Ibid., 291–92.

35 Ibid., 292.

36 Amy Sutherland, "What Shamu Taught Me about a Happy Marriage," *New York Times*, June 25, 2006, https://www.nytimes.com/2006/06/25/fashion/what-shamu-taught-me-about-a-happy-marriage.html.

37 Ibid.

38 Ibid.

39 Ibid.

40 Desmond Morris, *The Naked Ape* (McGraw-Hill, 1967), 9.

41 Ibid., 80.

42 Ronald Edwards, "The Evolution of Evolution," OUP Blog, April 19, 2016, https://blog.oup.com/2016/04/evolution-human-exceptionalism/.

43 Morris, *The Naked Ape*, Dell Publishing, 1999 repr. ed., iv.

44 Jeff Bailey, "Leroy Eldridge Cleaver (1935–1998)," *Encyclopedia of Arkansas*, https://encyclopediaofarkansas.net/entries/leroy-eldridge-cleaver-2743/.

45 Ibid.

46 "Stokely Carmichael (1941–1998)," American Radio Works, https://americanradioworks.publicradio.org/features/blackspeech/scarmichael-2.html.

47 Stokely Carmichael and Charles V. Hamilton, *Black Power: The Politics of Liberation* (Random House, 1967), 44.

48 Aaron Byungjoo Bae, "'The Struggle for Freedom, Justice, and Equality Transcends Racial and National Boundaries': Anti-Imperialism, Multiracial Alliances, and the Free Huey Movement in the San Francisco Bay Area," *Pacific Historical Review* 86, no. 4 (November 1, 2017): 691–722.

49 Bailey, "Leroy Eldridge Cleaver (1935–1998)."

50 *Island Trees v. Pico*, 457 U.S. 853, 897.

51 Eldridge Cleaver, *Soul on Ice* (Delta, 1968), 14.

52 Erin Blakemore, "Why the Communist Party Defended the Scottsboro Boys," History, February 18, 2025, https://www.history.com/articles/scottsboro-boys-naacp-communist-party.

53 Peter Dreier, "The Red Scare Took Aim at Black Radicals Like Langston Hughes," Jacobin, March 31, 2023, https://jacobin.com/2023/03/langston-hughes-red-scare-black-radicals-leftists-huac-red-baiting.

54 Ibid.

55 "Testimony of Langston Hughes (accompanied by his counsel, Frank D. Reeves) before the Senate Permanent Subcommittee on Investigations of the Committee on Government

Operations, Tuesday, March 24, 1953," NPR, https://legacy.npr.org/programs/atc/features/2003/may/mccarthy/hughes.html.

56 Ibid.

57 Ibid.

58 Ibid.

59 Ibid.

60 *Island Trees v. Pico*, 457 U.S. 853, 901.

61 "A Closer Look: At Dell Publishers," Sweet Savage Flame, https://sweetsavageflame.com/a-closer-look-at-dell-publishing/.

62 Keith L. Justice, *Bestseller Index: All Books, by Author, on the Lists of Publishers Weekly and the New York Times through 1990* (McFarland, 1998).

63 Lev Grossman and Richard Lacayo, "All-TIME 100 Novels," *Time*, October 16, 2005, https://entertainment.time.com/2005/10/16/all-time-100-novels/.

64 Megan Henricksen, "Kurt Vonnegut, 'Slaughterhouse-Five,'" The Banned Books Project, https://bannedbooks.library.cmu.edu/kurt-vonnegut-slaughterhouse-five/.

65 Betsy Morais, "The Neverending Campaign to Ban 'Slaughterhouse Five,'" *The Atlantic*, August 12, 2011, https://www.theatlantic.com/entertainment/archive/2011/08/the-neverending-campaign-to-ban-slaughterhouse-five/243525/.

66 Ibid.

67 Kurt Vonnegut, *Palm Sunday* (Delacorte, 1981), 5.

68 Ibid., 6–7.

69 *Island Trees v. Pico*, 457 U.S. 853, 900.

70 Danny Heitman, "Fiction as Authentic as Fact," *Wall Street Journal*, January 11, 2013, https://www.wsj.com/articles/SB10001424127887323936804578227971298012486.

71 David Holmes and Ferris Samara, "Was the Wild Frontiersman a Prolific Penman? A Stylometric Investigation into the Works of Davy Crockett," *Chance* 33, no. 2 (2020): 7–18.

72 Denis Dutton, "Decontextualized Crab; Nietzsche Dreams of Detroit," *Philosophy and Literature*, 16, no. 1 (1992): 239–49.

73 *Go Ask Alice* (Prentice-Hall, 1971), 159.

74 Casey Cep, "How a Mormon Housewife Turned a Fake Diary into an Enormous Best-Seller," *New Yorker*, July 25, 2022, https://www.newyorker.com/magazine/2022/08/01/how-a-mormon-housewife-turned-a-fake-diary-into-an-enormous-best-seller.

75 *Island Trees v. Pico*, 457 U.S. 853, 899.

76 *Pico v. Island Trees*, 638 F. 2d 404, 408.

77 Robert Penn Warren, "Malcolm X: Mission and Meaning," in *A Reader for Writers: A Critical Anthology of Prose Readings*, 3rd ed., ed. Jerome Walter Archer and Joseph Schwartz (McGraw-Hill, 1971), 513.

78 Jackie Mansky, "P. T. Barnum Isn't the Hero the 'Greatest Showman' Wants You to Think," *Smithsonian Magazine*, December 22, 2017, https://www.smithsonianmag.com/history/true-story-pt-barnum-greatest-humbug-them-all-180967634/.

79 Jonathan Swift, "A Modest Proposal," in *A Reader for Writers: A Critical Anthology of Prose Readings*, 3rd ed., ed. Jerome Walter Archer and Joseph Schwartz (McGraw-Hill, 1971), 469.

80 Plaintiffs Rule 9G Statement, District Court of the United States Eastern District, March 8, 1978.

81 Alice Childress, *A Hero Ain't Nothin' but a Sandwich* (Coward, McCann & Geoghegan, 1973), 9.

82 Chandrasekhar Krishnamurti and SSC Chakra Rao, "The Isolation of Morphine by Serturner," *Indian Journal of Anaesthesia* 60, no. 11 (2016): 861–62.

83 Steven R. Childers, "Opioid Receptors: Pinning Down the Opiate Targets," *Current Biology* 7, no. 11 (1997): R695–97.

84 Keith L. Dorrington and William Poole, "The First Intravenous Anaesthetic: How Well Was It Managed and Its Potential Realized?," *British Journal of Anaesthesia* 110, no. 1 (2013): 7–12.

85 "Opiate Addiction in the Civil War's Aftermath," Virginia Museum of History & Culture, https://virginiahistory.org/learn/opiate-addiction-civil-wars-aftermath.

86 Richard Askwith, "Last Aspirin Hero," *Daily Telegraph*, August 22, 1998, https://richardaskwith.co.uk/journalism/science-and-nature/last-aspirin-hero/.

87 "The History of Heroin: From King Tut to Cough Remedy," *Palm Beach Post*, https://heroin.palmbeachpost.com/history-of-heroin/.

88 Sean Gardiner, "Heroin: From the Civil War to the 70s, and Beyond," *City Limits*, July 5, 2019, https://citylimits.org/heroin-from-the-civil-war-to-the-70s-and-beyond/.

89 Alvin M. Shuster, "G.I. Heroin Addiction Epidemic in Vietnam," *New York Times*, May 16, 1971, 1.

90 *Island Trees v. Pico*, 457 U.S. 853, 898.

91 Childress, *A Hero Ain't Nothin' but a Sandwich*, 43.

4 Diagnosis: Censor

When I was six or seven years old, I said the word "darn" one day and my grandfather reprimanded me. He was thoroughly religious, an inveterate churchgoer, the sort of man who spreads the gospel in the Food Lion checkout line. My mother says he knew the Bible better than any minister. I tried to explain to him that "darn" isn't a bad word.

"Yes, it is," he said in his rolling mountain accent. "When you say that word, you're saying the other word in your mind, and that's what God hears."

Our old friend Daniel Defoe was even harsher, complaining in his 1697 "Essay Upon Projects" about the instability of the English language. Grammar was changing. Spelling was changing. About twelve thousand words had been added, many imported from other languages, especially French. People worried that this "Early Modern English," as linguists call it, was too unstable. They saw the new words as unruly, unrefined, barbarous. One class of additions made Defoe especially indignant: swear words. He saw them as a "Frenzy of the Tongue, a Vomit of the Brain," and as impertinent "as if a man shou'd *Fart* before a Justice or *talk Bawdy* before the Queen."[1]

I don't feel that strongly about cursing (or, if you're a Southerner like me, *cussing*). Naturally, I didn't grow up doing it. Kids would stop talking when they saw me approach, covering their mouths and saying, "Oops! I can't cuss around you." I don't hate cussing, and I don't think people who do it are horrible or vice-filled or hell bound. I just don't do it much myself.

That doesn't mean I don't see artistic value in doing it. We live in a time when there is more profanity than ever, with book titles such as *On Bullshit, You Are a Badass, Why Men Love Bitches, Beautiful Bastard*, and *The Great Glorious Goddamn of It All*. "Fuck" is still pixelated out, as in *The F—It List* or *The Subtle Art of Not Giving a F*ck*, though Tom Ford has a perfume called Fucking Fabulous. Network TV still confines itself largely to the softball swears "hell" and "damn," but on streaming services, you can hear pretty much anything. None of this should be bothersome. Words have power, but they are also tools. *We* control the power. If that power is used in the right way, what reason is there to quell it?

With an attitude like that, I would be a terrible censor.

***

The first censors, like the first of so much else, were Roman. Most people know this even if they don't *know* they know. How? It's in the Bible. According to Luke 2: 1–5,

> [1] And it came to pass in those days, that there went out a decree from Caesar Augustus that all the world should be taxed.
> [2] (And this taxing was first made when Cyrenius was governor of Syria.)
> [3] And all went to be taxed, every one into his own city.
> [4] And Joseph also went up from Galilee, out of the city of Nazareth, into Judaea, unto the city of David, which is called Bethlehem (because he was of the house and lineage of David:)
> [5] To be taxed with Mary his espoused wife, being great with child.

Later translations, like the New International Version and the New American Standard Bible, say that what Augustus ordered was a *census*. Servius Tullius (ca. 575–535 BC) was the first ruler to whip up one of these.[2] Responsibility for it rested with the consuls, the highest elected public officials of the Roman Republic, until 442 BC, when a pair of magistrates was appointed to take over the duty. Those magistrates were called censors, but they did more than count, as Cicero noted in his treatise *De Legibus*:

> Let the censors take a census of the people, according to age, race, family, and property. Let them have the inspection of the temples, the streets, the aqueducts, the rates, and the customs. Let them distribute the citizens, according to their tribes, fortunes, ages, and ranks. Let them keep a register of the equestrian and plebeian orders. Let them impose a tax on celibates. Let them guard the morals of the people. Let them permit no scandal in the senate. Let the number of such censors be two. Let their magistracy continue five years. Let the other magistrates be annual, but their offices themselves should be perpetual.[3]

Censors were keepers of the public morals or *Regimen morum*. This is the sense with which the word entered English in the 1590s, as well as "censure," meaning to criticize, judge, or reprimand.[4]

There have been a number of famous censors. We've already met some—Anthony Comstock, Henry VIII, the Watch and Ward Society, the Roman Catholic Church. Another was Norma Gabler, who in 1961, along with her husband, Mel, founded Educational Research Analysts, which is still in existence (its 1995-esque website promises "Public School Textbook Reform through Textbook Reviews"). From their home in Hawkins, Texas, the Gablers aimed "to rid schoolbooks of content they considered antifamily, anti-American and anti-God."[5]

Like about half the country, Texas adopts books statewide, meaning no text that isn't board-approved can appear in any classroom. In the 1960s, citizens who objected to a book could file a "bill of particular" detailing their complaint. The textbook committee would then hold hearings about the complaints, after which the board would decide whether to keep each book, reject it, or ask the publisher for revisions.[6] Worried by differences between her son's American history text and what she herself had learned in older books, Norma attended her first hearing in 1962, and afterward, she started reviewing books.[7] By 1970, she had made real progress. At her urging, science books were required to explicitly state that evolution was "a theory, not a fact." Publishers were also warned that no book would be adopted if it "contained offensive language that would cause embarrassing situations in the classroom."[8]

Some of the Gablers' efforts amounted to innocuous fact-checking, and they did uncover actual errors, such as a history text claiming that Senator John C. Calhoun of South Carolina had supported the tariff of 1816 (he had actually opposed it).[9] Their usual grouses, however, were ideological. They believed that the purpose of education was "the imparting of factual knowledge, basic skills and cultural heritage," which was best accomplished in schools that "emphasize a traditional curriculum of reading, math, and grammar, as well as patriotism, high moral standards, dress codes, and strict discipline, with respect and courtesy demanded from all students."[10]

That doesn't sound too limiting. The problem, though, was the Gablers' militarization. "What we're fighting is mental child abuse," Mel often said[11]— an attitude with little room for nuance. Then again, there *was* no nuance in the Gablers' definition of history: "facts rather than concepts" that are "taught as they were in older textbooks" in a "fair, objective and patriotic" manner.[12] History, of course, is more than facts. It includes analysis, synthesis, and understanding. You might argue that understanding can be manipulated, and you would be right. But the past twenty years or so have shown that facts, too, are vulnerable.

With their sensible clothes and fellowship-supper smiles, the Gablers were media sensations, both mainstream (they appeared on *60 Minutes*, *Today*, *Nightline*, *Good Morning America*, *Donahue*, *Freeman Reports*, *The David Frost Show*) and conservative (Jerry Falwell loved them). Misguided they may have been, but nobody got shot due to their efforts.

The same can't be said for Alabama-born Alice Moore.

***

A minister's wife and mother of four who sometimes wore strands of pearls that hung to her waist, Moore used her position on the Board of Education of Kanawha County, West Virginia, to espouse Gabler-like attitudes. In fact, the Gablers became mentors of sorts to Moore[13] when, in 1974, she challenged the board's textbook selections, including *The Autobiography of Malcolm X*, which Moore disliked because of its observation that "[a]ll praise is due to Allah that I moved to Boston when I did. If I hadn't, I'd probably still be a brainwashed black Christian."[14] She also targeted books containing passages by Allen Ginsberg, Sigmund Freud, and that cause célèbre of censors, Eldridge Cleaver, all of which she called "filthy, disgusting trash, unpatriotic and unduly favoring blacks."[15] She built up quite a following. Twenty-seven local ministers endorsed her, and more than twelve thousand people signed petitions insisting that the books not be adopted.[16] Yet the board did just that in June of 1974.

Big mistake.

Tensions mounted throughout the summer, with the district dividing itself into pro- and anti-textbook forces. On Labor Day, Rev. Marvin Horan thundered to a group of eight thousand protestors, "Now the thing we have to do is stay out of school until the books are gone. We must stay out of schools. The books must go!"[17] When schools opened the next day, attendance was down about 20 percent.[18] Picket lines started forming, resulting in work stoppages and business closings; thirty-five hundred coal miners went on strike.[19]

On September 6, Kanawha Circuit Court issued an injunction prohibiting protesters from interfering with the operation of the schools. The school board offered to remove the disputed books pending review by an eighteen-member board-appointed citizen committee. This was rejected, and protests escalated. Shots were fired, cars and homes firebombed, schools dynamited and vandalized, and eleven protesters arrested.[20] Twelve hundred students at George Washington High School walked out, insisting that the books be returned, while in another part of town, an anti-textbook protestor was shot and wounded.[21]

Superintendent Kenneth Underwood closed schools for four days. Still, the battle raged. During a rally, Rev. Charles Quigley prayed for God to kill the board members who had approved the books.[22] The Ku Klux Klan burned a cross in front of the district headquarters. Protesters attacked a CBS reporter and his film crew. Alice Moore herself got a round-the-clock bodyguard.[23]

The unrest was justified, in the eyes of the protestors, because of what the district intended to do with those accursed books. "They was going to teach my kids socialism and homosexuality," said David Callison.[24] "They was teaching situational ethics," said David Lucas.[25] "Satan is a roaring lion," said Phyllis Harmon-Higginbotham, "and he's out to steal, kill and destroy our children."[26]

The violence escalated again on October 9, 1974, when someone hurled dynamite through an elementary school window.[27] Then another school was attacked. Two nights later, protesters threw Molotov cocktails into a third school, and a fourth was firebombed a few nights after that. Fifteen sticks of dynamite were exploded near a gas meter at the Board of Education office.[28] By that point, a lot of people would have said, "Screw it. They're just books. We'll keep them out of the schools." Yet on November 8, the school board heroically voted to return them all.[29] When Reverend Horan was sentenced to three years in federal prison for his role in the bombings, the rampages came to an end.[30]

As for Alice Moore, her influence lingered. Remaining on the school board, she introduced guidelines for selecting future textbooks, which included

- "Textbooks for use in the classrooms of Kanawha County shall recognize the sanctity of the home";
- "Textbooks must encourage loyalty to the United States"; and
- "Textbooks must not defame our nation's founders or misrepresent the ideals and causes for which they struggled and sacrificed."[31]

Not wanting more tumult, the board agreed to them all. Moore remained a heroine and an inspiration to the far right, and in 2011, she received the Dr Robert Dreyfus Courageous Christian Leadership Award from Frontline Ministries.[32]

She died on July 5, 2007, at the age of eighty-three.

***

To some observers, Alice Moore would deserve the label of "America's top censor." Yet according to historian Adam Hochschild, that distinction belongs to Albert Sydney Burleson, a progressive Democrat (the term once meant something much different) who was instrumental in getting Woodrow Wilson elected to the presidency in 1912.[33] As a reward, Wilson appointed Burleson postmaster general in 1913.

Some of Burleson's achievements were laudatory. He expanded parcel post, rural free delivery, and air mail service. He was, unfortunately, also an ardent segregationist, forcing white and Black employees to sort mail in different areas, eat in different lunchrooms, and use different restrooms. In fact, he set up screens so that white employees didn't have to look at their Black counterparts.[34]

In 1914, World War I broke out in Europe. In his State of the Union address on December 7, 1915, Wilson spoke of American citizens "born under other flags … who have poured the poison of disloyalty into the very arteries of our national life" (i.e., German propaganda).[35] On April 2, 1917, Wilson asked Congress for a formal declaration of war on Germany. That same day, the chairman of the House Judiciary Committee, North Carolina's Edwin Y. Webb, introduced H.R. 291, A Bill to Punish Acts of Interference with the Foreign Relations, the Neutrality, and the Foreign Commerce of the United States, to Punish Espionage and Better to

Enforce the Criminal Laws of the United States, better known as the Espionage Act. Texas Senator Charles A. Culberson introduced a similar bill.

Tucked into that Senate bill was this provision:

> Whoever, in time of war, in violation of regulations to be prescribed by the President, which he is hereby authorized to make and promulgate, shall collect, record, publish, or communicate or attempt to elicit any information with respect to the movements, numbers, description, condition, or disposition of any of the armed forces, ships, aeroplanes, or war materials of the United States, or with respect to the plans or conduct, or supposed plans or conduct, of any naval or military operations, or with respect to any works or measures undertaken for or connected with the fortification or defense of any place, or any other information relating to the public defense or calculated to be or which might be useful to the enemy, shall be punished by a fine of not more than $10,000.00 or by imprisonment for not more than ten years, or both such fine and imprisonment; provided, that nothing in this section shall be construed to limit or restrain any discussion, comment or criticism of the acts or policies of the Government, or its representatives, or the publications of the same; provided, no discussion, comment or criticism shall convey information prohibited under this section.[36]

It was, in other words, a censorship clause.

A number of senators, Democrat and Republican, opposed this passage, arguing that it delegated too much power to the president; that it denied the right to trial by jury; and that it unconstitutionally abridged the freedom of the press.[37] William E. Borah of Idaho was the fiercest and most eloquent opponent:

> Once before in the history of the Government we undertook to establish something in the nature of an abridgment of speech and of the press. It was a complete and ignominious failure. It did not serve the objects and purposes of those who fathered it. It accomplished nothing in the way of that which they desired to accomplish. That was in 1798 [the Alien and Sedition Act]. Then during the Civil War we undertook again, in an indirect way, to establish a censorship by suppressing certain publications and to prevent the distribution of certain printed material coming supposedly, and in fact at that time conceded to be, from those who were in sympathy with the southern side of the contention. That was an ignominious failure, conceded to be such. It served no purpose whatever and accomplished no good whatever. The historians writing upon the subject and some of the men who enforced it, even, before they died conceded and acknowledged that their attempt to suppress these publications served no benefit and in no way aided the Government in its work.[38]

On May 12, Borah and his mates prevailed as the Senate voted, 39–38, to strike the passage. Wilson continued to fight, but in the end, Congress passed the bill sans censorship. It was signed it into law on June 15, 1917.

This was not a total victory for anticensorship forces, however, as the law stated that "[e]very letter, writing, circular, postal card, picture, print, engraving, photograph, newspaper, pamphlet, book, or other publication, matter or thing, of any kind, containing any matter advocating or urging treason, insurrection, or forcible resistance to any law of the United States, is hereby declared to be nonmailable."[39] What sorts of titles urged treason or insurrection? In Burleson's view, a lot. Foreign-language newspapers. Opinion journals. Socialist Party of America publications. Worst of all were "those offensive negro papers which constantly appeal to class and race prejudice."[40] From his desk in the Post Office Department headquarters in Washington, DC, Burleson shut down hundreds of such periodicals. By 1920, for instance, only one in ten socialist papers was still in operation.[41]

Burleson stayed in office until the last day of the Wilson administration, March 4, 1921, after which he lived in Texas until his death in 1937. Why is he America's top censor? The Gablers restricted more titles. Alice Moore caused more bloodshed. Yet neither of them was a high-ranking official in the United States government. The First Amendment states that "Congress shall make no law … abridging the freedom of speech, or of the press." The Espionage Act and its little brother, the Sedition Act of 1918, would seem to flout that mandate, leaving Burleson with a dubious duty to discharge.

By all accounts, he did so with relish.

***

Not all pro-censorship arguments are meritless. Parents, for instance, have the right to decide what media their children consume. A 2016 article for *The Federalist* quotes Kim Heinecke, who wrote to her children's school superintendent: "It is not a matter of 'sheltering' kids," said Heinecke, an Edmond, Oklahoma, mother of four who in 2016 challenged two books, Khaled Hosseini's *The Kite Runner* and Jeanette Walls's *The Glass Castle*, that her tenth-grade son was assigned to read. "It is a matter of guiding them toward what is best. We are the adults. It is our job to protect them—no matter how unpopular that may seem."[42]

Communities also have agency to chart their own course. In "In Defense of Book Banning," Mark Hemingway wrote that there is nothing nefarious in the removal of books from schools or libraries. Instead, "[y]our local community has simply decided that finite public resources are not going to be spent disseminating them. Judgments are made all the time about what goes on shelves for both practical and moral reasons. This is not book banning."[43]

Such an argument is reminiscent of the Island Trees school board. In a deposition dated November 21, 1977, Richard Ahrens said,

> We are the elected members of a board charged with the custody of thousands of youngsters during the school day. We stand in the shoes of their parents during that time. These students do not have the same rights to be exposed to obscenities as an adult. I will certainly not be an instrument of it. If they wish to read the "banned" books they are welcome to while not in school as long as their parents do not object. Most of these volumes are in the public library so there are alternative sources. As long as I have the legal right to exercise my discretion in the way I have I shall continue to do so. This is the essence of the concept of community standards and local control of school boards.[44]

Occasionally, censorship is not just acceptable but the right thing to do. In 1996, Congress passed the Communications Decency Act (CDA), a law that made it a crime for anyone to engage in online speech that was "indecent" or "patently offensive" if that speech could be viewed by a minor. The American Civil Liberties Union sued, arguing that the CDA was unconstitutionally vague and that it criminalized expression protected by the First Amendment.

The Supreme Court agreed and struck down the act. In his opinion, Justice John Paul Stevens wrote that "the interest in encouraging freedom of expression in a democratic society outweighs any theoretical but unproven benefit of censorship."[45] Congress tried again in 1998 with the Child Online Protection Act (COPA),* which narrowed the range of prohibited material. Again, the court said no.[46]

In 2001, Congress made a third attempt with the Children's Internet Protection Act, or CIPA, which required schools and libraries that rely on E-Rate—a federal system of discounts for internet access and other telecommunications—to install "a technology protection measure" on each of its computers with internet capability. In other words, those schools and libraries had to block access to websites that were obscene (as defined by *Miller v. California*), constituted child pornography (as defined by 18 U.S.C. 2256, a federal statute), or were harmful to minors. "Harmful" was defined as

> Any picture, image, graphic image file, or other visual depiction that — (i) taken as a whole and with respect to minors, appeals to a prurient interest in nudity, sex, or excretion; (ii) depicts, describes, or represents, in a patently offensive

---

* Not to be confused with COPPA, the Children's Online Privacy Protection Act. Passed in 1998, this law, which is still in effect, limits websites in the services they can offer children under age thirteen without parental consent.

way with respect to what is suitable for minors, an actual or simulated sexual act or sexual contact, actual or simulated normal or perverted sexual acts, or a lewd exhibition of the genitals; and (iii) taken as a whole, lacks serious literary, artistic, political, or scientific value as to minors.[47]

As with its predecessors, CIPA became the subject of a lawsuit, this time by an improbable plaintiff: the American Library Association. ALA argued that the law was unconstitutional because it "induces public libraries to violate their patrons' First Amendment rights" as a condition of receiving federal funds.[48] In 2002, district court judge Edward Becker agreed, ruling that CIPA was "facially invalid under the First Amendment" and ordering that the Federal Communications Commission and the Institute of Museum and Library Services "are permanently enjoined from withholding federal funds from any public library for failure to comply with" CIPA.[49]

One year later, in a 6–3 decision, the Supreme Court upheld CIPA. Writing for the majority, Chief Justice William Rehnquist observed that "[t]o fulfill their traditional missions of facilitating learning and cultural enrichment, public libraries must have broad discretion to decide what material to provide to their patrons."[50] Of course, a library that provides internet service cannot possibly review every single website before making it available. Judge Becker had reasoned, therefore, that "a public library enjoys less discretion in deciding which internet materials to make available than in making book selections."

Renquist rejected that distinction. "A library's failure," he wrote,

to make quality-based judgments about all the material it furnishes from the Web does not somehow taint the judgments it does make ... Most libraries already exclude pornography from their print collections because they deem it inappropriate for inclusion. We do not subject these decisions to heightened scrutiny; it would make little sense to treat libraries' judgments to block online pornography any differently, when these judgments are made for just the same reason.[51]

Filtering children's online experience may have been questionable twenty years ago, but it has strong backing now. In 2024, Congress passed a law banning TikTok in the United States—a law upheld by the Supreme Court,[52] though President Trump has been slow to enforce it.[53] Likewise, as of April 2025, twelve states— Connecticut, Louisiana, Texas, Maryland, Utah, Tennessee, Florida, Georgia, Minnesota, Arkansas, Ohio, and California—had passed laws restricting minors' use of social media, though some of those laws were blocked by courts.[54]

There is science to support the wisdom of such restrictions. The Mayo Clinic, for example, points out that social media can distract teens, disrupt their sleep, and expose them to "bullying, rumor spreading, unrealistic views of other people's lives and peer pressure."[55] Other studies link social media sites to rises in teen depression, anxiety, and suicide.[56]

Books may be the wrong place to flex restrictive muscles, but the internet is the perfect outlet. Rather than the passive information repository of Web 1.0, the current internet is a living thing, a conduit for social interaction. And haven't we always regulated our children's interactions? We regulate them because children, lacking worldliness, are no match for evil aims. Heck, even well-intentioned interactions can leave bruises. The Supreme Court was right to invalidate pre-CIPA bills that skewed too heavily toward compromising First Amendment liberties, and it was right to recognize that, in CIPA, Congress finally achieved the correct balance.

***

What, then, is the most accurate portrait of a censor: Kim Heinecke's worried parents? Richard Ahrens's in loco parentis? The Gablers' paper terrorists? Alice Moore's Christian soldiers? Sydney Burleson's bureaucratic fist?

It is a question that occupies Emily Knox, associate professor in the School of Information Sciences at the University of Illinois at Urbana-Champaign. Her 2015 study *Book Banning in 21st-Century America* focused on thirteen challenge cases in American public libraries and schools that took place between 2007 and 2011. It is one of the few studies that aims to understand, rather than lambaste, the Alice Moores of the world. Knox interviewed a number of these challengers. Her book discusses four recurring themes in their responses.

One is a sense of moral decay.[57] As we saw in chapter 1, a lot has happened in the past sixty years: a lot to stoke fear and efface trust. People who challenge books think that this blight was preventable—reversible, in fact, if certain books were done away with. These books play a dual role in challengers' worldviews. They are a symbol of decay, their obscenity reminding everyone of the Elysium that came before it, like the serpent in the garden. They are also a symptom of it—the destination of moral slippage. Challengers want to uphold the values of an earlier era, not to make a full return to the past but as a brake on society's rush to rot.[58]

A second concern is the role of public institutions in local communities. Here, Knox quotes the literary critic Michael Warner, who defines "public" as "a relationship among strangers that *must* consist of strangers."[59] Public, says Warner, is "self-organizing" and "only exists because of the powerlessness of the individual."[60] In other words, we depend on one another. We are interconnected. Circle of life.

Schools are part of the public sphere, as are libraries. Challengers lean heavily on the idea that because, say, *Slaughterhouse-Five* is available in public libraries, removing it from a school isn't so bad. (The Island Trees board mentioned this at every level of litigation.) Their worry, then, is not access but something more existential. The presence of an objectionable book in a library or on a school reading list means that the institution, and the community backing it, endorse that book. To Knox, then, censorship is a struggle for *knowledge*. "Forbidden knowledge," she writes, "is arcana Dei or knowledge for God alone," which "stands against legitimate knowledge that can be known by all."[61] Challenge cases, therefore, "focus on whether or not particular knowledge should be classified as public or legitimate."[62]

Many challengers see a connection between a school's curriculum and its library. For them, the library is an *extension* of the curriculum. For others, though, the two are separate. Curriculum is a place of orderly knowledge, while the library allows more freedom.[63] In the eyes of this latter group, if a book sits on a shelf awaiting discovery, that's a tacit acknowledgment and therefore OK. Assigning it as reading, however, is an active endorsement, which crosses a line by engendering mistrust in the teachers and administration.[64] And trust is paramount.

So are parents' wishes, which make up challengers' third source of anxiety. They tend to see parenting as not just a job, but a person's raison d'être. The primary responsibility of parents is to set boundaries and maintain control.[65] Challengers who are parents see their will as the highest authority. Not even the law trumps it. Even those who see book removal from the school library as a First Amendment violation "think that the district would still be upholding the First Amendment if a parent calls and requests that his or her child not be able to check out a particular book."[66]

One of these boundaries is the media that children consume.[67] To challengers, age limits are hard-and-fast boundaries with little room for interpretation. No moral relativism for them. Everything is rule-based, not cult-like, but commonsense. And because it's common, challengers resist the idea that they are imposing their beliefs on others. To them, most people think the way they do, and so anyone who doesn't is an outlier (in recent years, this has been upgraded to "a danger"). It is the school's job to insulate their children from these outliers, including other parents.[68] This outlook is predicated on a view of children as vessels to be filled. Knox quotes one challenger as saying, "We don't want to question the teachers' authority or the educational values that they bring forward. But we do want to be heard.... Rules need to be drawn and we need to put in all the good stuff while we can before we let the rest of the world fill them up."[69]

This dovetails with the fourth source of challenger angst: the innocence of childhood. Challengers have this notion that ideas are dangerous for young minds.[70] And if ideas are dangerous, then so are the people who promulgate them. This wasn't an issue in *Island Trees v. Pico*—for the school board, the books seemed to stand alone, with little emphasis on the authors—but it has become a battle cry for modern challengers, such as those opposed to Drag Queen Story Hour, a program started in San Francisco in 2015. Or supporters of legislation such as an

Idaho bill targeting "sex traffickers who 'condition' children through books or the availability of explicit material at libraries increasing the likelihood of pedophilia, 'rape, murder and child molestation'"[71] (i.e., librarians). In 2024, the group Moms for Liberty fought to remove five books from an upstate New York school, not simply because they were obscene, but because the quintet "normalizes violence and abuse of women and children, depicts rape, equates violence and pain with pleasure, [and] encourages and normalizes early sexual activity among minors."[72]

Books, of course, can be difficult or challenging, and sometimes scary. This is not, however, a threat to be guarded against. Kids need to be prepared for a threatening world, and books can help. For example, a book can give a child words to describe the indescribable. The ALA's *Intellectual Freedom Manual* tells the story of a fourteen-year-old girl who read Laurie Halse Anderson's award-winning novel *Speak*, in which ninth-grader Melinda Sordino is raped at a party.

After the girl finished it, she handed it to her mother and said, "This is what daddy has been doing to me."[73]

Permissiveness, of course, can go too far, and Steven Pico agrees that parental concerns have a place in the censorship discussion. "I never disparage parents who are advocating for their children's education," he told me. "Parents have a responsibility to be involved."[74] Problem is, book bans don't protect children. In fact, they make them defenseless. As an illustration, he invoked the 2023 effort in Glen Ridge, New Jersey, to ban *All Boys Aren't Blue*, a memoir by the Black queer activist George Johnson, as well as other LGBTQ+ books. The library trustees voted unanimously to retain every book, a decision that Johnson applauded: "Books that detail the truthful experiences of others build empathy, support and love. My book is simply my story. It details my first sexual experience. Kids need to know about agency, consent and that they have a right to say no."[75]

Another problem is that reasonable people can disagree over whether a book is too graphic, especially for older teenagers. One mom's trash is another mom's pleasure. I encountered this division myself vis-à-vis *Breaking Dawn*, Stephenie Meyer's fourth tale of the romance between vampire heartthrob Edward Cullen and his maddeningly warm-blooded beloved, Bella. My daughter Michelle, who was ten at the time, had borrowed the first three books from her teacher and enjoyed them. When she asked for *Breaking Dawn*, however, the teacher demurred, saying Michelle would need a note from her parents.

Upon hearing this, my older daughter, who had read the books years before, begged us to withhold our permission. Assuming this was an attempt to flaunt her privileged status as the firstborn, I asked her why. She wrinkled her nose and said, "It's full of sex."

Full of sex. I hadn't read the books, but you couldn't be a parent in the late 2000s without absorbing Twilight mania, and I hadn't seen any complaints that jibed with this assessment. Besides, Stephenie Meyer was a Mormon. Mormons are a lot of things, but "smut peddler" has not historically been one of them. Michelle's mother left the decision up to me, so I gathered a pen and paper and wrote the note. Perhaps I should have read the book first, but I didn't. Instead, I—get this—trusted the teacher's judgment.

Years later, I did read the series. Edward and Bella fall in love almost immediately, and their interactions are sexually charged. Yet they are careful not to consummate it because, being a vampire, he might lose control and kill her. Despite this complication, the two get married at the start of *Breaking Dawn*. Naturally, there is a wedding night. *This must be it*, I thought and settled in for a scorcher. Instead, the scene cut to the next morning, with Bella wearing a shredded nightgown, and Edward musing about the need to buy a new bed—literally, as chunks of wood were missing from the frame.

Not exactly *9½ Weeks*, is it?

Notes

1   Daniel Defoe, *An Essay upon Projects* (R. R., 1697), 248–49.
2   "Tullius, Servius," *A Dictionary of Greek and Roman Biography and Mythology*, ed. William Smith, https://www.perseus.tufts.edu/hopper/text?doc=Perseus:text:1999.04.0104:entry=tullius-servius-bio-1.
3   Cicero, "De Legibus (On Laws)," *Topostext*, https://topostext.org/work/752.
4   "Censor," *Online Etymology Dictionary*, https://www.etymonline.com/search?q=censor.
5   Douglas Martin, "Norma Gabler, Leader of Crusade on Textbooks, Dies at 84," *New York Times*, August 1, 2007, https://www.nytimes.com/2007/08/01/education/01gabler.html.
6   William Martin, "The Guardians Who Slumbereth Not," *Texas Monthly*, November 1982, https://www.texasmonthly.com/news-politics/the-guardians-who-slumbereth-not/.
7   Ibid.
8   Ibid.
9   Martin, "Norma Gabler."
10 Martin, "The Guardians."
11 Ibid.
12 Ibid.
13 Mike Selby, "The Textbook Wars of Kanawha County," *Cranbrook Daily Townsman*, March 28, 2017, https://www.cranbrooktownsman.com/our-town/the-textbook-wars-of-kanawha-county-5313339.
14 Trey Kay, Deborah George, and Stan Bumgardner, "Books and Beliefs: The Kanawha County Textbook Wars," American Radio Works, https://americanradioworks.publicradio.org/features/textbooks/books_and_beliefs.html.
15 Herbert N. Foerstel, *Banned in the U.S.A.* (Greenwood Press, 1994), 2.
16 Shirley Smith, "Kanawha County Textbook Controversy," *e-VW: The West Virginia Encyclopedia Online*, https://www.wvencyclopedia.org/entries/1064.
17 "The Great Textbook War: Transcript," American Radio Works, https://americanradioworks.publicradio.org/features/textbooks/transcript.html.
18 Smith, "Kanawha County Textbook."
19 Ibid.
20 Ibid.

21 Kay et al., "Books and Beliefs."

22 Ibid.

23 Ibid.

24 "The Great Textbook War: Transcript."

25 Ibid.

26 Ibid.

27 Kay et al., "Books and Beliefs."

28 Ibid.

29 Ibid.

30 Ibid.

31 Ibid.

32 Robert Knight, "Culture-War Heroine Gets Her Due," *Washington Times*, October 10, 2011, https://www.washingtontimes.com/news/2011/oct/10/culture-war-heroine-gets-her-due/.

33 Adam Hochschild, "America's Top Censor—So Far," *Mother Jones*, https://www.motherjones.com/politics/2022/10/hochschild-woodrow-wilson-censor-journalism/.

34 Ibid.

35 Daniel Moynihan, *Secrecy: The American Experience* (Yale University Press, 1998), 89.

36 65th Cong., 1st Session 1917, 766.

37 Thomas Carroll, "Freedom of Speech and of the Press in War Time: The Espionage Act," *Michigan Law Review* 17, no. 9 (1919): 621–65.

38 Congressional Record 55, pt. 2:2119 (May 11, 1917).

39 Espionage Act, 40 Stat. 217 (1917).

40 Hochschild, "America's Top Censor."

41 Ibid.

42 Jenni White, "Parents Shouldn't Force Kids to Read Smut," *The Federalist*, March 25, 2016, https://thefederalist.com/2016/03/15/parents-shouldnt-let-schools-force-kids-to-read-smut/.

43 Mark Hemingway, "In Defense of Book Banning," *The Federalist*, March 11, 2014, https://thefederalist.com/2014/03/11/in-defense-of-book-banning/.

44 Transcript of Richard Ahrens, 1977.

45 *Reno v. American Civil Liberties Union*, 521 U.S. 844, 885 (1997).

46 *Ashcroft v. American Civil Liberties Union*, 535 U.S. 564 (2002).

47 20 U.S.C. § 9134(f)(7).

48 *American Library Association, Inc. v. United States*, 201 F. Supp. 2d 401, 407 (E.D. Pa. 2002).

49 Ibid., 496.

50 *United States v. American Library Association*, 539 U.S. 194, 195 (2003).

51 Ibid., 208.

52 Amy Howe, "Supreme Court Upholds TikTok Ban," *SCOTUS Blog*, January 17, 2025, https://www.scotusblog.com/2025/01/supreme-court-upholds-tiktok-ban/.

53 Dace Potas, "Trump Delaying the TikTok Ban Is the Most Lawless Thing He's Done Yet," *USA Today*, June 25, 2025, https://www.usatoday.com/story/opinion/columnist/2025/06/25/trump-tiktok-ban-delay-extended/84323075007/.

54 Peter Gratton, "12 States with Teens' Social Media Regulation—Is Yours One of Them?," *Investopedia*, April 25, 2025, https://www.investopedia.com/states-with-social-media-regulation-for-teens-8757983.

55 "Teens and Social Media Use: What's the Impact?," Mayo Clinic, January 18, 2024, https://www.mayoclinic.org/healthy-lifestyle/tween-and-teen-health/in-depth/teens-and-social-media-use/art-20474437.

56 Elia Abi-Jaoude, Karline Treurnicht Naylor, and Antonio Pignatiello, "Smartphones, Social Media Use and Youth Mental Health," *Canadian Medical Association Journal* 192, no. 6 (2020): E136–41.

57 Emily Knox, *Book Banning in 21st-Century America* (Rowman & Littlefield, 2015), 67.

58 Ibid., 70.

59 Ibid.

60 Ibid.

61 Ibid., 11.

62 Ibid.

63 Ibid., 73.

64 Ibid., 74.

65 Ibid., 75.

66 Ibid., 72.

67 Ibid., 76.

68 Ibid., 80.

69 Ibid., 82.

70 Ibid.

71 Ian Max Stevenson, "'A Specter of Fear': Claims about Idaho 'Harmful' Books Rooted in QAnon Conspiracy Theory," *Idaho Statesman*, March 12, 2024, https://www.idahostatesman.com/news/politics-government/state-politics/article284635335.html.

72 Justin Rohrlich, "Moms for Liberty Goes to War with New York School over Five Library Books," *The Independent*, March 30, 2024, https://www.the-independent.com/news/world/americas/book-bans-public-schools-moms-for-liberty-trump-new-york-state-b2604694.html.

73 Pat Scales, "Intellectual Freedom and Young People," in *Intellectual Freedom Manual*, 10th ed. Martin Garnar and Trina Magi (American Library Association, 2021), 136.

74 Anthony Aycock, "Desperately Seeking Sources," *Missouri Review*, October 20, 2023, https://missourireview.com/desperately-seeking-sources-by-anthony-aycock/.

75 Julia Martin, "Glen Ridge Library Won't Ban LGBTQ Books as a Thousand People Show Up in Opposition," *Northjersey.com*, February 9, 2023, https://www.northjersey.com/story/news/essex/glen-ridge/2023/02/09/glen-ridge-library-nj-ban-lbgtq-books-protest/69889598007/.

5 Desperately Seeking Sources

When times are scary, so the saying goes, people respond by clamping down. Taking charge. Controlling what they can. In the 1970s, as we saw in chapter 1, a lot of scary stuff was happening. Anxiety over these occurrences was reflected in the decade's movies—*The Exorcist, The Texas Chainsaw Massacre, Jaws, The Omen, Halloween, Dawn of the Dead, The Amityville Horror*, and *Friday the 13th*, to name a few. These weren't minor films; they launched franchises, and in some cases, genres. People saw in them expressions of what sociologist Stanley Cohen called "moral panic," which is what results when

> [a] condition, episode, person or group of persons emerges to become defined as a threat to societal values and interests; its nature is presented in a stylized and stereotypical fashion by the mass media; the moral barricades are manned by editors, bishops, politicians and other right-thinking people; socially accredited experts pronounce their diagnoses and solutions; ways of coping are evolved or (more often) resorted to; the condition then disappears, submerges or deteriorates and becomes more visible.[1]

Counterculture, Satanism, serial killers, drug use, premarital sex, economic instability—all were present in that era's art, which, to worried parents, seemed perversely aimed at America's youth.

How did the country respond? By tying those apron strings as tight as possible.

***

Being a child is hard. It involves homework. Chores. Being nice to your siblings. Few people take you seriously. You have no agency, can make no decisions. You aren't allowed to drive or date or stay up past 9 p.m. Your entertainment peaked with Mr. Rogers. Yet these travails are trifles compared to kids of the early nineteenth century. Those who didn't die as infants were often put to work at an early age, risking their lives in coal mines and textile mills. Girls as young as five became nurses or maids to wealthy families. Others worked on farms or as street hawkers, or famously, chimney sweeps.

It was the Romantic poets who "invented" the notion of the "innocent child of nature."[2] Soon, doctors, writers, and other public intellectuals were chiming in with opinions on how to improve children's lot in life. In 1840, Lord Ashley, future 7th Earl of Shaftesbury, helped set up the Children's Employment Commission, which issued reports on the remorseless conditions in mines and other workplaces.[3] Such reports were echoed in Elizabeth Barrett Browning's "The Cry of the Children": "all day, we drag our burden tiring, / Through the coal-dark, underground—/ Or, all day, we drive the wheels of iron / In the factories, round and round." Or the novels of Charles Dickens (*Bleak House, Oliver Twist*), who at age twelve had been sent to work in a blacking factory and never forgot it.

Being a child got easier as the years progressed, thanks to improvements in child welfare, hygiene, nutrition, and education. By "easier," I mean survivable. Infant mortality dropped, but this raised another problem: what to do with all these children who hadn't died? By 1900, nearly all Western countries had laws prohibiting or restricting child labor, yet they were only loosely enforced. The United States census report from that year showed that nearly two million children—one of every six—had a job.[4] The National Child Labor Committee was founded in 1904 to advance "the rights, awareness, dignity, well-being and education of children and youth as they relate to work and working,"[5] but states opposed it, especially Southern states, whose farms and textile plants relied on young, underpaid laborers.

By the 1920s, women had been enfranchised and were working outside the home, making it increasingly common for children to spend their days at school, with peers, or on their own. This dip in parental supervision supercharged anxiety about children's moral development, leading to the formation of the American juvenile justice system.[6] Later, the upheavals of the 1960s "further eroded the protective membrane that once sheltered children from precocious experience and knowledge of the adult world," in the words of Marie Winn, author of *Children Without Childhood*.[7] Winn blamed television for quickening this decline, fretting that it let children "gorge on the fruit of knowledge, not only about sex but also about the complexities of life in general—Vietnam, Watergate, the energy crisis, famine."[8]

Of course, TV hasn't been the only information superfund highway. Books could also teach children a lot of what's what. This was especially true of an assertive new genre: YA fiction.

***

Children's books had existed since the seventeenth century. Early works for children were educational, instructing the young readers how to live virtuous lives. They were moralistic, such as Aesop's fables or *Tales of Mother Goose* (1697), or overtly religious, such as *Spiritual Milk for Boston Babes* (1656), written by John Cotton, a prominent minister in the Massachusetts Bay Colony. It was the first children's book printed in British North America.[9] (Only one first edition survives: in the New York Public Library.)

In the eighteenth century, children's literature became less didactic and more entertaining, and the nineteenth century saw the appearance of some classics:

- *Swiss Family Robinson* (1812),
- *Children's and Household Tales* by Jacob and Wilhelm Grimm (1812),
- *Alice's Adventures in Wonderland* (1865),
- *Tom Sawyer* (1876),
- *The Adventures of Pinocchio* (1883),
- *Treasure Island* (1883), and
- *The Jungle Book* (1894).

In the twentieth century, thanks to Harper & Row editor Ursula Nordstrom, who "believed in truth for children, even when it made adults uncomfortable," children were introduced to a new wave of magna opera, including *Stuart Little* (1945), *Goodnight Moon* (1947), *Charlotte's Web* (1952), *Where the Wild Things Are* (1963), *Harriet the Spy* (1964), *Freaky Friday* (1972), and *Where the Sidewalk Ends* (1974).[10]

Adolescents, of course, have different interests, different needs, than younger children. This is especially true of teenagers, a group that emerged as a distinct unit around the time of World War II. Until then, publishers did not distinguish between children's and adolescent books.[11] Teens had to be content with reading "up" (adult stuff) or "down" (Mother Goose, etc.). A few authors tried to straddle the young/old boundary. One was Edward Stratemeyer, who in the late 1800s began publishing adventure stories, first in boys' magazines, then as dime novels. He grew so prolific that, in 1905, he formed the Stratemeyer Syndicate, recasting himself as the Idea Guy and hiring ghostwriters to build out his frameworks into full-length novels.[12]

From this process came some of literature's most beloved serial characters, such as the Hardy Boys, the Rover Boys, Tom Swift, Nancy Drew, and the Bobbsey Twins. Stratemeyer paid his authors a flat rate while keeping the copyrights, and their perpetual earnings, for himself,[13] a model later used by romance, horror, and other genre publishers, as well as industry-unto-himself James Patterson, who usually starts with "a 50- to 70- page outline," then flips it to a coauthor to finish.[14]

Often overlooked in publishing histories, sandwiched as it is between the births of modernism (1920s) and postmodernism (1960s), the 1940s and 1950s were a transitional period. Richard Wright's *Black Boy* (1940), a book at the center of *Island Trees v. Pico*, previewed the mid-century fight for Black equality. George Orwell called out European fascism in *Animal Farm* (1945) and *1984* (1949). Shirley Jackson's grim story "The Lottery" (1948) satirized the tension between progress and tradition. Alfred Kinsey's *Sexual Behavior in the Human Male* (1948) and its 1953 sequel, *Sexual Behavior in the Human Female*, led Americans out of the bedroom and into the sizzling sixties. Benjamin Spock's *The Common Sense Book of Baby and Child Care* (1946) overturned the decades-old "spare the rod and spoil the child" parenting advice in favor of a "relaxed but clear-eyed posture," which "set the tone for the postwar era, shaping a generation that has yet to make its full and final impact on the United States."[15]

It wasn't just parents who were hungry for guidance. That newly defined teen demographic was as well. And where there's a market for something, culture will find a way to meet it. One of those ways was teen magazines, which started in the 1930s with *Compact*, aimed at older teens, and *Calling All Girls*, for younger ones. These titles merged into what would become *Young Miss*, or *YM*, which ran until 2004.[16] *Seventeen*, which is still going strong, began in 1944.[17]

These magazines were full of fashion and lifestyle advice, a genre that teenage fashion model Betty Cornell supercharged in 1951 with her book *Betty Cornell's Glamour Guide for Teens*. The book offered hairstyle, clothing, and food recommendations, as well as Talmudic pronouncements such as "Beautiful hair is about the most important thing a girl has"; "To walk gracefully one must move the leg in one piece"; and "The next time you get up to dance, pull in those tummy muscles, tuck in your fanny, pull up your rib cage, and then dance."[18] (My favorite: "If you don't know what foods are fattening, ask your chubby friends, because they *will* know.") For readers who couldn't get enough, Cornell produced a whole line of how-tos, including *Betty Cornell's Teen-Age Popularity Guide* (1953), *Betty Cornell's Teen-Age Knitting Guide* (1953), *Betty Cornell's All about Boys* (1958), and *So You're Going to be a Teen* (1963).

Cartoon representations of teendom were also popular, beginning when Archie Andrews, Betty Cooper, Veronica Lodge, and the rest of Riverdale's under-eighteen set appeared in the December 1941 issue of *Pep Comics*. Patsy Walker, who debuted in 1945, was a sort of female Archie, down to the red hair and dark-haired rival, Hedy Wolfe. Patsy's series ran for twenty years and spun off several more, including *Patsy & Hedy* and *Patsy & Her Pals*. Similar titles were *Buzzy* (1944), *Teena* (1944), *Katy Keene* (1945), *Millie the Model* (1945), *Leave It to Binky* (1948), and *Scribbly* (1948). Historians call these "teen humor comics," which segued into the romance comics genre of the late 1940s and beyond.[19]

For most historians, the first work of prose fiction to deal with typical teen concerns—growing up, fitting in, falling in love—was Maureen Daly's novel

Seventeenth Summer, which appeared in 1942. This makes it the inaugural young adult, or YA, book.* Daly began it when she was herself that surreal age, though it wouldn't be published for several more years. Born in Ireland in 1921, she and her family moved to the United States two years later, settling in Fond du Lac, Wisconsin.[20] At age fifteen, Daly entered a short story, "Fifteen," in a nationwide *Scholastic Magazine* contest, winning fourth place. The next year, she won first place in the *Scholastic* contest—as well as an O'Henry Award—with another story, "Sixteen," about two high schoolers who meet at a skating rink.[21]

Sticking with the same formula, she wrote *Seventeenth Summer* and entered it in a contest sponsored by the publisher Dodd, Mead & Company, which she won. Her prize? $1,000 plus publication, which occurred in 1942.[22] In a *New York Times* profile, Orville Prescott praised Daly's "sincerity, sound workmanship and authoritative knowledge of her subject," listing her among a group of "rising stars" that included Nelson Algren, Howard Fast, and Eudora Welty.[23] The book has been in print ever since.[24]

The story is straightforward. Seventeen-year-old Angeline "Angie" Morrow enters her final summer at home in 1940s Fond du Lac before leaving for college in the fall. Determined to hang out and have fun with friends, she instead falls for Jack Duluth, high-school sports hero, who shocks her at summer's end by proposing marriage. Jack isn't college material—he is bound for Oklahoma and his uncle's bakery business—and try as she might, Angie can't see a way to make it work. So, she gently turns Jack down.

Parts of the book haven't aged well. Certain boys are "fast." A nightclub pianist is "colored." One of Jack's buds, a guy called Swede, says he would "rather be a dead Chinaman" than go out on a cold night. Angie and her friends drink alcohol, and not on the sly—it is served to them in restaurants.

Yet it is easy to see why the book has such a devoted following: Angie herself. Her wit is reminiscent of Eloise Bridgerton. For instance, when she was getting to know Jack, Angie found him off-putting:

I could just see his father in shirt sleeves, folding food onto his knife and never using napkins except when there was company. And probably they brought the coffee pot right in and set it on the table. My whole mind was filled with a growing disdain and loathing. His family probably didn't even own a butter knife![25]

---

* Some sources award this title to Helen Boylston's 1936 novel *Sue Barton: Student Nurse*. I disagree, on the grounds that Sue was eighteen—a legal adult—and that the book, plus its six sequels, spend a lot of time on Sue's career, especially as it conflicts with later pressures on her to marry and have children. Sue Barton may not be an early YA heroine, but she is a feminist pioneer.

Plus she and her sister Lorraine talk about sex—I won't say "with abandon," but at least it's alluded to. Of how many other novels in the 1940s was that true?

Seventeenth Summer deals with serious subjects, but it does so with a light, upbeat tone. This was characteristic of YA books throughout the 1940s and 1950s. By the late 1960s, as the mood of the country darkened, so did writing for adolescents. Fiction began showing teens grappling with drugs, sex, violence, and other troubles:

- S. E. Hinton's *The Outsiders* (1967);
- Robert Lipsyte's *The Contender* (1967), featuring one of YA's first protagonists of color;
- Paul Zindel's *The Pigman* (1968);
- John Donovan's *I'll Get There. It Better Be Worth the Trip* (1969), another Ursula Nordstrom title and an early portrayal of same-sex attraction;
- Judy Blume's *Are You There God? It's Me, Margaret* (1970); and
- Robert Cormier's *The Chocolate War* (1974).

These are among some of literature's most frequently challenged books, a fact to which their authors have had varying reactions. Zindel said that he "ignore[s] critics usually."[26] Hinton was "pleased that people were shocked [by *The Outsiders*] ... I wanted something realistic to be written about teenagers."[27] Blume couldn't hide her exasperation: "I hate the idea that you should always protect children. They live in the same world we do. They see things and hear things. The worst is when there are secrets, because what they imagine, and have to deal with alone, is usually scarier than the truth."[28]

Cormier was more thoughtful on the subject. He wrote several essays in which he neither traduced censors nor lionized their opponents. Instead, he grappled with their ideas, searching for balance, acknowledging the impact on students, parents, teachers, and writers. In one of those essays, "A Book Is Not a House," he describes writing a masturbation scene for *The Chocolate War*—a scene he thought was authentic. When his fifteen-year-old daughter Chris, asked to read the work-in-progress, he removed that passage but re-inserted it to submit the book to editors, several of whom rejected it. Finally, one editor liked the book but suggested that Cormier consider removing that scene. "I knew instantly what I had done," Cormier wrote. "I had been willing to inflict that chapter on other people's 15-year-old daughters but unwilling to inflict it on my own daughter."[29]

Only one thing for it, then: "I removed the chapter."[30]

***

There is a tendency to assume that if teenagers are looking for information on sex, they must be engaging in it.[31]

That is certainly the stance of many conservative commentators, including Jenni White, who, in an article for *The Federalist*, cites a pair of studies, one of which "found that participants who reported frequent contact with sexually explicit material (SEM) had more casual sex partners and began having sex at younger ages."[32] Moreover, "SEM viewing frequency in women correlated with a lower age of first intercourse and a decrease in both sexual and relationship satisfaction among men."[33] The other study blamed racy movies for teens' sexual uninhibitedness. "Between the ages of ten and fifteen," the researchers wrote, "the tendency to seek more novel and intense stimulation of all kinds peaks. The wild hormonal surge of adolescence makes judicious thinking a bit more difficult."[34]

Books or no books, movies or no movies, I was not having sex as a teenager. Perhaps I excelled at keeping my "wild hormonal surges" in check. Perhaps, as a preacher's kid, I was noli me tangere. Whatever the reason, my sexual activity was zero, though my interest in sex was pi to a thousand places minus the decimal. Yet I was shockingly ignorant of the process. I knew little about consent. Identity. Acceptance. Communication. Honesty. I thought that blowjobs involved actual blowing. That "come" meant you stepped close to your partner. That AIDS was "the things that make you gay."[35] In the 1980s, there was no internet, *Cosmo* was strictly for girls, and Dr. Ruth—well.

How could I combat this information deficit?

Teens want sexual information. They need it. Pundits who worry about pornography are misguided. Pornography is not information; it is titillation. It is entertainment. It doesn't resemble real sex—ask anyone. This makes it of little use for what scholars call "information-seeking behaviors."

When people search for information, they usually have one of three goals: to seek answers, to reduce uncertainty, or to make sense of a situation. In other words, they have a *need*. An information need, according to the scholar Charles Cole, is "an adaptive human mechanism that drives humans to seek out, recognise, and then adapt to changes in their social and physical environments."[36] Silvania Miranda and Kira Tarapanoff, also information scholars, offer a more specific definition: information need is "a state or process started when one perceives that there is a gap between the information and knowledge available to solve a problem and the actual solution of the problem."[37] Researchers Denise Agosto and Sandra Hughes-Hassell have taken a long look into the everyday life information seeking, or ELIS, of teenagers. ELIS is "self-exploration and world exploration that helps teens understand themselves and the social and physical worlds in which they live."[38] Their model includes seven areas of teen development, each of which has its own ELIS characteristics: social, emotional, reflective, physical, creative, cognitive, and—censors, take note—sexual.[39]

As I have said, my parents were not useful in this area. They taught me many things—manners, open-mindedness, hard work. They were well educated and instilled in me a desire for the same. But we never discussed sex. Nor do I recall having any instruction in school, which is unsurprising. Sex education has always been a fraught topic. Few would argue that kids should know *nothing* about it. Yet where that knowledge should come from, and what it should entail, are not easily settled.

The idea of increasing public understanding of the subtleties of sexual intimacy was practically unknown until the early 1900s and the beginning of the social hygiene movement, a combination of public health awareness, medicine, and social work intended to help control sex work and "vice."[40] The movement was aimed at educating Anglo-Saxon white men, scaring them into only having "virtuous" sex with their wives, thereby reducing the family's exposure to STDs.[41] These had become rampant by the twentieth century. During World War I, for instance, they were the second most common reason for disability and absence from duty for American soldiers, being responsible for nearly seven million lost person-days and the discharge of more than ten thousand men.[42] (Only the Spanish influenza accounted for more loss of duty.)[43]

The Victorians had been famously close-mouthed about sexual matters, which reformers now saw as part of the problem. False modesty, they argued, only encouraged the problems to fester. Mary Ware Dennett's efforts had been a response to this. And there were others. One of the most prominent was the American Social Hygiene Association, formed in 1914 through the merger of three other groups: the American Federation for Sex Hygiene, the American Vigilance Association, and the New York Social Hygiene Society.[44] ASHA, as it was called, worked nationally as well as locally to publish instructional pamphlets, films, and newspapers and to encourage everyone to speak openly and without stigma about sex (a goal we still struggle with in the twenty-first century).

Before long, the government had gotten involved. In January of 1920, the US Bureau of Education and the US Public Health Service collaborated on the first-ever sex education survey among American high schools.[45] The survey sought information in three areas: the number of high schools teaching sex education, the content of sex education instruction, and the schools' attitudes on sex education. Out of almost sixty-five hundred responses, only 15 percent offered sex education "incidentally in subjects of regular curriculum" such as biology or sociology.[46] Another 25 percent provided "emergency" sex education in the form of "lectures, talks, sex hygiene exhibits, and pamphlets."[47] The rest offered nothing, though not for lack of wanting, as the study also found that 85 percent of principals thought there should be *more* sex education in schools.[48]

As the century progressed, sex education moved even further beyond mere disease prevention. In 1964, Dr. Mary Calderone, medical director for Planned Parenthood Federation of America, founded the Sexuality Information and Education Council of the United States (SIECUS), which became a recognized leader in the field of sexuality and sex education.[49] In 1972, the US Commission on

Population Growth and the American Future released a report acknowledging that "there seems to be a lag between the recognition of the importance of sexuality in human relationships and the development of ways to improve this aspect of our lives" and recommending "that funds be made available to the National Institute of Mental Health to support the development of a variety of model programs in human sexuality."[50] That same year, in the first national study on teen sexual activity, researchers John Kantner and Melvin Zelnick reported that 30 percent of 4,240 women ages 15–19 had had sex, though "only a minority correctly understood the risk of pregnancy in mid-cycle."[51] Three years later, the World Health Organization defined "sexual health" as "the integration of the somatic, emotional, intellectual, and social aspects of sexual being, in ways that are positively enriching and that enhance personality, communication, and love. Fundamental to this concept are *the right to sexual information* and the right to pleasure" (emphasis added).[52]

Not everyone celebrated this new openness around sex. Reactionary groups such as the John Birch Society and Christian Crusade fought the movement. One of Christian Crusade's pamphlets, *Is the School House the Proper Place to Teach Raw Sex?*, condemned the "rawness" of sex education, "the SIECUS SEXPOT," and the "revolutionary gospel" of SIECUS founder Mary Calderone.[53] It warned that unless sex ed is stamped out, "our children will become easy targets for Marxism and other amoral, nihilistic philosophies—as well as V.D.!"[54]

Such efforts seemed to have an effect. Gallup polls in 1969 and 1971 showed a drop in support for public school sex education from 71 percent to 65 percent.[55] A national survey conducted in 1977 showed that most Americans with traditional family values disapproved of sex education in public schools.[56] By the late 1970s, only 35 percent of private and public schools provided sex education, with widely varying content: birth control, for instance, was a growing interest.[57]

I entered middle school in 1985 and never received any sex education at all. Is it any wonder I turned to novels?

***

Mark Manson, author of *The New York Times* best-selling *The Subtle Art of Not Giving a F*ck*, lists three benefits of reading fiction: it promotes diversity, it increases empathy, and it offers a healthful escape ("like doing bench presses for your mind").[58] For teen readers, these boons run deeper. Harvard researcher M. G. Prezioso, for example, is "invested" in teens reading fiction "because it points us towards and enables this nuanced, textured understanding of the world we live in."[59]

What about sex? According to YA scholar Michael Cart, excluding sex from young adult books "is to agree to a de facto conspiracy of silence, to imply to young readers that sex is so awful, so traumatic, so dirty that we can't even write about it."[60] Information scientist Amy Patee agrees, arguing that sexual content offers young adults a "private, safe place to try on new feelings of sexual desire."[61] Fiction may be an atypical locus of sex education, but Patee sees it as an excellent one. She argues that if movies, fiction, and other mass media are the only sources available to some children, then we need to be less focused on their explicitness and more concerned with their accuracy.[62]

Moreover, scholars speak of the *right* to sexual knowledge. Sex is pretty important, no? Children shouldn't be expected not to learn about it. Schools may think they're fulfilling that right with biology-only (or, worse, abstinence-only) coursework, but it's all decontextualized, separated from emotional concerns such as love and respect. Fiction puts that context back in. As one teen in a research study commented,

> I think that books give you an incorporation of all aspects. From health you learn anatomy ... this is what happens, be safe. And then in terms of porn it's very vulgar, it's not very representative of real life sex. You know what I mean? I feel books incorporate all of that. Relationship aspects, dynamics between characters, it shows sex as the whole thing not just one specific scene or the biological aspect or something. So, I think it wholly encompasses everything.[63]

So, what kind of narrative works best for the sex education of young adults? Erin Farrow says that sexual content in YA fiction should be *warranted*.[64] That is, it should advance the plot or help with characterization. Teen readers are savvy. If a sex scene is superfluous or, worse, included just to sell the book, it will turn off most readers. A lot of YA fiction is written in the first person. First-person narratives offer a direct line to characters' thoughts, meaning any sexual portrayals are likely to focus just as much, if not more, on the internal stuff related to the act, such as questions of readiness and performance.[65] Intimate scenes, according to Pattee, should include character development "from anticipation to reflection."[66]

As for the act itself, how much detail should be included? Farrow says it's best to consider the reader. Sixteen- to eighteen-year-olds may have had some experience with sexual acts. Twelve- to fourteen-year-olds? Probably not. Thus, writing scenes for those two age groups will be completely different. At a minimum, the narrative should be "candid and sincere" but also sensitive and considerate.[67]

***

For me, the best writer about sex, the one from whom I learned the most, was not Susan Isaacs. (Why did Marcia cry?) It was not Ruth Harris. (Why did Jane cry, too? Does sex hurt? Is it like a football injury?) It was not Jackie Collins. (Seeing "pussy" in print was a thrill, but what the heck was that "magic button" stuff?) It was someone writing in an entirely separate genre, one that is at once fantastical and real, scary and consoling.

That writer was Stephen King.

My first King book was *Cujo*. Donna Trenton is a bored housewife whose fling with local poet/tennis player/furniture stripper Steve Kemp goes sour. Arguing with him for the gazillionth time, she reflects that "although she had seen his penis up close—had had it in her mouth—she had never really seen what his face looked like."[68] I read that line several times, trying to let it sink in. I knew about mouths. I knew about penises.

What I did not know was that the two could be contiguous.

As I read more King books, I noticed they all had varying degrees of sexual content. *Christine* offered a few backseat grindings. *Tommyknockers* had a line about someone's hymen bursting, which sent me to my mother's nursing dictionary. In *The Stand*, Nadine jerks off Harold, and he "cried aloud with the strength of his climax, unable to help himself. It was as if someone had touched a match to a whole network of nerves just under his skin, nerves that plunged deep to form the living webwork of his groin."[69] These lines were interesting but ephemeral. I needed something more sustained. More visceral. More instructive.

Then I read *IT*.

Published in 1986, *IT* is King's longest book (more than eleven hundred pages). It is also his best. The story of seven friends from Derry, Maine—Bill, Richie, Eddie, Beverly (Bev), Mike, Stan, and Ben—it sprawls across two time periods: 1958, when the self-styled Losers Club are kids; and 1985, when they are adults. In each time period, they battle a nameless, shape-shifting creature that assumes more than thirty forms, including a werewolf, a mummy, a giant eye, a giant spider, a witch, Frankenstein's monster, and, most famously, Pennywise the Dancing Clown.

In one of the 1985 sections, the grown-up Losers are summoned back to Derry to face the creature again. Bev lives in Chicago and is married to Tom, an unstable creep who nevertheless lights her fire. She moans at Tom's touch, grabbing his hand and shoving it between her legs. (Middle school me imagined his hand just above her knees, clenched like a tennis ball in a relay race.) King focuses on Tom's perspective: what he sees (her flushed face), what he feels (nails in his back, teeth in his shoulder), and what he hears (her scream at the end).

This imagery helped me picture what was going on. King, like Jackie Collins, can be coarse (lots of "ass" and "tits"), but he can also be lyrical, as in this line: "Sliding into her was like sliding into some exquisite oil."[70] A lot of instruction is tucked into this line. "Oil" doesn't mean Valvoline but something like frankincense, which is smooth and luxurious. How could something that soothing make Beverly bite and scratch? I didn't know, but it suggested sex was multifarious, sometimes confusing, and an assault on the senses (all true, as I would eventually discover).

In the second scene, Bev is in Derry with the reconstituted Losers' Club. As children, she and Bill had crushes on each other. Now, after an evening of reminiscing, Bill walks her back to her hotel room, where they tumble into bed. This time, King shows he can write from a woman's perspective:

Beverly felt her climax coming. She moved toward it, working for it, never doubting it would come. Her body suddenly stuttered and seemed to leap upward, not orgasming but reaching a plateau far above any she had reached with Tom or the two lovers she had had before Tom. She became aware that this wasn't going to be just a come; it was going to be a tactical nuke. She became a little afraid … but her body picked up the rhythm again. She felt Bill's long length stiffen against her, his whole body suddenly becoming as hard as the part of him inside herself, and at that same moment she climaxed—*began* to climax; pleasure so great it was nearly agony spilled out of unsuspected floodgates, and she bit down on his shoulder to stifle her cries.[71]

The language is idealized and a little performative. Yet it is reassuring. I like that, in the midst of facing the most terrifying monster in existence, these two seized the chance for release. It reminds me of the season 6 *M*A*S*H* episode "Comrades in Arms," where Hawkeye and Margaret are trapped in a hut that is being shelled. As explosions rattle the walls, the two embrace, full of fear, seeking comfort. Then they kiss. If fiction is an escape, such scenes are an escape-within-an-escape, warm and affirming, just what readers need to catch their breath. Fear strips you. It dehumanizes you. You'll do anything to wrest back that humanity. Is there anything more human than sex? Bill and Bev falling into bed wasn't harmful to middle school me; it was soothing. I felt encouraged.

To deny me access to that—well, I'd rather have faced the killer clown.

Notes

1   Stanley Cohen, *Folk Devils and Moral Panics* (MacGibbon and Kee, 1972), 1.
2   Linda Austin, "Children of Childhood: Nostalgia and the Romantic Legacy," *Studies in Romanticism* 42, no. 1 (2003): 75–98.
3   "Children's Employment Commissioners Report on Heaton," *Mining Institute*, https://mininginstitute.org.uk/research-education/archive-teaching-unit/e-childrens-employment-commissioners-report-on-heaton/.
4   Lori M. Campbell, "The Twentieth-Century Child," *Representing Childhood*, https://www.representingchildhood.pitt.edu/twentycent_child.htm.
5   Barbara Orbach Natanson, National Child Labor Committee Collection, *Library of Congress*, http://www.loc.gov/pictures/collection/nclc/background.html.
6   Campbell, "The Twentieth-Century Child."
7   Marie Winn, "What Became of Childhood Innocence," *New York Times Magazine*, January 25, 1981, 15–16.
8   Ibid.
9   "Spiritual Milk for Boston Babes," New York Public Library, https://www.nypl.org/events/exhibitions/galleries/childhood/item/5459.

10 Nell McShane Wulfhart, "The Fighter behind Many of the Most Beloved Children's Books of All Time," *Washington Post*, August 4, 2023, https://www.washingtonpost.com/books/2023/08/04/ursula-nordstrom-young-readers/.

11 Rita Koganzon, "The Age of Adolescence," *The Point*, May 23, 2023, https://thepointmag.com/criticism/the-age-of-adolescence/.

12 Margueritte Peterson, "Edward Stratemeyer: King of the Children's Series," *New Antiquarian*, May 28, 2018, https://www.abaa.org/blog/post/edward-stratemeyer-king-of-the-childrens-series.

13 Ibid.

14 Clay Skipper, "Here's How Author James Patterson Writes 31 Books at the Same Time," *GQ*, January 3, 2023, https://www.gq.com/story/james-patterson-routine-exellence.

15 Jay Parini, *Promised Land: Thirteen Books That Changed America* (Doubleday, 2008), 272.

16 James Bandler, "Conde Nast Acquires Teen Magazine YM," *Wall Street Journal*, October 7, 2004, https://www.wsj.com/articles/SB109708944526738188.

17 Kelley Massoni, *Fashioning Teenagers: A Cultural History of Seventeen Magazine* (Routledge, 2010), 9.

18 "Weird Words of Wisdom: A Million and One Tricks with a Strand of Pearls Edition," *Embarrassing Treasures*, November 21, 2012, https://embarrassingtreasures.com/tag/betty-cornell/.

19 Kelly Jensen, "The Teen Humor Comics of the 1940s," *Book Riot*, March 25, 2022, https://bookriot.com/the-teen-humor-comics-of-the-1940s/.

20 Sarah Raznor, "Fond du Lac Was the Birthplace of Young Adult Novels: Celebrating Maureen Daly," *Fond Du Lac Reporter*, May 13, 2019, https://www.fdlreporter.com/story/news/2019/05/13/maureen-daly-young-adult-author-fond-du-lac-wisconsin-revisits-seventeenth-summer/1167750001/.

21 Francis Booth, "Maureen Daly's Seventeenth Summer and the Birth of the Teenage Novel," *Ladies Literary Guide*, May 31, 2021, https://www.literaryladiesguide.com/literary-analyses/maureen-dalys-seventeenth-summer-and-the-birth-of-the-teenage-novel/.

22 "What Was the First 'YA' Book?," *Book Riot*, March 6, 2022, https://bookriot.com/the-first-ya-book/.

23 Orville Prescott, "A Handful of Rising Stars," *New York Times*, March 21, 1943, 46.

24 "What Was the First 'YA' Book?"

25 Maureen Daley, *Seventeenth Summer*, Books for Young Readers ed. (Simon & Schuster, 2024), 196.

26 "Paul Zindel Interview on Writing," *Paul Zindel*, http://www.paulzindel.com/finalpages/Interviews/int.writing.htm.

27 Gina Davis, "The Censorship Challenge," *Baltimore Sun*, February 12, 2006, https://www.baltimoresun.com/2006/02/12/the-censorship-challenge/.

28 Joyce Maynard, "Coming of Age with Judy Blume," *New York Times*, March 12, 1978, 80.

29 Robert Cormier, "A Book Is Not a House: The Human Side of Censorship," in *Censorship: A Threat to Reading, Learning, Thinking*, ed. John Simmons (International Reading Association, 1994), 67.

30 Ibid.

31 Anthony Aycock, "Desperately Seeking Sources," *Missouri Review*, October 20, 2023, https://missourireview.com/desperately-seeking-sources-by-anthony-aycock/.

32 Jenni White, "Parents Shouldn't Force Kids to Read Smut," *The Federalist*, March 25, 2016, https://thefederalist.com/2016/03/15/parents-shouldnt-let-schools-force-kids-to-read-smut/.

33 Ibid.

34 Ibid.

35   Aycock, "Desperately Seeking Sources."

36   Charles Cole, *Information Need: A Theory Connecting Information Search to Knowledge Formation* (Information Today, 2012), 189.

37   Silvania Miranda and Kira Tarapanoff, "Information Needs and Information Competencies: A Case Study of the Off-Site Supervision of Financial Institutions in Brazil," *Information Research* 13, no. 2 (2008), 13–26.

38   Denise E. Agosto and Sandra Hughes-Hassell, "Toward a Model of the Everyday Life Information Needs of Urban Teenagers, Part 1: Theoretical Model," *Journal of the American Society for Information Science and Technology* 57, no. 10 (2006): 1394–403.

39   Ibid.

40   Jessica Fillak, "The History of Sexuality Education in the United States," *Sexual Health Alliance*, June 8, 2021, https://sexualhealthalliance.com/nymphomedia-blog/the-history-of-sexuality-education-in-the-united-states.

41   Ibid.

42   John Frith, "Syphilis: Its Early History and Treatment until Penicillin and the Debate on Its Origins," *Journal of Military and Veterans' Health* 20, no. 4 (2012): 49–58.

43   Ibid.

44   "American Social Hygiene Association History and a Forecast," *VCU Libraries Social Welfare History Project*, https://socialwelfare.library.vcu.edu/programs/health-nutrition/american-social-hygiene-association-history-and-a-forecast/.

45   Newell W. Edson, "Some Facts Regarding Sex Instruction in the High Schools of the United States," *School Review* 29, no. 8 (1921): 593–602.

46   Ibid.

47   Ibid.

48   Ibid.

49   "About Us: History," *SIECUS*, https://siecus.org/about-us/#history.

50   "Population and the American Future: The Report of The Commission on Population Growth and the American Future," Center for Research on Population and Security, https://www.population-security.org/rockefeller/009_education.htm.

51   John Kantner and Melvin Zelnick, "Sexual Experience of Young Unmarried Women in the United States," *Family Planning Perspectives* 4, no. 4 (1972): 9–18.

52   Eli Coleman, "Working toward Sexual Health Promotion," American Sexual Health Association, https://www.ashasexualhealth.org/working-toward-sexual-health-promotion/.

53   Janice Irvine, *Talk about Sex: The Battles over Sex Education in the United States* (University of California Press, 2004), 51.

54   Ibid.

55   Valerie Huber, "A Historical Analysis of Public School Sex Education in America: A Historical Analysis of Public School Sex Education in America since 1900" (master's thesis, Cedarville University, 2009), 43.

56   Ibid.

57   Ibid.

58   Mark Manson, "Why You Should Read Fiction," https://markmanson.net/read-fiction.

59   Emily Boudreau, "Help Teens Connect to Fiction," Harvard Graduate School of Education, October 26, 2021, https://www.gse.harvard.edu/ideas/usable-knowledge/21/10/help-teens-connect-fiction.

60   Michael Cart, *Young Adult Literature: From Romance to Realism*, 2nd ed. (American Library Association, 2010), 144.

61   Amy Patee, "The Secret Source: Sexually Explicit Young Adult Literature as an Information Source," *Young Adult Library Services* 4, no. 2 (2006): 30–38.

62 Ibid.

63 Davin Helkenberg, "Young Women Encountering Information on Sexuality in Young Adult Literature," *Canadian Journal of Information and Library Science* 43, no. 2 (2020): 97–109.

64 https://theconversation.com/honest-and-subtle-writing-about-sex-in-young-adult-literature-48002.

65 Ibid.

66 Patee, "The Secret Source," 35.

67 Erin Farrow, "Honest and Subtle Writing about Sex in Young Adult Literature," *The Conversation*, September 25, 2015, https://theconversation.com/honest-and-subtle-writing-about-sex-in-young-adult-literature-48002.

68 Stephen King, *Cujo*, (Viking, 1981), 41.

69 Stephen King, *The Stand*, media tie-in ed. (Anchor, 2020), 902.

70 Stephen King, *It* (Viking, 1986), 110.

71 Ibid., 931.

6 To Cull a Mockingbird

Remember when Disney+ launched on November 12, 2019? There were, to put it mildly, problems. Content that should have been there wasn't. Devices that should have worked didn't. Many people sat and watched the spinning wheel of death, imagining what they would do if they could get their hands on Disney CEO Bob Iger. Customers who were brave—or pissed off— enough to call customer support stayed on hold for an hour or more.

Then there was the censorship.

Disney films have long drawn complaints of racist depictions. You probably know them from Reddit threads and YouTube sound-offs. The Siamese cats in *Lady and the Tramp*. The Dixieland ape in *Jungle Book*. A song in *Peter Pan*: "What Makes the Red Man Red?" *Dumbo*'s blackface crows. The entirety of *Song of the South*. Critics, too, have called out Disney for sexism. "In every princess movie," writes journalist Julia Esposito, "the woman's yearning for a man is idealized. The damsel must always be in distress, and the resolution is her knight in shining armor."[1]

With Disney+, the company saw a chance for redress. It added warnings to certain films that the movies "may contain outdated cultural depictions." Others were edited or altered to remove controversial scenes. A week after the launch, Jeannie Mai, a host of the talk show *The Real*, advocated going beyond on-screen disclaimers. "I think that racism is taught," she said, "and I think that Disney is responsible for educating us in so many ways, so why can't they educate us on the right thing to do by showing an edit?"[2] Mai's cohost, Loni Love, demurred, saying, "I think the teachable thing is 'that's the way it was back then.'"[3] Panelist Tamera Mowry-Housley agreed with Love: "I think it's the parent's responsibility. Once the parent sees that disclaimer … you then can use it as a teachable moment, you can educate your child."[4]

It is a debate that has continued with history, art, social media, Confederate Army monuments, and more. The debate highlights a censorship irony. The right is derided for thinking that if children are not exposed to certain acts or points of views, then those acts will never be committed, those views never adopted. Left-wingers, however, seem to think the same thing: if no one watches a film with racist scenes, then racism, like a weed deprived of water and light, will shrivel and die. This is not the way ideas work. *Island Trees v. Pico*, like other cases discussed in this book, like many acts of censorship in American history, came from the conservative end of the political spectrum.

Many. But not all.

***

It was my son Jace who got me into Harry Potter. As a teenager, he "lent" me his copy of the first book, by which I mean he shoved it into my hands and begged me to read it. Being unenlightened about the appeal of children's literature to adults and knowing that he would harass me until I had not just finished the book but could discuss it with him, I skimmed it, memorizing enough details to imply that I had read the thing immersively. When he offered me the second book, I demurred, saying I was too busy. In reality, I didn't *want* to read it. Over time, I felt guilty about my deception, and when I later got addicted to audiobooks, I decided to give The Boy Who Lived a second try.

Best. Decision. Ever.

Within a couple of months, I had listened to all seven Potter tomes. Then I returned to book 1 and started again. Naturally, we saw all the movies, and then I became an even bigger fan of J. K. Rowling's adult series starring the London-based detective Cormoran Strike and his partner, Robin Ellacott. Then things got weird. On June 6, 2020, Rowling retweeted an op-ed piece that included the phrase "people who menstruate." She ridiculed the phrase, writing, "I'm sure there used to be a word for those people. Someone help me out. Wumben? Wimpund? Woomud?"[5]

As a joke, it was mediocre. As a declaration of war, it was ideal. After a few days of backlash, Rowling wrote a long essay on her website in which she tried to clarify her comments. Her words came across as ill-informed, defensive, irrational. Fans argued with her, then vowed to stop supporting the Harry Potter machine. Daniel Radcliffe, Emma Watson, and other stars from the films spoke out against her. She was lampooned on talk shows. On April 1, 2024, Scotland's Hate Crime and Public Order Act, which criminalizes threatening, harassing, or abusive transphobic behavior, went into effect, prompting some observers to speculate that Rowling should be convicted under it. Her response? "I'm currently out of the country, but if what I've written here qualifies as an offense under the terms of the new act, I look forward to being arrested when I return to the birthplace of the Scottish Enlightenment."[6]

And on and on and on.

Conservatives call the outrage occasioned by Rowling's remarks "cancel culture." Liberals call it "actions have consequences." I call it nuts. Her tweets, and her essay, seem to me unnecessary and embarrassing, not to mention mean-spirited.

Jace? He was shaken by them.

He had always struggled to fit in at school. Then, as a teenager, he came out as a trans male. Milk was poured on him in the cafeteria. He was slammed against lockers. At home, his mother cried and called him "selfish" when he wanted to change his name. He found comfort in rereading the Harry Potter series. Harry, Hermione, Ron, Neville, Dumbledore, Sirius Black—they were his friends until Rowling's views tainted the association. "It's like my friends hate me now," he once told me.

I am still a fan of Rowling's work. In my mind, creation stands apart from creators. Books, plays, movies, paintings, and other creative work will exist centuries from now when everybody who made them no longer does. The work deserves to be praised or panned on its merits. Daniel Radcliffe, for one, seems to feel the same way. In an essay for the Trevor Project, he encouraged fans not to let the fallout over Rowling's tweets contaminate their relationship with the Harry Potter world. "If you found anything in these stories that resonated with you and helped you at any time in your life," he wrote, "then that is between you and the book that you read, and it is sacred."[7]

Jace disagrees—he'll never enjoy Rowling's work again—but he isn't bothered that I still like it. This cannot be said of other works seemingly ripe for cancellation.

Huck Finn, for example.

***

Mark Twain's *The Adventures of Huckleberry Finn* has been a lightning rod since it first appeared in the United States in February 1885. Sales were good—more than fifty thousand copies by May 6[8]—but critical opinion was divided. One reviewer called it "so flat, as well as coarse";[9] another deemed it "especially suited to amuse children on long, rainy afternoons."[10] Louisa May Alcott was more tart: "If [Twain] cannot think of something better to tell our pure-minded lads and lasses he had best stop writing for them."[11]

One thing that early detractors did not object to was the book's racial messaging. Rather, as Twain scholar Andrew Levy points out in *Huck Finn's America*, they worried about Twain's portrayal of children. The late 1800s saw lots of social achievements aimed at children. Public playgrounds, pediatricians, children's books, mandatory school attendance—these were measures of progress. Huck, dressed in rags, sleeping on doorsteps and stealing to survive, was an unsettling throwback. For Levy, Twain's novel was no mere adventure story but a disquisition on "literacy, popular culture, compulsory education, juvenile delinquency, at-risk children and the different ways we raise boys from girls, and rich from poor."[12]

Such were the concerns of the first group to ban the book, a group that may surprise you: the public library in Concord, Massachusetts. The ban was first reported in the *St. Louis Post-Dispatch* on March 17, 1885. A day later, the *New York Herald* offered a fuller account:

> One of the Library Committee, while not prepared to hazard the opinion that the book is "absolutely immoral in its tone," does not hesitate to declare that to him "it seems to contain but very little humor." Another committeeman perused the volume with great care and discovered that it was "couched in the language of a rough, ignorant dialect" and that "all through its pages there is a systematic use of bad grammar and an employment of inelegant expressions." The third member voted the book "flippant" and "trash of the veriest sort." They all united in the verdict that "it deals with a series of experiences that are certainly not elevating," and voted that it could not be tolerated in the public library.[13]

This was no localized controversy. Within a week, it had spread to the West Coast. In a March 29 editorial, the *San Francisco Chronicle* claimed that the moral panic was much ado about nothing: "The managers of this library evidently look on this book as written for boys, whereas we venture to say that upon nine boys out of ten much of the humor, as well as the pathos, would be lost."[14] As for the book's vulgarity, "there is not a line in it which cannot be read by a pure-minded woman."[15] (Ever the showman, Twain himself, in the April 4 *Hartford Courant*, thanked "a committee of the public library of your town" for the "generous action" of banning his book, as "it will cause the purchasers of the book to read it, out of curiosity, instead of merely intending to do so.")[16]

In 1902, public libraries in Denver and Omaha excluded *Huck Finn* for fear that the "immoral and sacrilegious" book would "put wrong ideas in youngsters' heads."[17] The Brooklyn Public Library banned it in 1905, removing it from the children's room because "Huck not only itched but scratched, and that he said sweat when he should have said perspiration."[18] (Again, Twain was ready with a retort: "Censorship is telling a man he can't have a steak just because a baby can't chew it.")[19]

In the late 1950s, a different concern started brewing: civil rights. Viewed through this lens, *Huck Finn*'s greatest sin was not its lawlessness but Jim's status as a runaway slave. The switch occurred seemingly overnight. As late as 1953, Ralph Ellison, celebrated author of *Invisible Man*, lauded Mark Twain for portraying Jim as "not only a slave but a human being, a man who in some ways was to be envied, and who expressed his essential humanity in his desire for freedom, his will to possess his own labor, in his loyalty and capacity for friendship and in his love for his wife and child."[20]

Five years later, however, Ellison no longer gave Twain the benefit of the doubt: "Jim's friendship for Huck comes across as that of a boy for another boy rather than ... of an adult for a junior; thus there is implicit in it not only a violation of the manners sanctioned by society for relations between Negros and whites, there is a violation of our conception of adult maleness."[21] Of Jim himself, Ellison was even pricklier, writing that the character "struck me as a white man's inadequate portrait of a slave."[22]

The New York City Board of Education was one of the first organizations to take action against *Huck Finn* based on race. In September 1957, citing "passages derogatory to Negroes," it dropped the novel from its approved textbook lists for elementary and junior high schools, though the book could still be taught in high school and purchased for school libraries.[23] In 1969, Miami-Dade Junior College followed suit, removing the book because it "creates an emotional block for black students that inhibits learning."[24] Arizona, Connecticut, Illinois, Michigan, Minnesota, North Carolina, Oregon, Pennsylvania, Tennessee, Texas, Virginia—all have banished *Huck Finn* at one time or another.[25] As recently as 2022, two schools in California pulled the censorship hat trick, banning Huck as well as *Of Mice and Men* and *To Kill a Mockingbird*.[26] That doesn't take into account all the efforts to change Twain's book over the years—efforts that are apparently ongoing. In 2011, Twain scholar Alan Gribben produced a new edition that removed the novel's 219 instances of the N-word and replaced them with "slave," a bit of expurgation that sprang from a "narcissistic contemporary belief that art should be inoffensive and accessible."[27]

Steven Pico has spoken to groups who wanted to ban *Huck Finn*, plus other classics that haven't aged well. He told one interviewer, "I've encountered feminists who advocate censorship and religious groups advocating censorship, and African-Americans who raise objections to *The Adventures of Huckleberry Finn* and *Gone with the Wind*."[28]

How do you feel about that? the interviewer might have asked, but she didn't have to.

"That does not anger me so much as it scares me," he said.[29]

***

In a 2016 essay, librarian and writer Jessica Colbert discusses weeding her University of Illinois library's LGBTQ collection and coming across a cringeworthy title: Janice Raymond's *The Transsexual Empire: The Making of the She-Male*. Though celebrated when it was published in 1979, the book's anti-trans vibe these days would make a lot of users uncomfortable. "All three of us working saw it," Colbert wrote, "and immediately had visceral reactions. 'Throw it in the trash! Rip it up! Banish it!'"[30]

Most librarians could tell similar tales. We know what to do with books that are outdated, but what about the unsavory ones? I don't mean Huck Finn and Harry Potter. Or Woody Allen's autobiography. Or *The Absolutely True Diary of a Part-Time Indian*, which has as many fine qualities as its author, Sherman Alexie, has creepy ones. In short, I do not mean good books that became tainted by changing social norms or their creators' misdeeds.

I mean books whose fundamentals are an affront to any right-minded individual. Books that were, in a sense, born bad. Books such as *The Anarchist Cookbook*, which has been linked to numerous terrorists, including Timothy McVeigh and the Columbine shooters, Eric Harris and Dylan Klebold. Or *The Turner Diaries*, whose author, William Pierce, has been called "America's foremost living Hitler admirer." Or *The Camp of the Saints*, which the Southern Poverty Law Center called "one of the top two books in white supremacist circles." Or *The Satanic Bible*. ('Nuff said.)

"Weeding," in librarian parlance, is another term for de-selection, the process of removing books or other items from the library collection. In many cases, this is done for prosaic reasons—shelf space, for instance. Librarians constantly add to their collections; they do *not* add to their buildings. Thus, old stuff is swept out to make room for the new. We also weed items that are obsolete (seen any cassette tapes in your library lately?) or damaged. (I don't mean a bent page or loose cover; I mean the book was dropped in a toilet. Or someone used a slice of pizza as a bookmark. Or a cat peed on it.) Also weed-worthy are books that haven't been checked out in forever, which could be replaced with more in-demand stuff.

In *The Weeding Handbook: A Shelf-By-Shelf Guide*, Rebecca Vnuk describes various "field-tested strategies." One of them is CREW, which stands for Continuous Review, Evaluation, and Weeding. CREW contains six guidelines under the acronym MUSTIE:

- M = *Misleading*: factually inaccurate;
- U = *Ugly*: beyond mending or rebinding;
- S = *Superseded* by a new edition or by a much better book on the subject;
- T = *Trivial*: of no discernible literary or scientific merit;
- I = *Irrelevant* to the needs and interests of the library's community; and
- E = *Elsewhere*: the material is easily obtainable from another library.[31]

Weeding, according to Vnuk, is not just something librarians do to pass the time—it's one of our primary duties. Library collections, after all, are not static; they change with the needs of the patrons. And it's important that they remain attractive and user-friendly. After all, "[w]ho wants to search through a dozen outdated or ragged books to find the one they are really looking for?"[32] Few people would see a problem with weeding in those circumstances.

Weeding that crosses the line into censorship is another matter.

"Librarian censorship" is a concept that enrages modern conservatives. Yet it has been understood, from the earliest days of the profession, to be one of our reluctant tools. In an 1895 speech, ALA president Joseph Nelson Larned advised those present to "judge books with an adequate knowledge and sufficient hospitality of mind; exercise a just choice among them without offensive censorship" but also to "defend [your] shelves against the endless siege of vulgar literature."[33] Thirteen years later, another ALA president, Arthur Bostwick, commented, "Books that distinctly commend what is wrong, that teach how to sin and tell how pleasant it is … are increasingly popular, tempting the author to imitate them, the publishers to produce, the bookseller to exploit. Thank Heaven they do not tempt the librarian."[34]

This attitude has continued into modern times. Writing in 1950, librarian and educator Leon Carnovsky commented, "I have never met a public librarian who approved of censorship or one who failed to practice it in some measure."[35] In 1995, former library school dean Guy Marco wrote: "Librarians, as gatekeepers, are authorized censors of their societies, and censorship is a library responsibility rather than a library problem."[36] A 2012 book, *True Stories of Censorship Battles in America's Libraries*, devotes some of those stories to these gatekeepers: the cataloger who "lost" newly bought books that she didn't approve of; the circulation clerk who checked out Alan Moore's *League of Extraordinary Gentlemen* over and over so that no children could; the school librarian who, when a student asked about an LGBT novel, responded, "This is a school library. If you are looking to read inappropriate titles, go to a bookstore."[37]

It is understandable, writes librarian Susan Patron, why librarians would exercise such caution—understandable but craven. Such librarians "have their ethics mixed up."[38] In Patron's view, it is not a librarian's job "to protect children from language or moral dilemmas raised in literature."[39] No, their job is to preserve access. Defend the right to read. Ensure that books, that "most deeply affecting way for children to encounter and explore moral ambiguity," are not the casualty of quidnuncs.[40]

Often, librarian "censorship" involves selection (i.e., not the decision to ditch a book but never to acquire it in the first place). In many instances, selection decisions are not political but practical. I've already mentioned one practical concern: space. No library can house everything. Another is money: no library can buy everything. As for content, the most important factor is quality control. For example, most libraries don't buy self-published books, as these have not undergone the rigorous editing and fact-checking that come with professional publishing. The library's mission is another consideration. For example, public libraries don't acquire scholarly texts, which are too specialized to interest the general public.

Some would say it doesn't matter *why* a book is not selected: lack of access is lack of access. Yet this is an unnuanced view. Library scholar Lester Asheim explains the difference:

The major characteristic which makes for the all-important difference seems to me to be this: that the selector's approach is positive, while that of the censor is negative. This is more than a verbal quibble; it transforms the entire act and the steps included in it. For to the selector, the important thing is to find reasons to keep the book. Given such a guiding principle, the selector looks for values, for strengths, for virtues which will over shadow minor objections. For the censor, on the other hand, the important thing is to find reasons to reject the book; his guiding principle leads him to seek out the objectionable features, the weaknesses, the possibilities for misinterpretation.[41]

Selection, in other words, "begins with a presumption in favor of liberty of thought; censorship, with a presumption in favor of thought control."[42]

The real problem with a library not making available *The Anarchist Cookbook* and similar titles is the precedent it sets. The escalating of tensions. The erosion of norms. Like court packing or eliminating the Senate filibuster, if one side can do it, so can the other. Jessica Colbert and her colleagues decided to dump *The Transsexual Empire* but not before she scrutinized her gut response, reconciling it with her views on intellectual freedom. She asked herself a series of questions:

> Would I weed it because I thought it supported an inherently oppressive system and set of ideas?
>
> Is it right to challenge books because they support an oppressive system?
>
> Does it actually change behaviors [or how] those ideas are ingrained in society?
>
> Do I not trust my patrons to engage critically with texts and ideas?[43]

In addition to being a librarian, I am also an adjunct instructor, teaching writing to college freshmen. For one assignment, I have my students write about something they disagree with or that makes them mad. They often write on contentious topics—abortion, gun control, racism. I teach them, when they are crafting an argument, to acknowledge, not ignore, the points of view that disagree with them. This strengthens their writing. When my students employ the tactic, they tend to include the same qualifier, using it so often, it has become a cliché: "Everyone is entitled to their opinion." The statement is the subject of essays from philosophers to radio hosts to mommy bloggers. It has an Urban Dictionary page. It has a Wikipedia entry.

It is an odious phrase. Why? I see it as a phatic expression, an empty utterance used reflexively to serve a social function, like "How are you?" or "Let's get together sometime." Logically, it cannot be true that all opinions are equally valid. Jamie Whyte, writing in *The Times*, believes that "insisting that you are entitled to your opinion cannot possibly give you any proper advantage in a debate."[44] Writer Patrick Stokes goes a step further, seeing a moral failure in the phrase: "The problem with 'I'm entitled to my opinion' is that, all too often, it's used to shelter beliefs that should have been abandoned. It becomes shorthand for 'I can say or think whatever I like.'"[45]

Of course, nobody can be stopped from *thinking* what they like. There is a difference between thought and speech. Opinion and expression. Prejudice and discrimination. We can only judge others by their actions, and if they don't act badly, the argument goes, those opinions will stay cloaked. Trouble is, they won't stay cloaked because people can't keep their mouths shut.

For one thing, they no longer have to. The past few years have seen to that with social media hot takes, combative press conferences, and extreme politicians. Second, Americans prize free speech more highly than most Western societies. It's part of our Enlightenment roots. Even when a truth is monstrously painful, the worse sin, for some of us, is having to keep mum about that truth.

Yet we can have a free society while still observing reasonable limits on expression. Before his 1995 attack on the Alfred P. Murrah Federal Building in Oklahoma City, Timothy McVeigh was a devotee of *The Turner Diaries*, a novel in which Earl Turner, the main character, sets off a truck bomb next to the FBI building in Washington, DC.[46] The novel's author, William Pierce, was a physicist and founder of the neo-Nazi group National Alliance, "the most dominant and dangerous hate group in America" for nearly thirty years.[47] The group didn't just hate minorities; it wanted to crush them. Pierce wrote about his desire to lock Jews, "race traitors" and other enemies of the "Aryan" race into cattle cars and send them to the bottom of abandoned coal mines. In 2001, he extolled McVeigh as "a man of principle."[48] Such opinions are like the One Ring, the Elder Wand, the Ark of the Covenant: too destructive to be wielded responsibly. No one has a valid claim, title, or guarantee to those beliefs.

No one, in short, is entitled to them.

***

I know what you're thinking: that McVeigh was a psycho and would have done what he did whether or not he had read *The Turner Diaries*. Maybe. But it's disingenuous to pretend that those sources had no effect on him. Words matter. We pledge allegiance to a flag because they matter. We utter marriage vows because they matter. We take oaths and swear on Bibles and teach children not to lie because they matter. People ban books, and others fight those bans, because they matter. And if words matter, then sometimes they can urge people to do things. Some of those things are good. Some are not.

Too many are not, it seems. A whole lot out there is straight-up dangerous, on the right and the left. The government can regulate only a little of it because of the First Amendment, which is good and proper. The rest falls to individuals, which isn't always bad. As we've just seen, there are views whose rejection is no great loss. When that rejection occurs, it isn't censorship; it is the marketplace of ideas working as it should.

Yet this is not what we usually mean by "censorship." It certainly isn't what anti-censors mean. They mean the suppression of ideas that are vibrant. That are powerful. That upend worldviews. In 1953, Supreme Court Justice William O. Douglas wrote: "Restriction of free thought and free speech is the most dangerous of all subversions. It is the one un-American act that could most easily defeat us."[49] That may be true, but it is a dangerous game to play. For every *Turner Games* that would be rightfully censored, there are a thousand *Down These Mean Streets* and *Black Boys* and *A Hero Ain't Nothing but a Sandwiches*—and, yes, a thousand *Huck Finns*—whose disappearance would be devastating.

Like nuclear weapons, it is war where even the winners lose.

Besides, you don't need censorship to protect children. You need patience. Encouragement. A commitment to critical thinking. One of the constants of children is that they ask questions. It is something they need to do. Asking questions is the essence of critical thinking. It is also a safety measure. When teens know they can ask about things—sex, for instance—they are less likely to experiment.

Parents, then, should strive to be "askable," a term coined by clinical psychologist Dr. Sol Gordon in the 1970s.[50] Askable parents are people who can talk to children about tough topics without irritation, impatience, or fear. They can muster information. They can articulate values. Being askable is not easy. It requires a change in outlook, a shift from protection ("You're too young for that") to empowerment ("What do you think it means?"). Children change every day. They have more flux than an electromagnet. Parents must be willing to change, too, varying their methods to allow the tween to grow, develop, and prepare for a successful adulthood.

Scholar Louise Musser argues that "[i]f students are to fully understand the history of many of our current social problems, they need to be better aware of the accepted practices and attitudes which were common in this country."[51] Critical thinking skills are important, Musser says, and those skills cannot be developed while limiting students' exposure to our troubling past. Such skills can be developed through discussion, which was Love and Mowry-Housley's point regarding the expurgation of films on Disney+. Blogger Patrick Coleman makes a similar argument, applauding Disney for making that option available through (mostly) non-censorship:

[I]t gives me an opportunity to talk about fairness and honesty. I can ask [my children] to consider if the depictions of people of color would make the people they depict happy or sad? I can ask if it feels like fun or bullying? I can ask if they believe it's okay and talk about how the world has changed, and how it continues to struggle to change.[52]

In this era of rage tweets, deepfakes, and cancel culture, we need all the discussion we can get.

Notes

1   Julia Esposito, "The Problematic History of Disney," *34th Street*, November 30, 2020, https://www.34st.com/article/2020/12/walt-disney-problematic-pixar-racism-2020-ignorance-sleeping-beauty.

2   Todd Garrin, "Jeannie Mai Says 'Offensive' Disney+ Content Should Be Edited Out: 'Racism Is Taught,'" *Yahoo! Entertainment*, November 18, 2019, https://www.yahoo.com/entertainment/jeannie-mai-says-offensive-disney-content-should-be-edited-out-racism-is-taught-215838919.html.

3   Ibid.

4   Ibid.

5   "'Transgender Women Are Women': Daniel Radcliffe Responds to J.K. Rowling's Controversial Comments," *CBS News*, June 9, 2020, https://www.cbsnews.com/news/daniel-radcliffe-responds-jk-rowling-transphobic-tweets/.

6   "JK Rowling in 'Arrest Me' Challenge over Hate Crime Law," *BBC*, April 2, 2024, https://www.bbc.com/news/articles/c51j64lk2l8o.

7   "'Transgender Women Are Women,'" *CBS News*.

8   Robert B. Brown, "One Hundred Years of Huck Finn," *American Heritage* 35, no. 4 (1984), https://www.americanheritage.com/one-hundred-years-huck-finn.

9   Ibid.

10 Ibid.

11 Nat Hentoff, "The Trials of Huckleberry Finn," *Washington Post*, March 17, 1995, https://www.washingtonpost.com/archive/opinions/1995/03/18/the-trials-of-huckleberry-finn/56d34227-2ba8-4636-bdb5-7d1e5ba56d83/.

12 Andrew Levy, *Huck Finn's America: Mark Twain and the Era That Shaped His Masterpiece* (Simon & Schuster, 2014), xxii.

13 "'Huckleberry Finn' in Concord," *New York Herald*, March 18, 1885, https://twain.lib.virginia.edu/huckfinn/nyherald.html.

14 "Ruling Out Humor," *San Francisco Chronicle*, March 29, 1885, https://twain.lib.virginia.edu/huckfinn/sfchron2.html.

15 Ibid.

16 *Hartford Courant*, April 4, 1885, https://twain.lib.virginia.edu/huckfinn/harcour1.html.

17 Brown, "One Hundred Years of Huck Finn."

18 "The Adventures of Huckleberry Finn," *Time*, September 26, 2008, https://entertainment.time.com/2011/01/06/removing-the-n-word-from-huck-finn-top-10-censored-books/slide/the-adventures-of-huckleberry-finn/.

19 Ibid.

20 Ralph Ellison, "Twentieth-Century Fiction and the Black Mask of Humanity," in *Shadow and Act* (Random House, 1964), 51.

21 Ralph Ellison, "Change the Joke and Slip the Yoke," in *Shadow and Act* (Random House, 1964), 58.

22 Ibid.

23 Leonard Buder, "'Huck Finn' Barred as Textbook by City," *New York Times*, September 12, 1957, 1.

24 "The Adventures of Huckleberry Finn by Mark Twain," *Banned Library*, June 26, 2016, https://www.bannedlibrary.com/podcast/2016/6/26/banned-61-the-adventures-of-huckleberry-finn-by-mark-twain.

25 Ibid.

26 "Banned Books 2022—The Adventures of Huckleberry Finn," *Marshall Libraries*, https://www.marshall.edu/library/bannedbooks/the-adventures-of-huckleberry-finn/.

27 Michiko Kakutani, "Light Out, Huck, They Still Want to Sivilize You," *New York Times*, January 6, 2011, https://www.nytimes.com/2011/01/07/books/07huck.html.

28 Debra Lau *Whelan, NCAC Talks to the Man* behind Pico v. Board of Ed, Nat'l Coal. Against Censorship, July 9, 2013, https://ncac.org/news.

29 Ibid.

30 Jessica Colbert, "Weeding vs. Censorship: A Personal Experience," *Hack Library School*, May 2, 2016, https://hacklibschool.wordpress.com/2016/05/02/weeding-vs-censorship-a-personal-experience/.

31 Rebecca Vnuk, *The Weeding Handbook: A Shelf-by-Shelf Guide* (American Library Association, 2015), 6.

32 Ibid., 1.

33 Joseph Larned, "Presidential Address, Lake Placid Conference," in *The Library and Society: Reprints of Papers and Addresses*, ed. Arthur Bostwick (H. W. Wilson, 1920), 417.

34 Arthur Bostwick, "The Librarian as a Censor," in *Library Essays: Papers Related to the Work of Public Libraries* (H. W. Wilson, 1920), 139.

35 Leon Carnovsky, "The Obligations and Responsibilities of the Librarian Concerning Censorship," *Library Quarterly* 20, no. 1 (1950): 21–26, https://www.journals.uchicago.edu/doi/10.1086/617600.

36 Guy A. Marco, "Two False Dogmas of Censorship," *New Library World* 96, no. 7 (December 1, 1995): 15–19.

37 Valerie Nye and Kathy Barco, eds., *True Stories of Censorship Battles in America's Libraries* (American Library Association, 2012).

38 Ibid., 19.

39 Ibid.

40 Ibid., 20.

41 Lester Asheim, "Not Censorship but Selection," *Wilson Library Bulletin* 28 (September 1953): 63–67.

42 Ibid., 64.

43 Colbert, "Weeding vs. Censorship."

44 Jamie Whyte, "Sorry but You Are Not Entitled to Your Opinion," *The Times*, August 9, 2004, https://www.thetimes.com/best-law-firms/profile-legal/article/sorry-but-you-are-not-entitled-to-your-opinion-gpbbnzjlspd?region=global.

45 Patrick Stokes, "No You're Not Entitled to Your Opinion," *The Conversation*, October 4, 2012, https://theconversation.com/no-youre-not-entitled-to-your-opinion-9978.

46 Jo Thomas, "Behind a Book That Inspired McVeigh," *New York Times*, June 9, 2001, https://www.nytimes.com/2001/06/09/us/behind-a-book-that-inspired-mcveigh.html.

47 "National Alliance," *SPLC*, https://www.splcenter.org/resources/extremist-files/national-alliance/.

48 Thomas, "Behind a Book That Inspired McVeigh."

49 William O. Douglas, "The One Un-American Act," *Vassar Alumnae Magazine* 38, no. 4 (1953): 2–4.

50 Dee Wedemeyer, "For Teen-Agers, a Different Kind of Sex Education," *New York Times*, March 10, 1977, 30.

51 Louise S. Musser, "Censoring Sexist and Racist Books: Unjustified and Unjust," *Children's Literature Association Quarterly* 9, no. 1 (1984): 36–37.

52 Patrick A. Coleman, "Disney+ Isn't Hiding Old Racist Movies. And That's Good for Parents," *Fatherly*, November 12, 2019, https://www.fatherly.com/play/disney-isnt-hiding-old-racist-movies-and-thats-good-for-parents.

7 Battle of the Books

sland Trees v. Pico wasn't the first case of library censorship in United States history.

It wasn't the first case in New York history.

Heck, it wasn't even the first case in Nassau County history.

In 1949, Canadian-born writer and conservative activist Lucille Cardin Crain, in partnership with the oil magnate William F. Buckley Sr.—plus his son, the Yale-attending, *National Review*-founding, Gore Vidal-feuding William Jr.—started a quarterly newsletter called *Educational Reviewer*. The publication's purpose was to "cite passages and page numbers from books which might 'subvert' the school child."[1]

For its first issue, the *Reviewer* focused on Frank Abbott Magruder's *American Government: A Consideration of the Problems of Democracy*, which had been used in high schools for nearly four decades. It charged Magruder with "advocating collectivism"—that is, communism—and puffing up the Soviet Union.[2] When conservative radio broadcaster Fulton Lewis criticized the book to his sixteen million listeners, worried parents started pressuring school boards to ban it. Such attacks were documented in Texas, Arkansas, Indiana, New Jersey, the District of Columbia—and Port Washington, New York, which is on Long Island.[3]

A few years later, in August 1954, a woman named Maude Willdigg began a campaign against a book held by Hillside Grade School in New Hyde Park, in North Hempstead. The book was *Russia* by Vernon Ives. Published in 1943, the slim volume, intended for elementary-school readers, offers an "objective treatment" of the Union of Soviet Socialist Republics.[4] Willdigg, however, thought the book gave a "very flattering comparison between the United States and Russia" and "lies from beginning to end."[5] She demanded that the New Hyde Park School Board ban this and several other titles. The board refused, so Willdigg took it as a "hostage." Then in September, a second book, *Our Country* by Lucy Sprague Mitchell and Dorothy Stall, was spirited away by another townsperson, Elinor Warren, who argued that, despite its title, the book "doesn't give the child a true picture of our country."[6]

That was enough for Associate State Education Commissioner Frederick J. Moffitt, who urged the New Hyde Park board to ban *Russia*, deeming it "controversial."[7] The State Textbook Review Commission was called in to review the book. One member, Harper Sibley, thought it harmless. She panned the controversy, saying, "Our country is so great we can stand a little something. Our bodies are strong to withstand germs, so our body politic can withstand a little too."[8] Despite this testimonial, the commission upheld the ban in March 1955, not because the book was seditious, as Willdigg had charged, but because it has passages that are "untrue" or "almost certain to evoke untrue inferences."[9]

A third contretemps began on March 1, 1962, when *Newsday* reported that a number of books had been banned from the Bethpage High School library. The ban included works by Ernest Hemingway, William Faulkner, Albert Camus, John Steinbeck, and others.[10] No reason was given for the ban until a day later, when it was disclosed that the books had been locked in Principal Frank Sabatella's office for *four years* on the advice of Evelyn Gibson, the school librarian, who had "checked with the State Education Department and compiled lists of books to be examined."[11] Whether Gibson did this of her own accord or at the behest of the school's Book Evaluation Committee, which had been created to "get smut off the shelves," was unclear.[12]

Either way, the reaction was precipitate. On March 2, Sabatella said that he would consider letting honors students access the books.[13] On March 6, Superintendent Charles Bryan promised to clear things up "in no time flat."[14] Some editorials called the ban "silly," "disgusting," and "a wet blanket on the fire in the minds of our young"; others defended Sabatella as "a fine man" who was simply trying to do the right thing.[15] (No one, it seemed, came to Mrs. Gibson's defense.)

And there were other incidents. In one study of Nassau County libraries, John Farley reported that forty-two of fifty-four librarians—78 percent—had fielded at least one book complaint or protest.[16]

Pico v. Island Trees would be the mother of them all.

***

Richard Ahrens, he of the boyish good looks, was first elected to the Island Trees Board of Education on August 14, 1972, amid a "bitter, years-old war fought by moderate and conservative factions" for control of the board.[17] A coast guard veteran, Ahrens described himself as a "traditionalist" who was opposed to high taxes, "open classrooms," and other progressive education measures.[18] (Years later, when he ran for a seat on the Nassau County Legislature, Ahrens argued for a "mandate that all county workers speak English on the job" and to "penalize illegal immigrants who send their children to public schools.")[19]

Almost immediately, a series of controversies began to consume the school board. In 1973, moderates took control and fired Superintendent of Schools Edwin

Klotz, a conservative hire from the previous year. Klotz later filed a $1 million lawsuit for defamation of character.[20]

In 1974, with the election of NYPD officer Frank Martin, conservatives retook the board. Ahrens became president, Martin vice president. That December, the board denied tenure to John Turano, a science teacher at Island Trees Junior High, despite the teacher being recommended for tenure by his department chair, his principal, and the Island Trees superintendent, Richard Morrow.[21] Turano claimed that this act was racially motivated—he was Italian American—which led to a hearing before the State Division of Human Rights.

In 1976, the state human rights commissioner, Werner Kramarsky, ordered the board to reinstate John Turano, writing that "Ahrens' admissions and alleged bigoted remarks require more than mere denials, apologies or claims of intended humor to justify" Turano's dismissal (apparently, the board chair had told a "joke" about Italians at a meeting that Turano attended.)[22] Ahrens promised to comply "under no circumstances," vowing instead to appeal the decision he called "the biggest farce I've seen in years."[23]

Another dispute, this one involving an elementary school teacher, Rose Leggio, who was approved for tenure on August 17, 1976, but then later "excessed," went to the Appellate Division of the Supreme Court of New York, which ruled in her favor.[24] There was the attempt to shutter the school newspaper (see chapter 2), as well as several days of student demonstrations over a strict new attendance policy. During one protest, six students were arrested on charges of criminal trespass. One was charged with juvenile delinquency.[25]

Absent this tinderbox environment, things might have been different. Perhaps, freed from partisan tiffs, from sit-ins and walk-outs, from the swinging sixties that became the sinful seventies, from tension and tempers, and too much sex, from the press up his ass and that meddling Werner Kramarsky, Ahrens might have decided that he had had enough of the book bans and thrown in the towel. But he had capitulated with the student newspaper, the *Bulldog*, and had that earned him any goodwill? Nope.

Perhaps Richard Ahrens thought, *Damned if I'm backing down this time.*

***

Steven Pico filed his complaint—the document that initiates a lawsuit—in New York State Supreme Court in Mineola, the seat of Nassau County, as a class-action lawsuit challenging the book removals on state and federal constitutional grounds, as well as the prohibition on classroom use. (In New York, the state-level trial court is called, incongruously, the Supreme Court. New York's highest court, which in other states is usually called the supreme court, is the Court of Appeals.) This removal, the plaintiffs contended, abridged their rights under the First Amendment to the US Constitution; Section 1983 of Title 42 of the US Code;

and Article 1, Section 8 of the New York Constitution, which asserts that "[e]very citizen may freely speak, write and publish his or her sentiments on all subjects, being responsible for the abuse of that right; and no law shall be passed to restrain or abridge the liberty of speech or of the press." It also, they claimed, violated the academic freedom of Island Trees' teachers and librarians under federal and New York law.

The board filed its answer on January 24, denying the plaintiffs' accusations and offering a number of defenses. Most were procedural, but the first would form the backbone of the board's argument all the way through the Supreme Court: "In doing the acts complained of in the Complaint herein, defendant was duly authorized by, and acted under, the authority of the provisions of Section 1701, 1709 and 1710 of the Education Law of the State of New York."[26] (Translation: *We got this. Stay out of it.*) On August 16, the case was moved from state court to federal court, and both sides began their preparations.

Representing the plaintiffs was a trio of attorneys from the New York Civil Liberties Union: Alan Levine, Alan Azzara, and Steven Hyman. Founded in November 1951, the NYCLU had an enviable track record, winning high-profile cases involving political expression, students' rights, prisoners' rights, and more. It got abortion decriminalized in New York three years before *Roe v. Wade*.[27] Its Project on Civil Liberties and Mental Illness "created an entirely new area" of law, including the landmark closure in 1975 of Willowbrook, a wretched facility on Staten Island for people with intellectual and developmental disabilities.[28] (Senator Robert Kennedy called Willowbrook a "snake pit" in 1965; and in 1972, it was the subject of an ABC News exposé hosted by a bushy-haired, steely-eyed Geraldo Rivera.)[29]

Up against this juggernaut was forty-eight-year-old George Lipp, the quintessential small-town lawyer. Lipp handled a little of everything: divorces, wills, real estate closings, minor criminal matters. He had represented the Island Trees School Board for five years, negotiating with the unions and advising it on student discipline. Lipp appeared with his clients in the US District Court for the Eastern District of New York on February 3, 1978. It was not a trial but a hearing. Both sides had asked for summary judgment, meaning that they wanted fifty-year-old Judge George Pratt, a Corning, New York, native who would go on to preside over several ABSCAM[2] trials, to dismiss the case in their favor without a trial. (ABSCAM was a 70s-era FBI sting operation leading to the convictions of seven United States congressmen on charges of bribery and corruption.)

At issue, said Lipp, was "local control of school policy."[30] Not only did the board have full authority to set the curriculum, he argued, but it also had the "right to use its own personal philosophy with regard to educational suitability"[31] of books and other materials—a philosophy that reflected the will of the community, as Ahrens was fond of saying. In his November 1977 deposition, Ahrens pointed out that, at Lipp's request, the board had sent a questionnaire to all 4,719 mailing addresses in the Island Trees district, asking the recipients' opinions on the book bans. "Of those responding," Ahrens said, "508 or 59% supported the board while 353 or 41% did not."[32] (Ahrens often cited these figures in press interviews, using them to contend that the board had a mandate to toss the books. Whether a little more than half the population constitutes a mandate is open for debate.)

Levine countered that, authority or no, the board can't ban a book "simply because its views offend us or the majority of the community."[33] This, he argued, would violate teachers' academic freedom and students' constitutional right to "free and uninhibited inquiry."[34] Judge Pratt wondered whether students could ask about the books in class and whether teachers were free to respond. Yes, said Lipp, noting that the board "is not prohibiting a discussion of the barrio, the ghetto, drugs or the sordid social scene depicted by these books."[35] The hearing lasted an hour, after which Pratt said he would issue his ruling later. Known for his sharp wit and courtroom zingers, Pratt promised that his decision would not be based on the books' content.

"If we have to decide on the merits of the books," he said, "God help us."[36]

***

The ruling arrived 180 days later, on August 2, in a ten-page opinion that covered four issues:

1 subject matter jurisdiction (i.e., whether the court had the authority to rule on this matter);
2 class certification (i.e., whether this should be a class-action lawsuit);
3 the constitutionality of removing or restricting the library books; and
4 the constitutionality of striking the books from the curriculum.[37]

Pratt made short work of the first two. He quoted the US Supreme Court in stating that local governing bodies "can be sued directly ... for monetary, declaratory, or injunctive relief" when there is an allegation of unconstitutional acts.[38] He denied class certification by pointing out that, though the five plaintiffs opposed the board's actions, "there is reason to believe that at least some students, and perhaps even a majority of parents, in the district feel otherwise."[39]

As for issue four, Pratt observed that, though it is possible for a student to have a valid academic freedom claim under the "right to receive" doctrine (more on that in chapter 8), such a claim won't work in this case because "[n]o teacher has joined in, nor do the plaintiffs establish that any teacher currently desires to use any of the restricted books in the curriculum."[40]

This left issue three: the constitutionality of removing or restricting the library books.

Pratt began by noting that the plaintiffs relied on three recent federal cases, all of which denounced library bans: *Minarcini v. Strongsville City School District* (1976), *Right to Read Defense Committee of Chelsea v. School Committee of the City of Chelsea* (1978), and *Salvail v. Nashua Board of Education* (1979). In *Salvail*, a Nashua, New Hampshire, school board ordered the removal of the feminist magazine *Ms.* from a high school library. When a coalition of students, alumni, teachers, and concerned citizens sued, the court ruled that the board had "failed to demonstrate a substantial and legitimate government interest sufficient to warrant" the magazine's banishment.[41]

The judge in *Right to Read*, Joseph L. Tauro, was more flamboyant. After "several weeks of discovery, a six day [!] bench trial and post trial submission of memoranda," he ordered the leaders of Chelsea (Massachusetts) High School to return the poetry anthology *Male and Female Under 18* to the school's library, writing:

> The library is "a mighty resource in the marketplace of ideas" ... There a student can literally explore the unknown, and discover areas of interest and thought not covered by the prescribed curriculum. The student who discovers the magic of the library is on the way to a life-long experience of self-education and enrichment. That student learns that a library is a place to test or expand upon ideas presented to him, in or out of the classroom. The most effective antidote to the poison of mindless orthodoxy is ready access to a broad sweep of ideas and philosophies. There is no danger from such exposure. The danger is mind control.[42]

In *Minarcini*, which Tauro quoted when he called a library "a mighty resource," the Strongsville (Ohio) City School District rejected faculty requests to acquire Joseph Heller's *Catch-22* and Kurt Vonnegut's *God Bless You, Mr. Rosewater* as textbooks. It also ordered *Catch-22* and Vonnegut's *Cat's Cradle* to be removed from the school library. Finally, it prohibited any use of these books in class discussions or for supplemental reading. The District Court ruled in favor of the school board on all counts, but the Sixth Circuit Court of Appeals sided with the plaintiffs on the issue of library removal, calling a school library "a storehouse of knowledge" and "an important privilege" that "is not subject to being withdrawn by succeeding school boards whose members might desire to 'winnow' the library for books the content of which occasioned their displeasure or disapproval."[43]

Pratt was not persuaded by this troika. For him, the most relevant case was one on which George Lipp focused and which we have already discussed: *Presidents Council, District 25 v. Community School Board* (1972)—the case in which another New York school district banned Piri Thomas's *Down These Mean Streets*. That case was decided by the Second Circuit, meaning that federal courts in New York were bound by its dictates, as opposed to *Minarcini*, *Right to Read*, and *Salvail*, which, being from other jurisdictions, held only *persuasive* authority. In other words, Pratt could ignore them if he wanted to.

Alan Levine had argued *Presidents Council* before the Second Circuit. He knew it didn't favor his clients, so he tried to distinguish it, meaning he argued that its facts were different enough from the facts of *Pico* that it didn't have to be followed. According to Pratt, however, it did. Like *Presidents Council*, he wrote, the Island Trees dispute was an administrative issue, not a constitutional one. There was "no religious question, either free exercise or establishment; nor was there a ban on the teaching of any theory or doctrine; nor has there been a restriction imposed on classroom discussion, or a penalty inflicted on any teacher or librarian."[44] Removing the books might have "reflect[ed] a misguided educational philosophy," but it was not "a sharp and direct infringement" on anybody's rights.[45] Levine had argued that the First Amendment required federal courts to forbid school boards from yanking library books on the basis of content, but Pratt disputed this, saying that one of the purposes of public education was "indoctrinative, to transmit the basic values of the community."[46] According to *Presidents Council*, a book that was "improperly" selected could be removed "by the same authority which was empowered to make the selection in the first place."[47] *Presidents Council*, in other words, was the way to go.

Summary judgment for the defendants.

***

Reactions to the ruling were mixed. Island Trees board member Frank Martin hailed it as a win for local government: "This case was a direct attack on local control of school districts [...] If you take away from local school boards, the responsibility and authority to decide on curriculum, then it's no better than a legal body that's put there to order pencils."[48] Thomas Shannon, executive director of the National School Board Association, agreed, saying that somebody has to make a decision, "and what better group of people than the locally elected representatives in the community."[49]

For Justine Schachter, a board member of the county public library, confidence in Ahrens and his mates was misplaced. "Nobody is contesting anything they ever do," she said. "I'm terribly disappointed."[50] William North, of the Freedom to Read Foundation, was harsher, calling the Island Trees book bans "the harbinger of another McCarthy era."[51]

Within twenty-four hours of Pratt's decision, the NYCLU announced that it would appeal to the Second Circuit. Attorneys hate to lose, of course, but this was different. This was history. "This is the first decision which sanctions a school board making a determination based on their own philosophical and moral beliefs," said Alan Azzara. "Everybody doesn't live like the people in Island Trees, and at some point, their children will have to learn that people riot and loot and take drugs."[52]

His unspoken addition: *and read books.*

Notes

1   Jack Nelson and Gene Roberts Jr., *The Censors and the Schools* (Little, Brown, 1963), 40.
2   Ibid., 41.
3   Ibid., 42.
4   Bill Butler, "School Board Bars 'Book-Burning,'" *Newsday* (Nassau ed.), October 24, 1954, 7.
5   Ibid.
6   Bill Butler, "NHP Woman Takes 2nd Book as 'A Poor Selection,'" *Newsday* (Nassau ed.), September 25, 1954, 5.
7   Ibid., 11.
8   Bill Butler, "School Book 'Burned' in Hyde Park Is Called 'Innocuous,'" *Newsday* (Nassau ed.), December 22, 1954, 18.
9   "State Uphold Book Ban—For New Reason," *Newsday* (Nassau ed.), March 22, 1955, 7.
10 Joseph Gelmis, "LI School Library Bans 11 Top Writers," *Newsday* (Nassau ed.), March 1, 1962, 3.
11 Joseph Gelmis, "School to Review Ban on Top Authors' Books," *Newsday* (Nassau ed.), March 2, 1962, 21.
12 Ibid.
13 Ibid.
14 "School Acting to 'Clear Up' Book Banning," *Newsday* (Nassau ed.), March 6, 1962, 21.
15 "Bethpage's Book Ban Denounced by Readers," *Newsday* (Nassau ed.), March 7, 1962, 47.
16 John J. Farley, "Book Censorship in the Senior High School Libraries of Nassau County, New York" (PhD dissertation, New York University, 1964), 78–79.
17 Dan Hertzberg, "Island Trees Voters Dig in Once More," *Newsday* (Nassau ed.), May 31, 1974, 17.
18 Ibid.
19 John T. McQuiston, "Elections Could Threaten Republicans' Control of Nassau County Legislature," *New York Times*, September 8, 1997, https://www.nytimes.com/1997/09/08/nyregion/elections-could-threaten-republicans-control-of-nassau-county-legislature.html.
20 Hertzberg, "Island Trees Voters Dig in Once More," 17.
21 Michele Ingrassia, "School Firing Ruled Bias," *Newsday* (Nassau ed.), September 2, 1976, 5.
22 Ibid.
23 Ibid.
24 *Leggio v. Oglesby*, 69 A.D.2d 446, 419 N.Y.S.2d 118 (1979).
25 "Controversial Rules Are Modified a Bit," *Newsday* (Nassau ed.), April 1, 1977, 21.
26 Defendants' answer to the complaint, January 24, 1977.
27 *"New York Civil Liberties Union: Championing Civil Rights and Civil Liberties for 50 Years"* (New York Civil Liberties Union, 2003), 18, https://assets.nyclu.org/publications/nyclu_pub_50_years.pdf.
28 Ibid., 19.
29 "The Closing of Willowbrook," *Disability Justice*, https://disabilityjustice.org/the-closing-of-willowbrook/.
30 Michele Ingrassia, "Judge Delays Ruling on School Book Ban," *Newsday* (Nassau ed.), February 3, 1978, 19.
31 Ibid.
32 Transcript of Richard Ahrens, 1977.
33 Ingrassia, "Judge Delays Ruling on School Book Ban," 19.
34 Ibid.
35 Ibid.

36 Ibid.

37 *Pico v. Island Trees*, 474 F. Supp. 387 (1979).

38 Ibid., 393.

39 Ibid.

40 Ibid., 397.

41 *Salvail v. Nashua Bd. of Ed.*, 469 F. Supp. 1269, 1275 (D.N.H. 1979).

42 *Right to Read Defense Committee v. School Committee of the City of Chelsea*, 454 F. Supp. 703, 715 (D. Mass. 1978).

43 *Minarcini v. Strongsville (Ohio) City School District*, 541 F. 2d 577, 581 (6th Cir. 1976).

44 474 F. Supp. 387, 397.

45 Ibid.

46 Ibid., 396.

47 Ibid., 397.

48 T. J. Collins, "Island Trees Book Ban Upheld," *Newsday* (Nassau ed.), August 3, 1979, 5.

49 Ibid.

50 Ibid., 23.

51 Ibid., 5.

52 Ibid., 23.

8 Hello, Newman

On February 6, 1980, the Second Circuit handed down its long-awaited ruling. The town had been waiting, awash in unease. It wasn't brother versus brother but parent versus child, the latter wanting unfettered access to any book at any time, the former saying, "Well, wait a minute." Angry letters, overheated speeches, cries of "Censorship!" and rejoinders of "Trust us" had filled the air for months. The world was watching. It was time to find out the fate of the embattled school board in this little Vermont town.

Vermont? Isn't Island Trees in New York?

Yes. Yes, it is. But I am talking now about another case, *Bicknell v. Vergennes*. It is forever aligned with *Island Trees v. Pico*. Same court. Same issues. Same precedents. Same day. Journalists at the time connected the two cases, as did the justices who wrote the opinions. Yet few writers nowadays discuss them together. Few writers, in fact, discuss *Bicknell* at all. This might be because of David Bicknell himself, who was also a student body president but, unlike his Nassau County counterpart, seems not to have become a five-decade defender of the right to read.

No doubt the outcome of the case had something to do with that.

The saga began on February 16, 1978, when *The Burlington Free Press* reported on a year-long campaign by six parents in the city of Vergennes (population: 2,242) to remove two books from the high-school library: Patrick Mann's *Dog Day Afternoon*, the novelization of the blockbuster Al Pacino movie that was itself based on a real-life bank robbery; and James Lawrence's *Rebel Hawke*, a *Shaft* wannabe set during the Revolutionary War. One of these parents was fifty-six-year-old Kittredge Haven, a real estate salesman and self-described "patriotic conservative type,"[1] who said he and the librarian, Elizabeth Phillips, were at odds over the merits of *Dog Day Afternoon*, which Haven called "hard core pornography."[2] (Perhaps this was due to the reason for the bank robbery: to get money to pay for one character's gender affirmation surgery.)

Bicknell responded at a March 8 school board meeting, reading a statement prepared by the student council: "An author doesn't always choose to depict a chaste fantasy. The author has license to write about life as it really is (that is, crime, violence, war and other lifestyles)."[3] Harold Leach, a parent who joined Haven in the complaint, asserted that "this book does not meet the standards set forth by an educational society," while another parent in attendance pushed back with "if you've done a good job in parental guidance, you ought to have a little more faith in your youngsters than this"[4]—an argument that seems not to have been made against the Island Trees board. Nor did Island Trees librarians make the dispute about themselves like Vergennes's Elizabeth Phillips, who urged the board not to ban *Dog Day Afternoon* (she had already agreed to remove *Rebel Hawke*), saying, "The library is a place where fear is out of place and to make me afraid to buy certain books because they might offend somebody is not right."[5]

The board voted unanimously to form a committee of citizens who would review all books before they are added to the library's collection, but it postponed a decision on *Dog Day Afternoon* until March 22, when a motion to remove it failed thanks to a 3–3 vote. Board chair Lawrence Gelbo would have been the tiebreaker, but he refused to vote, saying, "I couldn't live with myself if it had gone either way."[6] Afterward, he considered resigning as board chair, claiming to be "hurt" by the board's inability to come up with a compromise.[7]

The board got another chance on April 5, when it considered a complaint about *The Wanderers*, Richard Price's coming-of-age story collection about seventeen-year-old Richie Gennero and his Bronx gang. Phillips again took the book's side, saying that its reviews were excellent, though she admitted it contained seedy language and sexual scenes.[8] Leach was less diplomatic, calling the book "nothing but filth."[9]

The board voted to ban *The Wanderers*. It also took another crack at *Dog Day Afternoon*, though this one wasn't banned but moved to a "restricted shelf," which amounted to exile in the principal's office.[10] David Bicknell announced that the student council would consider legal action.[11]

The board's other action was to bypass the review committee and just order Phillips not to buy any more novels "until further vote of the board."[12] On June 12, the board added that Phillips could not buy *any* books except "Dorothy Canfield Fisher, science fiction and high interest-low vocabulary" without board approval[13]—another indignity for Phillips, who hadn't agreed with the formation of the review committee. "I would assume," she had said that previous March, "that the concept of review would be illegal—that would be censorship."[14] I imagine a twinkle in her eye as she then said, "If the main quality of good judgment is being careful not to offend anybody, then I don't have good judgment."[15]

"Enough is enough," said Bicknell. Joined by eight students, five parents, the Right to Read Defense Committee of Vergennes, and the redoubtable Phillips (who would later be forced to resign), he sued the school board in the US District Court for Vermont on September 28, claiming that

- the book removals and freezing of library acquisitions were First Amendment infringements;
- both actions violated the school's Library/Media Policy of "free access to library materials," and thus the students' due process rights; and
- the actions abridged teachers' and librarians' due process rights.[16]

The court sided with the board on August 24, 1979, dismissing the plaintiffs' complaint, and Bicknell appealed. In February of 1980, a three-judge panel of Jon Newman, Walter Mansfield, and Charles Sifton of the Second Circuit heard the appeal. On October 2, in a 2–1 verdict, with Sifton dissenting, they upheld the dismissal. Newman wrote:

> Appellants do not dispute that the Board has the power to remove these two books because of their language. Their point is that the decision to remove is unlawful when the determination of whether the books are vulgar or indecent is made solely on the basis of Board members' personal tastes and values. But so long as the materials removed are permissibly considered to be vulgar or indecent, it is no cause for legal complaint that the Board members applied their own standards of taste about vulgarity.[17]

Personal tastes and values. Remember that bugbear as we examine the Second Circuit's analysis of the Island Trees affair.

***

Appellate courts aren't like you see on TV. Prosecutors are not fiery, à la Jack McCoy. Defense counsel isn't brimming with Matlockian charm. Witnesses don't throw acid onto district attorneys' cheeks, which is how Gotham DA Harvey Dent became Two-Face, one of Batman's deadly enemies. Defendants don't bum-rush judges, as happens in the real world from time to time.

No, appeals begin in the driest way possible: a written brief. The side that loses at trial submits this brief, or argument, explaining why it should have won. The other side then submits a rebuttal. The judges read these briefs before holding oral arguments, an event that is like a trial but more boring, as both sides' attorneys just stand around debating legal minutiae and jousting with the judges, who then retire to decide who won. Months later, they announce their ruling with a written opinion representing the majority view. Other judges are free to write their own concurring or dissenting opinions. These lack the force of law, but they can make for provocative reading.

For the Island Trees plaintiffs—now, at the appeals level, called *appellants*—the triumvirate of Azzara, Levine, and Hyman handled the work, joined by two other attorneys, Richard Emery and Arthur Eisenberg. Though only in his mid-thirties, the Cornell-educated Eisenberg had already argued a dozen or so cases before the US Supreme Court. He was brought in to help develop the First Amendment argument in *Pico v. Island Trees*, which he called "one of my favorite cases" when we spoke by phone. Though in his eighties, his voice sounded like a man in middle age, with the timbre I imagine carrying him to victory in so many of those oral arguments.

As he and his partners began working on the appellants' brief, Eisenberg realized that it needed some punching up. The board's actions, he told me, "did not translate easily into a First Amendment claim." According to the First Amendment, government officials cannot discriminate against expression based on content or viewpoint. This works imperfectly with library collections, which, as we've seen, necessarily involve some content judgments.

The attorneys therefore came up with two theories that they hoped would be more persuasive. One, Eisenberg said, was that the First Amendment requires library officials to advance principles of *pluralism* in selecting materials. Officials cannot exercise their authority to remove books in pursuit of narrow political orthodoxy. The second theory was what Eisenberg called the "principle of procedural regularity," meaning that where First Amendment rights are at stake, the government must act with some degree of consistency. They can't just do stuff and then justify it later.

The resulting brief, of which Eisenberg was the lead author, was a masterpiece of reason, analysis, and graceful writing. It contained little legalese and tortuous syntax. It wasn't in a hurry. The meat of the brief was these three arguments:

1   The Island Trees board violated the First Amendment by removing the books merely because they were "offensive";
2   Although schools can teach proper language, they cannot ban books simply for containing bad language; and
3   The book bans, insofar as they were prompted by religious objections, violated the religious establishment clause of the First Amendment.

Argument three was the shortest, only a page long. Noting that, in *Epperson v. Arkansas*, the Supreme Court had held that book bans are unconstitutional if they are based on religious or moral objections to the books, Eisenberg argued that such objections had been present in this case from the beginning. He quoted the board's March 19, 1976, press release—"If we were to offend the religious and moral standards of even one parent or child, we would be unworthy of the public trust"—before pointing out that the board disapproved of *The Fixer* and *Slaughterhouse-Five* because they were, respectively, "antisemitic" and "antireligious."[18]

Argument two quoted Ahrens complaining about *A Hero Ain't Nothin' but a Sandwich*—"you can't try to teach proper English and allow the students to read things that are improper"—before observing that, though such usage might confuse elementary-school students, it seems nonsensical that high-school students can't understand that dialogue in books is not intended as a grammar lesson. "If they are that unsophisticated," wrote Eisenberg, "what serious modern author will they be able to read?"[19]

As for the books' language being offensive, Eisenberg cited Guidelines of the New York Board of Regents, which urged that literature "be judged as a whole" and that inclusion should be based on "whether the book presents life in its true proportions, whether circumstances are realistically dealt with, and whether the book is of literary value."[20] The Island Trees ban, he argued, did not do this. Instead, it was an attempt to "sanitize the libraries and insulate students from the real world," which Eisenberg called "a futile and dangerous effort."[21]

And even if sanitization were a worthy goal, the law demanded that it be met with narrower means than banning books. Here, he quoted the Supreme Court case *Elrod v. Burns* (1976), regarding political speech of public employees: "If the State has open to it a less drastic way of satisfying its legitimate interests," it may not use a method that "broadly stifles the exercise of personal liberties."[22] Criticizing Judge Pratt's reliance on *Presidents Council*, he pointed out that the ban in that case was not as severe, as it only removed books from a library.[23] The Island Trees board also excised a book, *The Fixer*, from a class curriculum. This was more, not less, restrictive, and therefore unlawful.

With argument one, Eisenberg addressed the board's main contention—that it had ultimate authority over all aspects of the district schools, including curriculum and library selection—head-on. Yes, he conceded, the board does have a lot of authority, but it is not unlimited. He discussed *Meyer v. Nebraska* (1923), a case challenging a Nebraska state statute that prohibited the teaching of a foreign language in any school below eighth grade. Justice James Clark McReynolds delivered the court's opinion, which invalidated the statute. Though "the desire of the legislature to foster a homogenous people with American ideals" is understandable, McReynolds wrote, "a desirable end cannot be promoted by prohibited means."[24] Other cases were cited having to do with compulsory flag salutes, prohibitions on teaching evolution (*Epperson v. Arkansas*), and wearing black armbands to protest war (the famous 1969 case of *Tinker v. Des Moines*). These cases, Eisenberg argued, show a clear rejection of the same "pall of orthodoxy" that the Island Trees ban would impose.[25]

Turning specifically to books, Eisenberg raised some of the issues I discussed in chapter 6 regarding selection vis-à-vis removal, with the latter being worthy of constitutional protection. With selection, "practical limitations of time, shelf space, money and class hours suggest that not every book can be bought and not every idea can be taught."[26] Schools will therefore always have some latitude to make such decisions.

Things get trickier, however, when books are *removed* from a library. Though the Island Trees board claimed it was concerned about the books' quality, it made none of the usual efforts to ascertain that quality. It read no book reviews. It consulted no evaluative sources. It sought no advice from school professionals. It ignored the recommendations of its own review committee. The board's actions and words, Eisenberg pointed out, lead to the conclusion that "no purpose other than the imposition of orthodoxy prompted defendants' actions."[27]

In such a case, Eisenberg noted, "the federal judiciary has an obligation to exercise its authority for the protection of basic First Amendment values."[28] Judge Pratt had not seen a distinction between adding books and removing them. Therefore, he had ruled that judges had *no* obligation or authority to get involved.

Would the Second Circuit agree?

***

The board's answer brief, written by George Lipp, is a sloggier read than Eisenberg's. The prose is less flowing, more affected. Nevertheless, it makes a strong argument. Lipp concentrated on three questions:

1 Should the federal courts intervene when a school board bans or removes books based on vulgarity, bad taste, and irrelevance?
2 Are such prohibitions unconstitutional if the board allows the ideas inside the books to be taught?
3 Is it "irrational" to rely on school board members' "value concepts" when making decisions about books?

As with the appellants' brief, the school board, now called the *appellees*, began with a summary of the facts. It was a summary slanted to make the board look measured, diligent, and dutiful, just as Eisenberg's summary portrayed the board as capricious, wrongheaded, and insular. Lipp highlighted, for instance, Frank Martin's objection to "the presence of ethnic slurs" in some of the books,[29] which was not a focus of any news coverage. Such a mention made the board look benevolent, caring, and waaaay ahead of its time. (Four decades later, in 2021, linguist John McWhorter called slurs "our newest profanity.")[30]

To support the first point—that federal courts should stay out of school library decisions—Lipp leaned into New York State law. He quoted Section 1709 of the Education Law, which gave the boards of education of union free school districts the power

- "to prescribe the course of study" for students;
- "to prescribe the text-books to be used in the schools";

- "to take charge and possession of" books and other school property; and
- to "have all the powers reasonably necessary to exercise powers granted" by the New York legislature.[31]

He spent most of the brief arguing the second point: that the eleven book removals were not a constitutional issue. He rejected the charge that the board was "indoctrinating" students by painstakingly discussing the difference between a secondary school and a university. The latter is a true "marketplace of ideas," while the former "acts *in loco parentis* with respect to minors."[32] In other words, high schoolers lack the same academic freedom rights as college and graduate students. Then, in a move that modern conservatives would recognize, Lipp argued that the *real* un orthodoxy would be "[n]ot to permit a board of education to utilize its own values and … those of the community in its decision" regarding books and curriculum.[33]

Next, Lipp dredged up the *Presidents Council* decision, insisting that it is *not* materially different from the Island Trees case, as Eisenberg had argued, and should therefore be followed. Lipp acknowledged that in *Presidents Council* teachers were not prohibited from assigning *Down These Mean Streets* as outside reading, whereas the Island Trees dispute included such a prohibition. Yet he called this encroachment "miniscule." If the mere assignment of a book as outside reading was unconstitutional, he argued, then its "power to control curriculum is meaningless."[34]

Finally, Lipp addressed the "right to know" or "right to receive" doctrine, which wasn't new but had seldom been applied in a school setting. Eisenberg had not brought this up, "but since most *amici** have," Lipp wrote, "a response is indicated."[35] The right, as its name implies, is an individual's guarantee to have access to certain information. It was derived from a series of cases culminating in *Virginia State Board of Pharmacy v. Virginia Citizens Consumers Council, Inc.* (1976), which held that prescription drug consumers may receive advertising information about the drugs because the First Amendment is intended to protect the hearers as well as the speakers of protected speech, including commercial speech.[36]

The right had never previously been asserted in a case involving student access to library books.

Citing the trial judge in *Bicknell v. Vergennes*, and reminding the court that Judge Pratt had dismissed the right-to-know principle as "diffuse, speculative and factually unsupported," Lipp declared there was "absolutely no justification in

---

* *Amici curiae* is Latin for "friends of the court." It refers to third parties such as nonprofits, professional associations, and trade groups with an interest in the case who file their own briefs supporting one side or the other.

constitutional law for the extension of such a doctrine to public school students."[37] Case by case, he undermined the doctrine, seemingly slamming the door on it with these words: "Since there appears to be no question but that the board of education may regulate the curriculum (even to the extent of deciding what books to shelve) it is difficult to see how Appellants can posit a far greater right—that of a student to receive whatever information he chooses."[38]

Was this enough to persuade the Second Circuit?

* * *

It was not.

The same three-judge panel that decided *Bicknell* ruled this time in favor of the students. The opinion acknowledged that courts cannot possibly rule on every squabble in every school across the country, nor should they. Why? "Everyday administration of a school's curriculum or a school library does not, either directly or indirectly, impinge on the free expression of ideas."[39]

Yet the Island Trees case was more than the usual selecting and discarding of library materials. Rather, it was "an unusual and irregular intervention in the school libraries' operations" in which the board acted in an "erratic, arbitrary and free-wheeling manner."[40] The books were removed from the library not because school officials had read them and become concerned but on the basis of excerpts "collected by anonymous readers whose editorial comments revealed political concerns reaching far beyond the education and well-being of the children."[41] (Remember that declaring a book obscene on the basis of excerpts alone had been disallowed by Judge August Hand in the *Ulysses* case.) This approach, in the court's view, was "calculated to create public uproar."[42]

Moreover, by injecting these issues "into the School board election, a labor dispute [1978 teachers union strike], public meetings … and then into a district-wide plebiscite," the board signaled "that freedom of expression in the District would be determined in some substantial measure by the majority's will."[43] In other words, the court saw evidence of procedural and substantive irregularities, which, coupled with the board's stated emphasis on its own moral and political views, suggested that its actions were "not in the interests of the children's well-being, but rather for the purpose of establishing those views as the correct and orthodox ones for all purposes in the particular community"[44]—a constitutional no-no if ever there was one.

Judge Sifton, writing for the majority, remanded the case back to the district court for a trial. The board appealed to the en banc court, or full complement of ten Second Circuit judges, which split down the middle in a 5–5 vote. This meant that the panel decision would stand. In both cases, Mansfield voted the same: for the school board. Sifton voted the same: for the students.

The difference was Newman. In his concurring opinion, Judge Newman agreed that school authorities have broad discretion to remove books based on vulgar language and explicit sex. The Island Trees removals, however, seemed to be "the sort of clearly-defined, school-wide action that carries with it the potential for impermissible suppression of ideas."[45] In a 2003 law journal article, Edward Rubin wrote that, for Newman, the real impact of the book removals was to "disparage the ideas that the books expressed."[46] This made the removals "an act of expressive speech by the government"—an act that was odious to Newman, who wrote that "[t]he symbolic effect of ... removing a book solely because of its ideas will often be more significant than the resulting limitation upon access to it."[47]

The board had maintained that it objected only to the books' vulgarity and sexual content, but Newman thought that Steven Pico had introduced enough evidence of an improper political motive that a trial was needed to suss out the truth. Hence, his vote to remand. This is opposed to *Bicknell*, in which Newman, writing for the majority, noted, "There is no suggestion that the books were complained about or removed because of their ideas, nor that the Board members acted because of political motivation."[48] No doubt there *were* political motives. The history of censorship in the 1970s suggests that was often the case. If so, then the Vergennes board did a better job of shutting up about it than the Island Trees board.

Litigation, like football, is a game of inches.

Asked for his opinion, Kurt Vonnegut called the Second Circuit's ruling "a victory for the Constitution, not for my book."[49] True, the Island Trees affair probably didn't hurt his sales, yet he clearly took it personally. Naturally, being Vonnegut, he couldn't resist a bon mot: "There's nothing about sex in [*Slaughterhouse-Five*] because it's something I don't understand."[50]

Notes

1   Bonnie McCardell, "'Patriotic Conservative' Wants More Control over Library Picks," *Burlington Free Press*, March 12, 1978, 1B.
2   Bonnie McCardell, "Parents Object to 2 Library Books," *Burlington Free Press*, February 16, 1978, 2B.
3   Bonnie McCardell, "Vergennes to Form Book Review Panel," *Burlington Free Press*, March 9, 1978, 1B.
4   Ibid.
5   Ibid., 8B.
6   Bonnie McCardell, "Board Chief May Resign in Book Flap," *Burlington Free Press*, March 24, 1978, 1B.
7   Ibid., 2B.

8   Bonnie McCardell, "'The Wanderers' Banned from Library," *Burlington Free Press*, April 6, 1978, 1B.

9   Ted Tedford, "Vergennes Wrestles with Censorship Controversy," *Burlington Free Press*, April 30, 1978, 3A.

10 Ibid.

11 McCardell, "'The Wanderers' Banned from Library," 4B.

12 Louis Berney, "Students Sue to Get Books Back in School's Library," *Times Argus*, September 28, 1976, 16.

13 *Bicknell v. Vergennes*, 475 F. Supp. 615, 618 (D. Vermont, 1979).

14 Bonnie McCardell, "Librarian Seeks Alternative to Book Review Committee," *Burlington Free Press*, March 26, 1978, 4B.

15 Ibid.

16 *Bicknell v. Vergennes*, 475 F. Supp. 615.

17 *Bicknell v. Vergennes*, 638 F. 2d 438, 441 (2nd Cir., 1980).

18 Brief of appellants, Pico v. Island Trees, Second Circuit Court of Appeals, 1979, 36.

19 Ibid., 28.

20 Ibid., 29.

21 Ibid., 30.

22 Ibid., 31.

23 Ibid.

24 *Meyer v. Nebraska*, 262 U.S. 390, 401 (1923).

25 Brief of appellants, 17.

26 Ibid., 19.

27 Ibid., 22.

28 Ibid., 24.

29 Brief of appellees, Pico v. Island Trees, Second Circuit Court of Appeals, 5.

30 John McWhorter, *Nine Nasty Words* (Avery, 2021), 8.

31 Brief of appellees, 7–8.

32 Ibid., 16.

33 Ibid., 18.

34 Ibid., 22.

35 Ibid., 27.

36 *Va. Pharmacy Bd. v. Va. Consumer Council*, 425 U.S. 748 (1976).

37 Brief of appellees, 27.

38 Ibid., 29.

39 *Bicknell v. Vergennes*, 638 F. 2d 404, 414.

40 Ibid.

41 Ibid., 416.

42 Ibid.

43 Ibid.

44 Ibid., 417.

45 Ibid., 434.

46 Edward L. Rubin, "Jon Newman's Theory of Disparagement and the First Amendment in the Administrative State," *New York Law School Law Review* 46, no. 1 (2003): 249–77.

47 Ibid., 258.

48 *Bicknell v. Vergennes*, 638 F. 2d 438, 441.

49 Noel Rubinton, "So It Goes: Ruling Pleases Vonnegut," *Newsday* (Nassau ed.), October 4, 1980, 3.

50 Ibid.

9 Supreme Court, B!t¢hes!

There are two stereotypes of preachers' kids: goody-goody or hellion. Straitlaced or screwup. Demon or angel. I was the goody-goody. Kept my room clean. Made straight As. Never smoked, drank, or cussed. Went to college, then grad school, then more grad school. Became a librarian, an English teacher, and a writer. The nerdy trifecta. At church all the time. Couldn't just sing in the choir; I had to sing solos. Couldn't just appear in a play; I had to take a prominent role. Sunday school teachers looked to me to explain thorny passages. On Youth Sundays, I couldn't hide out as an usher but, lucky me, instead delivered the sermon. My father used to say my actions could get him fired because church members had eyes on my sister and me. *Always.* So, I knew a thing or two about duty. Still, of course, I screwed around a lot. Threw dirt clumps at passing cars. Pushed Walmart shopping carts into ditches. Broke into the church one night to scare our youth minister, who was working late.

Maybe what I needed was a mission.

Steven Pico had a mission. A calling. A quest. At age seventeen! It took him eight years, and though it was exhilarating, parts were unpleasant, such as being called a "communist" in public. What he won't forget was the silence of his teachers. Only one ever spoke to him about the book bans, whispering to him one day after class that he was doing the right thing.

"I will never be able to forget that she felt the need to whisper," he said ruefully.[1]

***

It is hard to get a case before the Supreme Court. The justices accept only 100–150 of the 7,000 appeals they receive each year, a process called "granting a writ of certiorari."[2] There are a few reasons why a writ is granted, according to the Rules of the Supreme Court of the United States:

1　A United States court of appeals has entered a decision in conflict with the decision of another United States court of appeals on the same important matter; has decided an important federal question in a way that conflicts with a decision by a state court of last resort; or has so far departed from the accepted and usual course of judicial proceedings, or sanctioned such a departure by a lower court, as to call for an exercise of this Court's supervisory power.

2   A state court of last resort has decided an important federal question in a way that conflicts with the decision of another state court of last resort or of a United States court of appeals.

3   A state court or a United States court of appeals has decided an important question of federal law that has not been, but should be, settled by this Court, or has decided an important federal question in a way that conflicts with relevant decisions of this Court.[3]

In 1980, school library censorship was an unsettled area of law. There were the conflicting Second Circuit opinions in *Pico* and *Bicknell*; the 5–5 en banc split in *Pico*; and the pro-ban case of *Presidents Council* versus the three "right to know" cases of *Minarcini*, *Right to Read*, and *Salvail*. It was the sort of scenario when the court tends to step in.

And step in it did.

The Supreme Court of the 1970s and 1980s is often called a "transitional" court. In 1982, the year of the *Island Trees* decision, it consisted of nine justices: William J. Brennan Jr.; Byron R. White; Thurgood Marshall, America's first African American justice; Harry A. Blackmun; Lewis F. Powell Jr.; William H. Rehnquist; John Paul Stevens; Sandra Day O'Connor, America's first female justice; and Chief Justice Warren E. Burger.

Burger, a conservative justice, was appointed in 1969 by President Richard Nixon. He took over from Earl Warren, who had held the position since 1953. The Warren Court is widely considered the most liberal court in United States history.[4] Many of the rights we now take for granted were established by the Warren Court. In 1953, it ended school segregation with *Brown v. Board of Education*. A decade later, it guaranteed the right to counsel for indigent defendants (*Gideon v. Wainwright*). Sexual rights were bolstered by *Griswold v. Connecticut* (1965) and *Loving v. Virginia* (1967), which awarded constitutional protection to birth control and interracial marriages, respectively. *Miranda v. Arizona* (1966) required police officers to issue so-called Miranda warnings—the right to remain silent, the right to an attorney—before questioning criminal suspects.

In addition to Burger, Nixon got the chance to appoint three more conservative justices: Blackmun (1970), Powell (1972), and Rehnquist (1972). He hoped these appointments would shift the court to the right, and it did, though that didn't prevent another of the court's marquee liberal decisions: *Tinker v. Des Moines* (1969), in which some high school students were suspended for wearing black armbands to school to protest the Vietnam War. The court ruled that "neither teachers nor students shed their constitutional rights to freedom of speech or expression at the schoolhouse gate"[5]—a ruling that would be key in *Island Trees v. Pico*.

Other left-leaning decisions were *New York Times v. United States* (1971), protecting publication of the Pentagon Papers; *Erznoznik v. City of Jacksonville* (1974), allowing a film that contained nudity because an "offended viewer readily can avert his eyes"; *United States v. Nixon* (1974), rejecting Nixon's claim of executive privilege for his Watergate communications, which led to his resignation; and *Regents of the University of California v. Bakke* (1978), upholding affirmative action in college admissions. And there was *Roe v. Wade* (1973), with which you may be familiar.

***

On the eve of oral arguments before the Supreme Court, both sides were feeling the pressure. For Frank Martin, now the Island Trees board president, it was crucial that the board retain its book-banning power. "When it's young," he told *The Washington Post*, quoting a child psychiatrist who likened a child's mind to an oak sapling, the tree "has to be protected from the winter. A child's mind is the same way. During the formative years, you can't give it too much stimuli."[6] Besides, as an ex-cop, he knew that the streets weren't as bad as Piri Thomas and Eldridge Cleaver made out. Their books, he said, were written "to sell, to be spectacular and dramatic."[7]

For the students, the books were a stand-in for how they wanted to be treated: like they had some sense. *Of course*, they could be trusted with challenging literature. One letter to the editor of *Newsday* summed up this position: "It seems to be the opinion of the board that our young people should not have the right to develop informed opinions based on exposure to a wide variety of viewpoints. Apparently the board does not believe in informed opinion, just opinion…. Once again Island Trees is the laughingstock of Long Island!"[8]

And it was more than the books. If the board prevailed, there would be no basis for federal judicial review in future cases. An entire area of accountability would be forestalled, leaving no check on local government power. Besides, wrote A. M. Kane in a 1980 op-ed, the book bans were a smokescreen to cover the board's other failures, such as low SAT scores. "As long as school boards place parochial concerns before national issues and requirements of the broader society," she wrote, "local control imposes a barrier to the full development of society."[9]

With so much riding on the court's decision, how did the attorneys—George Lipp, Alan Levine, and Arthur Eisenberg—prepare?

For Lipp, the first hurdle was existential. "I'm a small-town lawyer," he told *Newsday*. "I know what I am."[10] What he was was a guy who lacked a big law firm's money. Its expertise. Its battle scars. Yet this didn't deter him. For one thing, he had defied the odds just by getting the Supreme Court to accept the case: "a 1-in-30 legal feat."[11] For another, after five years of handling the case throughout the lower courts, who knew it better than he did? It was this logic that led Martin to assert that he never considered replacing Lipp with someone more experienced. The man, he said, "has earned his place before the Supreme Court."[12]

So, he got to work.

The first thing to do was write his brief, the written summary of his clients' position: that a state board of education has sole authority to manage the schools in its district, including deciding what resources should be in the schools' libraries. A brief, according to the Supreme Court's rules, must be fifty pages or less.[13] After both sides file their initial briefs, they can submit shorter second briefs that respond to each other's positions. In addition, the US government, represented by the solicitor general, can file a brief aligning with one or the other party. The court can also permit amicus curiae, or "friend of the court," briefs.

Lipp cranked out his forty-four-pager during a nineteen-day crucible at his winter home in Venice, Florida. "There were two or three nights running when I didn't get any sleep," he said.[14] It opens with this grandiose statement: "The decision of the Court requires the striking of a delicate balance between the conflicting interests at stake in a manner that will not compel the federal court system to continuingly address the specifics of actions such as those complained of."[15] Translation: *Butt out, justices. This ain't your fight.*

Again and again, Lipp hammered the idea of community values and respect for authority. On the question of the Island Trees board's political motives, rather than decrying them, Lipp leaned in, writing that "the board is a political subdivision of the state and all school systems carry on some form of political indoctrination in the better sense of the word."[16] In a preview of arguments that modern-day politicians often make, Lipp argued that even if the board *was* wrong, it is up to voters, not the courts, to correct them. Giving jurists a say "would be to disregard [the board members'] electoral mandate."[17]

In one passage, Lipp emphasized just how important Island Trees was: "There is no post office address known as Island Trees. There is no Village ... no separate fire department or police force."[18] The only "distinctive identity," therefore, is the school district, which "acts *in loco parentis* with respect to minors."[19] In other words, the district cares. It would not willingly transmit the wrong values to its charges—values that approve of these eleven bad books. And even if the books were all right, the court shouldn't enjoin the board from removing them due to "the need for extreme caution in involving itself in the decision making processes of the public schools."[20] It especially shouldn't question "content-based decisions" that are necessarily, and therefore permissibly, matters of personal judgment.

One thing absent from Lipp's brief is a discussion of the books themselves. This was not an oversight. "I'm just ignoring them," he explained at the time.[21] Why? To Lipp, the case was never about intellectual freedom. The board members had read the books before voting on the removals, which in his mind was enough to show that they weren't simpletons trampling all over the First Amendment. No, he saw the case as one of institutional power. The board had the power, so the court should let them exercise it. Let the NYCLU get bogged down in lit crit. He would stick to the law, which he thought favored his client.

Unlike Lipp, Eisenberg and Levine were veterans of the high court. To them, though, this was not just another case. It was, as Eisenberg told me, "a frontier First Amendment issue, unique, ground-breaking litigation." Levine likewise was eager, having failed to restore *Down These Mean Streets* to the library shelves in *Presidents Council, District 25 v. Community School Board*. The two attorneys were a smart match. As he had at the Second Circuit, bookish Eisenberg took the lead on writing, which cued up Levine, wired and effusive, to handle the oral argument. They worked long hours over Christmas, shirking family duties and living on peanuts and soda, submitting their thirty-seven-page brief a couple of hours before the noon deadline on December 31, 1981.[22]

As had been the case at the Second Circuit, Eisenberg's brief was crisper, more compelling. He reiterated the board's missteps in removing the books:

1 Its objections had been not to the whole books but to excerpts.
2 Its ban was imposed without professional corroboration (i.e., without reading reviews or consulting experts). In fact, the members had disregarded the recommendations of their own review committee.
3 The ban was absolute: books weren't just removed from the library—they couldn't be assigned or recommended.
4 The board never looked for other objectionable books in the library (this observation was not made at the district or circuit levels, but it's an interesting one).[23]

He acknowledged the board's commitment to transmitting its values to Island Trees students, agreeing that this is a necessary thing. He also agreed with Lipp that it wasn't in anyone's interest for courts to make regular rulings on libraries' collection management decisions.

This ruling, however, was anything but regular. The board, Eisenberg argued, used "the force of government to censor unpopular expression and those who seek to express—or be exposed to—differing perspectives."[24] This "exclusive emphasis on the values of the Island Trees community ignores [board members'] obligation to prepare students for the world beyond Island Trees."[25] Steven Pico echoed this idea when I talked to him. Think back, he said, to the authors who were removed. Richard Wright, Langston Hughes, Alice Childress—these were among the twentieth century's most prominent Black writers. Bernard Malamud was one of America's greatest Jewish writers. *Laughing Boy*, winner of the 1929 Pulitzer Prize, was about the Navajo nation. Take away these writers, and how would forty-three hundred white children be exposed to other cultures? They wouldn't, that's how.[26]

If Lipp ignored the removed books' contents, Eisenberg embraced them. For instance, he reminded the court that the board had banned *The Fixer* and *Slaughterhouse-Five* for being antisemitic and antireligious, respectively, before writing: "If the First Amendment means anything, it means that no agency of the state, least of all one charged with the duty to educate, may prevent students from reading a book because it mentions an unpleasant historical fact."[27] (This is happening today with so-called educational gag orders. In Florida, for example, the 2023 Stop WOKE Act prohibited "instruction that could make students feel uncomfortable about a historical event because of their race.")[28]

Bottom line: school boards have power. But not more power than the United States Constitution.

***

With both sides' briefs submitted, the next step was oral arguments, which are typically scheduled for Mondays, Tuesdays, and Wednesdays, October through April.[29] Heard on March 2, 1982, *Island Trees v. Pico* was "one of the hottest tickets in town."[30] Each side was given six passes to the 213-seat courtroom, but those were quickly used up. Steven Pico was there, as was board president Frank Martin. Patrick Hughes and Richard Melchers, two other board members, were also there, as was Barbara Bernstein, director of the Nassau chapter of the New York Civil Liberties Union. Others had to joust for a seat. "We can't take everybody in the world," said Chief Marshal Alfred Wong, who said he felt like a ticket manager at a Broadway theater.[31] Lawyer Alan Azzara said he was swamped with requests. "What do they think this is," he said, "a rock concert?"[32]

Appearing before the Supreme Court is not like the lower courts, where you spend a lot of time arguing what the law is. The high court is concerned with what the law *should be*. Moreover, it has the power to turn "should be" into "is." Such power, says former solicitor general Paul Clement, gives the court a mystique unmatched in American jurisprudence—that and its building, where the justices sit almost on top of the lawyers arguing before them. "If the Chief Justice were to reach out and you were to reach out," said Clement, "you can just about touch fingertips."[33]

Attorneys often prepare for a Supreme Court appearance by practicing before groups of colleagues who play the role of the justices. Levine and Eisenberg did this, as did Lipp, who also turned to Hollywood, taking pointers from the 1981 movie *First Monday in October*.[34] The film stars Jill Clayburgh as Ruth Loomis, a young conservative who, after becoming the first female Supreme Court justice, clashes with Walter Matthau's Daniel Snow, an older liberal jurist. (Released two days after Ronald Reagan nominated Sandra Day O'Connor to become the court's actual first woman justice, the film got mixed reviews. Janet Maslin opened hers in typical tart fashion: "What if the latest Supreme Court Justice were a woman? And what if that woman were a terrible pill?")[35]

During oral arguments, each side has thirty minutes to present its case.[36] Lipp hoped to be allowed a five-minute opening statement, but he was interrupted almost immediately by Chief Justice Burger, who asked, "In your view, does it make any difference what is in the books?"[37] Remember: this was a topic Lipp had avoided in his brief. Standing before the Court, however, he replied that, yes, it makes a difference. "Books must be viewed as a whole," he said, "but there were passages in each one triggering the action."[38]

Justice O'Connor returned to that idea some minutes later. Could a school board, say, "remove from student exposure all references in the library to a particular ideology?"[39] Would *that* be worthy of judicial review? Lipp acknowledged that a board could not engage in "a comprehensive and obvious attempt to sanitize a whole body of thought."[40] However, he went on, that is not what happened here. Island Trees removed "nine books out of thousands"[41]—hardly an obliteration.

OK, said Justice Stevens. What about one book? What about the removal of one book that, say, contained "disparaging remarks about Jews and blacks?"[42] Should the courts get involved over one book? This is the sort of thing the Supreme Court does in every oral argument: it puts the onus on the complaining party. It says, all right, you're standing here, telling us we can't intervene in your decision to remove books in your school. When could we intervene? What should be the standard for review?

Lipp didn't have a good answer.

Eventually, Justice Marshall got onto the topic of standards. Did the board, in its decision to remove the books, "act on the basis of any standards or any indication of just what rules it thought it was applying?"[43] After all, it appointed a book review committee and then largely dismissed its recommendations. Why?

Lipp tried to argue that standards weren't needed because of all the "imponderables"—morals, ethics, and so on. To standardize these, he said, would be "an unmanageable task."[44]

That didn't satisfy Marshall. A minute or two later, he asked, "Do you concede that when a school board puts a book in its library, it puts a stamp of approval on that book?"

Lipp: I say that there is some imprimatur.
Marshall: It wants the students to read everything they can, good and bad?
Lipp: Good and bad with regard to style, with regard to content, but not with regard—
Marshall: Or good and bad with regard to the standards which you don't have.[45]

A few minutes later, it was Levine's turn. Like Lipp, he had barely begun speaking before the questions started coming. One of them was a question that had also been asked of Lipp: suppose there is a book that has been found to violate criminal obscenity laws. Could that book be removed from a school library? Lipp had struggled with his answer. Levine's, however, distilled his whole argument beautifully:

> The judgment of a jury is, first of all, a judgment that a book has fit into a very narrow exception to First Amendment protection, the obscenity standard. The exception to First Amendment protection asserted by the [school board] here is a very broad one. They assert the power to ban books that give offense. That doesn't resemble the obscenity standard at all.[46]

In response to another question, Levine elaborated:

> [T]he right to read a book is so clearly inherent in First Amendment analysis that even though most book cases have been brought by book sellers, or book publishers, surely if the state deprived the citizenry of reading a book, the citizenry would have a right—a First Amendment right to protest that action.[47]

Later, Levine faltered in the same way as Lipp: articulating a clear standard for when a court should intervene. However, he got off a few good one-liners in the process:

> [I]f the courts abdicate, if the federal courts say that anything school boards say and do about books is beyond judicial review, then you leave people remedyless for the assertion of very important rights … I don't think that a school board can cloak its political concerns in the mantle of educational suitability. They may say that, and they may want the [Supreme] Court to believe that is what went on here, but they did in fact make some very explicit political judgments.[48]

Those judgments were, of course, the removal of Eldridge Cleaver's *Soul on Ice*—Cleaver was a member of the Black Panthers—as well as *A Hero Ain't Nothing but a Sandwich*, for the George Washington passage.

As for *A Reader for Writers*, Levine was no doubt delighted when, in a final set of remarks, Lipp acknowledged that it was removed due to one of its selections, Jonathan Swift's "A Modest Proposal," being "in bad taste." Perhaps the justices couldn't believe their ears either. "Would it be permissible," came the inevitable question, "for them to take every book out of the library they thought was in bad taste? What does bad taste mean?"[49]

What, indeed.

***

The question before the Supreme Court had sounded simple: does the First Amendment prohibit boards of education from removing books from school libraries? On June 25, 1982, a few days before Paul Sochinski's high-school commencement, the court delivered its answer. By then, Steven Pico had finished his degree at Haverford College and was working at the nonprofit National Coalition against Censorship. I'll let him tell it: "The Court ruled 5–4 in my behalf. The decision was not a sweeping condemnation of book banning which many had hoped for. We won by the skin of our teeth."

What did he mean "skin of our teeth"?

An appellate court opinion consists of two main parts. One part is the holding, or ruling, which is the court's decision on the outcome of the case. Is the lower court ruling affirmed? Reversed? Something else? The second part is the analysis: a discussion of the legal reasoning that underpins the holding. The reasoning is crucial because it becomes binding on all future cases unless the opinion is later overruled.

If all nine justices agree on everything about a case, that's easy: the court issues a single unanimous opinion. Things get tricky, though, when one or more justices agree on the *holding* but not the *reasoning*. Those justices then write separate concurring opinions, which are useful in understanding those justices' ideologies. Concurring opinions, however, are not binding.

Justices who disagree with the holding are free to write dissenting opinions, which are also nonbinding. Often, one justice writes such an opinion, and others who voted against the majority join it. In *Island Trees v. Pico*, however, all four dissenting justices—Powell, Rehnquist, O'Connor, and Chief Justice Burger—wrote their own opinions. Moreover, two justices—White and Blackmun—wrote separate concurrences, meaning they agreed with the holding but not the reasoning. This left only the plurality of Stevens, Brennan, and Marshall to represent the official opinion of the court.

That opinion was written by the seventy-six-year-old Brennan. I spoke to Maria Warren, a former prosecutor who has taught law for two decades, who called Brennan "one of the most influential liberal forces on the high court of the twentieth century." Born to Irish immigrants in Newark, New Jersey, Brennan learned those liberal values at a young age. His father was a labor leader at a time when many signs still hung on shop doors indicating that "no Irish need apply."

Brennan took that sensibility to Pennsylvania's Wharton School and then to Harvard Law School, where he represented indigent clients as a member of Harvard's Legal Aid Society. After Harvard, he ended up on the other side, representing management at the prestigious Newark firm of Pitney, Hardin & Skinner. He served as a trial judge from 1949 to 1951 before being appointed to the Supreme Court of New Jersey. On October 15, 1956, he was given a recess appointment to the US Supreme Court by President Dwight Eisenhower and sworn in the following day.

Brennan was "characterized by a love of humanity," according to former prosecutor Warren, as interested in the life of the Supreme Court's janitor as in the other justices. An unflappable negotiator, he evinced great warmth and charm, plus a nonpareil commitment to compromise. Besides *Island Trees v. Pico*, he wrote a number of landmark opinions. One was *Baker v. Carr* (1962), which stated that apportionment—the determination of how many members each state sends to the House of Representatives—was an appropriate question for federal courts, setting the stage for later cases that ensured "one person, one vote."[50] In *New York Times v. Sullivan* (1964), he ruled that for a statement to be defamatory, it must contain "actual malice," meaning that it had to be made with knowledge of its falsity or "reckless disregard" for its truthfulness.[51] *Green v. County School Board of New Kent County, Virginia* (1968)[52] and *Keyes v. School District No. 1* (1973)[53] furthered the cause of school desegregation. And in *Plyler v. Doe* (1982),[54] his opinion ensured access to public schools for undocumented alien children.

(He had his limits, of course, such as upholding the convictions of Samuel Roth in 1957 and Ralph Ginzburg in 1968 for peddling obscenities. As Brennan read his Ginzburg opinion in court, his neck got "redder and redder." Why? "Brennan has a daughter, and while he is a libertarian in other matters, he becomes a censor of materials that might harm the purity of his daughter.")[55]

Looking at the makeup of the Supreme Court in the early 1980s, oddsmakers probably did not give Steven Pico much of a chance. Brennan and Marshall were the liberals, while Rehnquist, Burger, O'Connor, and Powell formed the conservative bloc. This left Stevens, Blackmun, and "Whizzer" White—he had played halfback in the NFL from 1938 to 1940[56]—as the centrists, though White was sometimes right of center: he dissented in *Miranda v. Arizona*; dissented in *Roe v. Wade*; and, in *Bowers v. Hardwick* (1986), upheld the criminalization of oral and anal sex between consenting adults.[57] (This opinion was overturned in 2003.)[58]

According to Pico, the reason the court agreed to take up his case was because the four dissenters thought they could convince a fifth to join them.[59] But who? Not Marshall, who was so in sync with Brennan that clerks called them "Justice Brennanmarshall" behind their backs.[60] Stevens and Blackmun were probably unreachable as well.

That left White.

Maybe the conservatives assumed he was theirs; maybe they lobbied him hard. Either way, Brennan "outmaneuvered" them, writing an opinion that White could "tacitly accept,"[61] though White did so in spartan fashion, agreeing that the case should go to trial but not endorsing the First Amendment "dissertation" that Brennan included.[62]

Brennan began his opinion by reviewing the facts of the case before distilling all the issues into two questions:

1 Does the First Amendment limit the discretion of the Island Trees school board to remove library books from its schools?
2 If so, is there a "genuine issue of fact whether [the board] might have exceeded those limitations?" (In other words, does the case need to go to trial?)

School boards, Brennan observed, "have a substantial legitimate role to play in the determination of school library content."[63] Yet that authority "must be exercised in a manner that comports with the transcendent imperatives of the First Amendment."[64] What does he mean by "transcendent"? He means that though courts should stay out of routine school business, "the First Amendment rights of students may be directly and sharply implicated" by library book removals.[65]

This is due to an argument that Judge Pratt rejected back in district court: the right to receive information. Brennan wrote that the court has repeatedly recognized this right, which he called "an inherent corollary of the rights of free speech and press."[66] First, the right "follows ineluctably from the *sender's* First Amendment right to send [ideas]. More importantly, the right to receive ideas is a necessary predicate to the *recipient's* meaningful exercise of his own rights of speech, press, and political freedom."[67] This principle applies to students as much as anyone else, and especially in a library. Quoting another case, *Keyishian v. Board of Regents* (1967), Brennan wrote that "'students must always remain free to inquire, to study and to evaluate, to gain new maturity and understanding.' The school library is the principal locus of such freedom."[68]

As for Island Trees' right to remove books, Brennan thought that the members "rightly possess significant discretion to determine the content of their school libraries. But that discretion may not be exercised in a narrowly partisan or political manner."[69] Intent, in other words, is key. The Constitution doesn't permit ideas-based discrimination, and if that is what the board intended with its removals, then that is an obvious violation. Such actions, he wrote, "stand inescapably condemned by our precedents."[70]

So, was that the board's intent? Brennan worried that it might have been. Like Judge Sifton writing for the Second Circuit, Brennan found the board's actions curious. "This would be a very different case," he wrote, "if the record demonstrated that petitioners had employed established, regular, and facially unbiased procedures for the review of controversial materials."[71] Instead, they "ignored 'the advice of literary experts,' the views of 'librarians and teachers within the Island Trees School system,' the advice of the Superintendent of Schools, and the guidance of publications that rate books for junior and senior high school students."[72] Basically, the evidence did not "rule out the possibility that petitioners' removal procedures were highly irregular and *ad hoc*—the antithesis of those procedures that might tend to allay suspicions regarding petitioners' motivations."[73]

Bottom line: we're goin' to trial.

Only three justices—Marshall, Blackmun, and Stevens—joined Brennan in circumscribing the right of school boards to remove library books, though Blackmun did not sign on the plurality opinion, as he rejected Brennan's "right to receive information." The conservatives rejected everything, seemingly agreeing with Rehnquist, who found Island Trees' actions "hard to distinguish from the myriad choices made by school boards in the routine supervision of elementary and secondary schools";[74] that no ideas were suppressed; and that no rights of free speech and expression were infringed. Justice White, as discussed above, was the swing vote, preferring not to pick a winner but to play for overtime.

Remember: a game of inches.

Notes

1   Steven Pico, "An Introduction to Censorship," *School Library Media Quarterly* 18, no. 2 (1990): 84–87.
2   "Supreme Court Procedures," *United States Courts*, https://www.uscourts.gov/about-federal-courts/educational-resources/about-educational-outreach/activity-resources/supreme-court-procedures.
3   Supreme Court Rule 10(c).
4   Jim Beam, "A Tumultuous Time: Remembering Chief Justice Warren and Perhaps the Most Liberal Supreme Court in US History," *American Press*, July 8, 2023, https://americanpress.com/2023/07/08/a-tumultuous-time-remembering-chief-justice-warren-and-perhaps-the-most-liberal-supreme-court-in-us-history/.
5   *Tinker v. Des Moines*, 393 U.S. 503, 506 (1969).
6   Charles Babcock, "Book Banning Spreads," *Washington Post*, May 9, 1982, https://www.washingtonpost.com/archive/politics/1982/05/10/book-banning-spreads/8f892694-9de3-4faa-8d20-f168dd0ff7dc/.
7   Ibid.
8   "Book Ban in Island Trees," *Newsday* (Nassau ed.), March 26, 1976, 77.
9   A. M. Kane, "Stop Protecting Children from Ideas," *Newsday* (Nassau ed.), November 7, 1980, 66.
10 "Preparing for the High Court," *Newsday* (Nassau ed.), January 10, 1982, 4.
11 Ibid.
12 Ibid., 26.
13 "Supreme Court Procedures."
14 "Preparing for the High Court," 27.
15 Petitioners' brief, Island Trees v. Pico, United States Supreme Court, December 2, 1981, 9.
16 Ibid., 10.
17 Ibid., 11–12.
18 Ibid., 17.
19 Ibid.
20 Ibid., 22–23.

21 "Preparing for the High Court," 27.

22 Ibid.

23 Respondents' brief, Island Trees v. Pico, United States Supreme Court, January 5, 1982, 7–9.

24 Ibid., 14.

25 Ibid., 24.

26 Anthony Aycock, "Desperately Seeking Sources," *Missouri Review*, October 20, 2023, https://missourireview.com/desperately-seeking-sources-by-anthony-aycock/.

27 Ibid., 33.

28 Vimal Patel, "Republicans Target Social Sciences to Curb Ideas They Don't Like," *New York Times*, November 21, 2024, https://www.nytimes.com/2024/11/21/us/florida-social-sciences-progressive-ideas.html.

29 "Supreme Court Procedures."

30 Rita Ciolli, "Scramble for Seats in Book-Ban Case," *Newsday* (Nassau ed.), March 2, 1982, 11.

31 Ibid.

32 Ibid.

33 "What's It Like to Argue in Front of the Supreme Court?," *Harvard Law Today*, January 10, 2023, https://hls.harvard.edu/today/whats-it-like-to-argue-in-front-of-the-supreme-court/.

34 "Preparing for the High Court," 4.

35 Janet Maslin, "The Screen: 'First Monday in October,'" *New York Times*, August 21, 1981, 54.

36 "Supreme Court Procedures."

37 Transcript of oral arguments, Island Trees v. Pico, United States Supreme Court, March 2, 1982, 4.

38 Ibid.

39 Ibid., 9.

40 Ibid., 10.

41 Ibid.

42 Ibid.

43 Ibid., 22.

44 Ibid., 26.

45 Ibid., 27.

46 Ibid., 29.

47 Ibid., 32.

48 Ibid., 49–57.

49 Ibid., 59.

50 *Baker v. Carr*, 369 U.S. 186 (1962).

51 *New York Times Co. v. Sullivan*, 376 U.S. 254 (1964).

52 *Green v. County Sch. Bd. of New Kent County*, 391 U.S. 430 (1968).

53 *Keyes v. School Dist. No. 1*, 413 U.S. 189 (1973).

54 *Plyler v. Doe*, 457 U.S. 202 (1982).

55 Nat Hentoff, *Speaking Freely* (Knopf, 1997), 137.

56 "Byron 'Whizzer' White," *CU Athletic Hall of Fame*, https://cubuffs.com/honors/cu-athletic-hall-of-fame/byron-whizzer-white/1.

57 *Bowers v. Hardwick*, 478 U.S. 186 (1986).

58 *Lawrence v. Texas*, 539 U.S. 558 (2003).

59 Pico, "An Introduction to Censorship," 86.

60 Del Dickson, ed., *The Supreme Court in Conference, 1940–1985: The Private Discussions behind Nearly 300 Supreme Court Decisions* (Oxford University Press, 2001), 10.

61 Pico, "An Introduction to Censorship," 86–87.

62 *Island Trees v. Pico*, 457 U.S. 853, 883.

63 Ibid., 869.

64 Ibid., 853.

65 Ibid.

66 Ibid., 867.

67 Ibid.

68 Ibid., 868–69.

69 Ibid., 870.

70 Ibid., 872.

71 Ibid., 874.

72 Ibid.

73 Ibid., 875.

74 Ibid., 920.

10 Keep Suing, Keep Fighting

There is a maxim among lawyers: hard cases make bad law. Richard Stone, writing for the New York Education Department in 1982, took it a step further, saying *Island Trees v. Pico* proves that "particularly hard cases make no law." By this, he meant that "[t]he almost unanimous reaction thus far to the *Island Trees* decision is that the Court has failed to resolve the issue, that the Court was 'deadlocked' and that the Court has failed to provide any useful guidelines for school boards and for the lower Courts."[1]

Genevieve Lakier, professor of law at the University of Chicago, agreed when I spoke to her. She said the Supreme Court had been trying to balance two contradictory interests: first, that inquisitive students should be exposed to many ideas; and second, that local school boards have a mandate, as well as carte blanche, to control that exposure. "The line that the court draws is a very fine one," Lakier mused—too fine to be the final word.

Part of the problem, she said, is that no one knows quite what to do with plurality opinions. Although such decisions are binding, they set a weak precedent. For example, in *Muir v. Alabama Educational Television Commission*, a case decided just three months after *Pico*, the US Court of Appeals for the Fifth Circuit dismissed the earlier ruling. *Muir* is a combination of two cases, both involving public television stations that canceled their scheduled broadcasts of "Death of a Princess," a British docudrama based on the true story of Princess Mishaal bint Fahd Al Saud, a member of the House of Saud who confessed to committing adultery in 1977 at the age of nineteen. She and her lover were executed: firing squad for her, beheading for him.

The stations were sued for the cancellations, with plaintiffs claiming violations of their First Amendment rights. At one point, the plaintiffs "suggest[ed] that while it is a proper exercise of editorial discretion for a [station] initially to decide not to schedule a program, it is constitutionally improper for the [station] to decide to cancel a scheduled program because of its political content."[2] Sound familiar? The court rejected this analogy to *Pico*, remarking that the case was "of no precedential value as to the application of the First Amendment."[3] No fewer than thirty other cases have criticized *Pico* or limited its impact. (These are all by lower courts, none of which has the power to overrule the case. Only the Supreme Court itself can do that.)

By 1995, the Fifth Circuit had warmed to *Pico*. In *Campbell v. St. Tammany Parish School Board*, it considered the decision of a Louisiana school board to scotch Jim Haskins's book *Voodoo and Hoodoo* from the parish libraries. Haskins was an educator and "one of America's most prolific children's book authors," according to his obituary.[4] *Voodoo and Hoodoo* offers a history of these West African practices, along with—this must be the part people objected to—"a presentation of 'spells,' 'tricks,' 'hexes,' [and] 'recipes' [that] outline, in how-to form, the way to bring about particular events."[5]

The court discusses *Pico* at length, ultimately deciding that, "[e]ven though the constitutional analysis in the Pico plurality opinion does not constitute binding precedent, it may properly serve as guidance."[6] Noting that Justice White did not explicitly reject the First Amendment argument but merely declined to examine it, the court ruled that a right to receive information from libraries *does* exist—in its jurisdiction, anyway. Thus, it reversed the removal and ordered a trial.

There were other blows against book bans. Also in 1995, a Kansas school board nixed from its library Nancy Garden's novel *Annie on My Mind*, which concerns a romance between two teenage girls, Annie and Liza. Several board members objected to the "glorification" of homosexuality, which can lead to death, destruction, disease, and other problems. That wasn't the most extreme view: one member thought the library should reject *all* fiction in favor of "factual books like the Bible."[7] In *Case v. United School District No. 233*, the district court noted that *Pico* was not binding, yet it decided to follow Justice Brennan's ruling because it "is the only Supreme Court decision dealing specifically with the removal of books from a public school library."[8]

A final example is *Counts v. Cedarville School District* (2003). In this case, two Arkansas parents, Billy Ray and Mary Nell Counts, sued on behalf of their fourth-grade daughter, Dakota, whose school had restricted access to the Harry Potter series due to concerns that the books "might promote disobedience and disrespect for authority" and that they include "witchcraft" and "the occult."[9] The district court sided with the Counts family, quoting *Pico* in its assertion that "[t]he right to read a book is an aspect of the right to receive information and ideas, an 'inherent corollary of the rights of free speech and press that are explicitly guaranteed by the Constitution.'"[10]

***

By now, you're probably wondering what I think of all this. Am I on the side of censors? Readers? School boards? Free speech activists? Do I agree with Steven

Pico, who might have seen the actions of the Island Trees school board as "Hell is empty and all the devils are here"?[11] Or am I sympathetic to the board, who might have regarded its critics as "full of sound and fury, signifying nothing?"[12]

I will tell you.

In chapter 5, I sketched a history of America's effort to protect childhood innocence. Such protection was often the impetus behind book bannings of the 1970s, and it remains one for certain actions in the 2020s—parents' rights bills, for example. In 2023, sixty-two such bills were filed in statehouses nationwide.[13] The year before, it was eighty-five.[14] For the most part, these bills codify common sense, giving parents a voice in matters of student discipline, instruction, and health care.

Yet there are overreaches, such as this statement from a new Ohio law: "Upon request of the student's parent, a student shall be excused from instruction that includes sexuality content and be permitted to participate in an alternative assignment."[15] The law defines "sexuality content" as "any oral or written instruction, presentation, image, or description of sexual concepts or gender ideology provided in a classroom setting."[16]

More outspoken was the Texas State Board of Education, which in 2023 "overwhelmingly rejected the inclusion of several American Library Association policies in the state's librarian certification requirements."[17] Why? ALA "has a long history of circumventing parental rights to fill local and school library shelves with pornographic, racist, and leftist propaganda" and also "prides itself on bypassing state laws that protect students from indoctrination and grooming."[18]

As I said in a previous chapter, children do not need protection from ideas. Would-be censors assume that if no one reads about sex, drugs, witchcraft, or boys kissing boys, then those acts will never be committed. Censorship, in their minds, prevents the spread of vulgarity and obscenity. It's a path to a purer society.

This is magical thinking, of course. Judges may wrestle with the contours of propriety, but we don't, not if we abandon political posturing and hero complexes and instead use our common sense. I know what pornography is, and so do you. I'll join you in keeping kids from it. Otherwise, I don't care to get involved.

But, you may say, what about all the stuff that's borderline? The thing about borders is, they should be available. Monitored? Sure. But available. What's waiting on the other side is something spectacular, and you can't blame travelers for wanting to go there. We just need to watch out for them as they do. So give me access over absence. Enrichment over embargo. "Are we there yet?" over "When are you coming back?"

And standards of decency change over time. One era's vulgarity is a later era's masterpiece. For instance, the shower stabbing in the movie *Psycho* is one of history's scariest movie moments. Yet what alarmed many 1960 viewers was the scene just before it, when Marion Crane shreds evidence about the $40,000 she stole and, not wanting to leave the incriminating scraps in the trash can, flushes them down the toilet. No mainstream movie had ever shown a toilet, which was "thought to be offensive," says film historian David Thomson. "Hitchcock said 'well this is silly' and he got away with it."[19]

Steven Pico has stayed abreast of censorship trends. He saw the fearmongering in his community in 1975, and he sees it across conservative America today. "I hate this idea that books are dangerous," he told me, then paused, considering. "What is the most dangerous thing that can enter a school today?" He paused again, waiting for me to answer.

"A gun," I said.

"Right. They don't want to talk about the gun, so they're weaponizing the books."[20]

He made the fear of obscenity sound made-up, an instrument of mob rally, a rationale for martial law of the mind. I'm not so sure. Nowadays, we know about hippies. Rock 'n' roll is four generations old. We are awash in true crime shows and podcasts—heck, we can watch it happen on social media. Sex is written about as frankly as a trip to Food Lion. Fifty years ago, however, a lot of that was new. I can see how people feared an escalation of Yeats's World War I-era words: "Things fall apart; the centre cannot hold; / Mere anarchy is loosed upon the world." We have the same fears now, courtesy of COVID-19, the wars in Ukraine and Gaza, inflation, and other domestic ills. The average person is powerless against these problems.

One thing they can do: ban books.

Is that the right response? Nope. Was it the right response in Nassau County, New York? Certainly not. Yet I don't think it was a covert power grab. *Newsday* covered the Island Trees book bans from start to finish, and missing from those seven years' worth of articles was a lot of conspiracy theorizing. Residents quoted in those articles mostly accuse the board of being misguided, not power hungry. Board members themselves seemed genuinely to think that they were doing the right thing. They said it in courthouse depositions, and they said it to the newspapers. In March 1976, after the famous "just plain filthy" press conference, the board members took questions from the media. They were, according to George Vescey of *The New York Times*,

> friendly and open and—except for a few complaints about the behavior of the media—they seemed willing to listen to the personal opinions of one reporter, who said he would be proud to have his early teen-age daughters read works by Mr. Malamud, Langston Hughes, Kurt Vonnegut Jr., Richard Wright and others on the review list.
>
> "But what about the anti-Semitic remarks in "The Fixer?" asked Louis Nessim, a board member, referring to graphic remarks about incest, mutilation and other violence.
>
> "I think this book would make anybody more upset about persecution because of these examples," the visitor said.

"But if these words were eliminated," [board president Frank] Martin asked, "the book would be just as good, wouldn't it?"[21]

In May 1982, a month or so before the Supreme Court's ruling, Martin talked to *The Washington Post* about the impact of "bad" books on impressionable young minds. "[I]f just one Island Trees student is adversely affected," he said, "I would be totally negligent."[22] He recalled reviewing and rejecting a social studies text that described the late jazz musician Louis Armstrong as a famous Black person. "Hey," he said, "I like Louis Armstrong's music, but dammit, it doesn't belong in a social studies textbook, especially when they're taking space away from the Second World War or American history."[23]

Short-sighted? Yes. Smoke screen for despotism? I don't hear it. We know how it sounds when a person lies. To my ear, Martin and his colleagues were not lying.

They were just plain wrong.

***

The Supreme Court's decision did not immediately calm any turbulence in Nassau County.

Steven Pico was, of course, elated: "It's a message to the censors around the country that school boards have a responsibility to encourage students to think freely. The Supreme Court is saying that it is the job of a board of education to teach young people how to think, not what to think."[24] One can imagine him jumping around the room, dousing his co-plaintiffs in champagne.

Also pleased was Alice Childress, author of *A Hero Ain't Nothin' but a Sandwich*. "It is a victory," she said. "People have to justify their challenges to books."[25] Less celebratory was Bernard Malamud: "The sad thing is that [the board members] are unmoved by literature; nor do they understand its relation to the health and moral vigor of a democracy."[26] Judy Blume didn't have a dog in the fight, but when she heard what happened, "she burst into tears," saying, "Thinking is one of our inalienable rights and I'm so glad that right has been upheld."[27]

Technically, the court's ruling simply overturned Judge Pratt's award of summary judgment to the Island Trees board. In other words, it was allowing a trial—unless the board dropped the case. "We have no apology to make," said Frank Martin. "We feel we acted for the good of the students of Island Trees."[28] Maybe so. Yet pressing ahead to trial would have consequences. George Lipp thought the board would prevail, but he was concerned about the effect on its members. "They will be put in cages by all that publicity," he said.[29] Ivan Gluckman, attorney for the National Association of Secondary School Principals, echoed this. "Each member's entire life could be open to scrutiny," he said before adding: "If I were a board member, my attitude would be to leave the books alone."[30]

And that is what the board did. Two months after the decision, in August of 1982, it voted to return the books to the library shelves on one condition: they had to be slapped with a "Parental Notification Required" warning. Attorney Arthur Eisenberg objected immediately. "We believe [the board] moved to restore the books in part owing to the recognition that the First Amendment limits the capacity of school boards to ban books because they don't like the ideas expressed in them," he said, noting that "to single out the books for special treatment again" means "the constitutional defect is not necessarily cured."[31]

In other words: *Nice try, but it's not enough.*

One person who agreed with Eisenberg was New York Attorney General Robert Abrams, who said the board's new restriction would violate a state law on the confidentiality of library records[32]—a law that Steven Pico told me he helped pass. The conflict dragged on, with some twelve hundred residents petitioning the board to stop fighting and give up. In early 1983, it did, restoring the books with *no* restrictions, though with one last kvetch. "It was proper to remove the books," said Patrick Hughes, one of four board members who voted to return them, "but we've spent too much time on this. It's time to put it behind us."[33] Christina Fasulo, one of the "nay" votes, was even less gracious. "Until the day I die," she said, "I refuse to budge on my position. Since when is it demeaning to take filth off library shelves?"[34]

The group with the least to say about the case's outcome was current Island Trees students. "The books are the farthest thing from their minds," said one student about his classmates.[35] "I don't think anyone cares," agreed another. "Half the books I wouldn't read anyway. They just sit on shelves."[36] Anyone who thought administrators might mention it during that year's graduation were disappointed. "That's Island Trees for you," said Nilda Moretti, who had opposed the book ban. "Nobody's mentioning a landmark decision. History's being made here, but nobody's interested."[37]

These days, censors wield a weapon they largely ignored in the 1970s: state legislatures. It began, according to Laura Pappano, the same as in Island Trees: with a list—the Krause List, to be exact.[38] Matthew Krause was an attorney who was elected to the Texas House of Representatives in 2013. In 2021, as chair of the Texas House Committee on General Investigating, he sent a list of some 850 books to several school districts as well as the Texas Education Agency, demanding that each district tell him how many of these books it possessed, what those books cost, and which other books it owned that "might make students feel discomfort, guilt, anguish, or any other form of psychological distress because of their race or sex or convey that a student, by virtue of their race or sex, is inherently racist, sexist, or oppressive, whether consciously or unconsciously."[39] Some districts responded; some did not. Krause never explained his request, including how he compiled his list, and he never followed up with districts that didn't comply. He had been a legislator in good standing for nearly a decade, but this move seems to have ended his political career: by 2023, he was out of office.[40]

Yet the spirit of the list seemed to catch on, as other states began passing library-unfriendly bills. In 2023, more than 150 bills were introduced with goals such as usurping collection development responsibilities, removing access to certain types of information, and otherwise restricting library access. Of those bills, 20 (13 percent) were signed into law.[41] In 2024, 128 such bills were introduced, with 7 (5 percent) becoming law.[42]

The downward trend is encouraging, but more work remains. John Chrastka, executive director of the lobbying firm EveryLibrary, is at the forefront of that work. He divides people into four categories: believers, who are "already our supporters"; questioners, who "want to know how the library addresses issues they care about"; people who are "suspicious of government and taxes in general, not just the library" (library leaders don't like discussing taxes, but "we have to talk about" them, Chrastka says, "because everybody else is"); and, finally, those who "just aren't going to vote for the library."[43] Different techniques appeal to different groups, but what they all have in common is urgency. "All too often," Chrastka muses, "the only people who've thought about public libraries are the librarians. That's what we have to change."[44]

* * *

The efforts of John Chrastka and his colleagues aside, courtrooms are still the most significant anticensorship battlegrounds. The Supreme Court has not reconsidered *Pico* in more than forty years. I think it will. It *has* to. Book ban lawsuits are spreading through the system, and judges are flying blind, making guidance-free rulings just as they did before 1982. All it takes is one ultra-determined litigant to push through a test case, a *Pico* 2.0.[45]

In 2025, it appeared that case might be *Little v. Llano County*.

The case began in 2021, when a group of Llano County, Texas, residents wanted certain books to be removed from the public library system—books they saw as "obscene" and "pornographic." These included Maurice Sendak's *In the Night Kitchen* (a book often banned because the main character, Mickey, appears in the nude), Robie H. Harris and Michael Emberley's *It's Perfectly Normal* (a sex education book for preteens), and Dawn McMillan's *I Broke My Butt*.

In total, seventeen books were removed. Library officials said this was done as part of the normal weeding process (we discussed weeding in chapter 6), though that doesn't explain why the library board was dissolved and restocked with the book challengers; why the OverDrive e-book service was canceled; or why librarian Suzette Baker, who had opposed the book removals, was fired.[46] There was also a failed effort to close the Llano County library entirely.[47]

Seven Llano County residents sued. Led by former speech-language pathologist Leila Green Little, they claimed that the book removals were content-based and therefore violated their First Amendment rights. The district court ruled in favor of the plaintiffs, and the book banners appealed to the Fifth Circuit Court of Appeals. On June 6, 2024, a three-judge panel upheld the district court's decision, ruling that governments cannot remove books from a public library to keep patrons from accessing certain ideas.[48]

This victory, however, was fleeting. Less than a month later, the en banc court nullified the panel's ruling and ordered a new hearing, which took place on September 24, 2024. ("En banc," French for "on the bench," means that all judges on a court rehear a case after a panel's decision. This is done when the court believes a case to be especially complex or important.)[49] At that hearing, Llano County's attorney, Jonathan Mitchell, asserted that "library curation decisions are government speech" and therefore not bound by the First Amendment. Arguing directly against *Pico*, he said that failing to include a book in a library collection is "no different from a government that decides to withdraw or remove all handguns from a government-owned store" and "no different from a governmental unit that decides to remove or cancel abortion services that were previously offered at a government-owned hospital."[50]

Such an argument had failed in other book banning cases. Yet, on May 23, 2025, the Fifth Circuit accepted it, overturning the district court's ruling by a vote of 10–7. "Supreme Court precedent sometimes protects one's right to receive someone else's speech," wrote Judge Stuart Kyle Duncan in the majority opinion. "Plaintiffs would transform that precedent into a brave new right to receive information from the government in the form of taxpayer-funded library books. The First Amendment acknowledges no such right."[51]

As part of the ruling, Duncan turned back the court's anti-censorship *Campbell* decision, writing,

> Yes, cases protect your right to receive information from other people, but none gives you the right to demand it from the government [...] for good reason. People could tell libraries not only which books to keep but also which to buy. Courts would endlessly split hairs over a library's motives for removing a book. And, most obvious, removing a library book does not deny anyone the chance to read it. [...] People who want the book can buy it or borrow it from somewhere else.[52]

He did not, of course, have the power to overrule *Pico*, which was decided by a higher court, yet he certainly criticized it, calling the ruling "splintered," "highly fractured," and "of no precedential value" vis-à-vis the First Amendment.

Bottom line: the ruling gave libraries in Texas, Louisiana, and Mississippi—the states covered by the Fifth Circuit—the green light to remove books for any reason.

It was a disappointing defeat for the plaintiffs, and in the aftermath, they faced the same choice as the Island Trees school board: accept the decision or appeal to the Supreme Court. On June 17, they notified the Fifth Circuit that they intended to appeal. Remember: the Supreme Court can choose which cases to accept, and it doesn't accept a lot. Yet many observers thought Little v. Llano County had a good chance of making the docket.

For one thing, the Fifth Circuit's en banc reversal of its own panel's ruling suggested the need for the high court to step in.

Second, the current Supreme Court has been eager to revisit earlier precedents. In the past few years, it curtailed abortion protections,[53] ended the judicial policy known as Chevron deference,[54] and canceled affirmative action in college admissions,[55] all of which were long-standing, seemingly bedrock principles. Why not target *Pico*, especially because it wasn't a decisive ruling to begin with?

Third, unlike most book ban cases, *Little* pertained not to a school library but a public one. Public libraries, according to UCLA professor Eugene Volokh, are not like school libraries. In his blog *The Volokh Conspiracy*, he wrote, "I tentatively think a *public school* is entitled to decide which viewpoints to promote through its own library: School authorities can decide that their library will be a place where they provide books ... essentially as supplements to the school curriculum (over which the school has broad authority)."[56]

Public libraries, however, "are much more about giving more options to readers, rather than about teaching particular skills and attitudes to students."[57] Moreover, they serve a greater number of people: an entire county population rather than just a school system. Llano County isn't large, only about twenty thousand citizens, but the Fifth Circuit also covers cities such as Houston, Dallas, and New Orleans. That's *millions* of people whose right to read has been compromised.

In his dissenting opinion, Judge Stephen Higginson of the Fifth Circuit noted that the majority ruled on the right to receive information—finding, as did five of the nine *Pico* justices, that such a right doesn't exist in a library context—but *not* on the right to be free from the prescription of "what shall be orthodox in politics, nationalism, religion, or other matters of opinion."[58] In other words, the government can't tell people what to think or feel, or whom to support, or where or how to worship.

Higginson distinguished between the government's mission as *educator* and its role as *sovereign* before noting that, according to Chief Justice Rehnquist's dissent in *Pico*, "the government-as-educator role was limited in scope and did not extend to the shelves of the public library."[59] He then quoted Justice Blackmun: "[W]hile it is not clear to me ... whether a State operates its public libraries in its 'role as sovereign,' surely difficult constitutional problems would arise if a State chose to exclude 'anti-American' books from its public libraries—even if those books remained available at local bookstores."[60]

As for the assertion that library collections represent government speech, *Pico* didn't discuss that at all, and Judge Higginson didn't think much of it, either. Yet it is the sort of idea that the Supreme Court might have embraced. The plaintiffs could counter that, because the county tried to fire the librarian and disband the library board, perhaps "free speech" wasn't its overriding concern.

Another argument that might have swayed the high court was a religious one (i.e., that certain books must be removed from libraries because they infringe on the religious freedom of one group or another). Religion was not part of this case or *Pico*, but such concerns have exploded at the Supreme Court. In fact, it seems to invite them. In the past decade, the court has ruled, under the banner of religious liberty, that a company can deny its employees insurance coverage for contraceptives,[61] that a high-school football coach was unjustly terminated for kneeling on the field in private prayer after games,[62] and that a maker of wedding cakes can refuse service to a same-sex couple.[63]

Why not a ruling that Christians don't have to tolerate *Slaughterhouse-Five*?

Finally, in the Fifth Circuit opinion, Judge Duncan tried to calm everyone down. "No one is banning (or burning) books," he wrote. "If a disappointed patron can't find a book in the library, he can order it online, buy it from a bookstore, or borrow it from a friend."[64] Llano County is small and rural. Many of its residents may not have the purchase option. For them, a book being unavailable in a library is a de facto ban. The organization EveryLibrary agrees, writing that the Fifth Circuit's opinion "reveals an indifference to the lived reality of millions of Americans for whom public libraries are their only or primary means of access to books."[65] Besides, if someone for whom the book is inappropriate can easily get it elsewhere—if, in fact, the court is *urging* them to get it elsewhere—then what does removal accomplish? Not protection, that's for sure.

Alas, after a number of amicus briefs filed by PEN America, the ALA, and the National Coalition Against Censorship—joined by Steven Pico himself—the Supreme Court rejected the case on December 8, 2025. "This means," wrote Leila Little in an email to me, "that public library patrons have no First Amendment rights to access information. [It] means we now live in a censorship state."

No one knows what will happen now that Leila's four-year journey is over. Yet one thing is sure: there will always be those who rise up against censorship. Who take the side of readers. Of frightened kids. Of writers who can no longer speak for themselves. Writers like Kurt Vonnegut, who, after that 1977 press conference announcing the lawsuit, wrote in Steven Pico's copy of *Slaughterhouse-Five* to keep doing what he was doing.

Keep suing.

Keep fighting.[66]

Notes

1 Robert Stone, "School Libraries and the First Amendment: An Analysis of Island Trees" (internal memo, New York State Education Department, 1982), 12.
2 *Muir v. Alabama Educational Television Commission*, 688 F. 2d 1033, 1044 (5th Cir., 1982).
3 Ibid., 1045.

4   Mel Watkins, "James Haskins, an Author on Black History, Dies at 63," *New York Times*, July 11, 2005, https://www.nytimes.com/2005/07/11/books/james-haskins-an-author-on-black-history-dies-at-63.html.

5   *Campbell v. St. Tammany Parish School Board*, 64 F. 3d 184, 185 (5th Cir., 1995).

6   Ibid., 189.

7   *Case v. Unified School Dist. No. 233*, 908 F. Supp. 864, 871 (D. Kan. 1995).

8   Ibid., 875.

9   *Counts v. Cedarville School District*, 295 F. Supp. 2d 996, 1002 (W.D. Ark. 2003).

10 Ibid., 999.

11 William Shakespeare, *The Tempest*, ed. David Bevington, 4th ed. (HarperCollins, 1992), 1.2.252–53. (References are to act, scene, and line.)

12 William Shakespeare, *Macbeth*, ed. David Bevington, 4th ed. (HarperCollins, 1992), 5.5.30–31. (References are to act, scene, and line.)

13 Bella DiMarco, "Legislative Tracker: 2023 Parent-Rights Bills in the States," *Future Ed*, https://www.future-ed.org/legislative-tracker-2023-parent-rights-bills-in-the-states/.

14 Ibid.

15 Ohio Code § 3313.473(B)(1)(b).

16 Ibid., (G)(5).

17 Jordan Boyd, "Texas Board of Education Refuses to Adopt American Library Association's Anti-Parent Policies," *The Federalist*, April 26, 2023, https://thefederalist.com/2023/04/26/texas-board-of-education-refuses-to-adopt-american-library-associations-anti-parent-policies/.

18 Ibid.

19 Meg Shields, "Alfred Hitchcock and the Terrors of the Bathroom," *Film School Rejects*, August 14, 2017, https://filmschoolrejects.com/alfred-hitchcock-terrors-bathroom/.

20 Anthony Aycock, "Desperately Seeking Sources," *Missouri Review*, October 20, 2023, https://missourireview.com/desperately-seeking-sources-by-anthony-aycock/.

21 George Vescey, "Giving Books an 'F,'" *New York Times*, March 28, 1976, 16.

22 Charles Babcock, "Book Banning Spreads," *Washington Post*, May 9, 1982, https://www.washingtonpost.com/archive/politics/1982/05/10/book-banning-spreads/8f892694-9de3-4faa-8d20-f168dd0ff7dc/.

23 Ibid.

24 Rite Ciolli, "Top Court Restricts Ban of Books by School Board," *Newsday* (Nassau ed.), June 26, 1982, 13.

25 Ibid.

26 Ibid.

27 Ibid., 7.

28 Ibid., 13.

29 Ibid., 7.

30 Ibid.

31 Margaret L. Weeks, "Island Trees Board Returns Nine Banned Books to Shelves," *Education Week*, August 25, 1982, https://www.edweek.org/education/island-trees-board-returns-nine-banned-books-to-shelves/1982/08.

32 Michael Winerip, "L.I. School Board Ends Its Fight to Ban Books," *New York Times*, January 31, 1983, B7.

33 Ibid.

34 Ibid.

35 James Bernstein, "For Graduates, Book Ban Is 'No Big Deal,'" *Newsday* (Nassau ed.), June 28, 1982, 17.

36 Ibid.

37   Ibid.

38   Laura Pappano, "The Magic Pebble and a Lazy Bull: The Book Ban Movement Has a Long Timeline," *The Hechinger Report*, January 15, 2024, https://hechingerreport.org/the-magic-pebble-and-a-lazy-bull-the-book-ban-movement-has-a-long-timeline/.

39   Ibid.

40   Ibid.

41   "Legislation of Concern in 2024," *EveryLibrary*, https://www.everylibrary.org/billtracking2024.

42   Ibid.

43   Dave Shumaker, "EveryLibrary's John Chrastka Talks Midterms Aftermath," *Information Today* 36, no. 1 (2019): 14–15.

44   Ibid., 15.

45   Anthony Aycock, "How a Single Court Case Could Determine the Future of Book Banning in America," *Literary Hub*, June 17, 2025, https://lithub.com/how-a-single-court-case-could-determine-the-future-of-book-banning-in-america/.

46   Lisa Peet, "Library Collection Decisions Not Protected by First Amendment Says Fifth Circuit Court," *Library Journal*, May 29, 2025, https://www.libraryjournal.com/story/library-collection-decisions-not-protected-by-first-amendment-says-fifth-circuit-court.

47   William Melhado, "Llano County Library Supporters Declare Victory as Officials Decide Not to Close All Branches," *Texas Tribune*, April 13, 2023, https://www.texastribune.org/2023/04/13/llano-county-library-books/.

48   *Little v. Llano County*, No. 23-50224 (5th Cir. June 6, 2024).

49   Aycock, "How a Single Court Case Could Determine the Future of Book Banning in America."

50   Transcript of Oral Argument: Little v. Llano County, *Free Speech Arguments—Can Public Libraries Remove Books Based on Viewpoint? (Little v. Llano County)*, September 24, 2024, https://www.ifs.org/blog/free-speech-arguments-episode-18-little-v-llano/.

51   *Little v. Llano County*, No. 23-50224 (5th Cir. May 23, 2025).

52   Ibid.

53   *Dobbs v. Jackson Women's Health Organization*, 597 U.S. 215 (2018).

54   *Loper Bright Enterprises v. Raimondo*, 603 U.S. 369 (2024).

55   *Students for Fair Admissions, Inc. v. President and Fellows of Harvard College*, 600 U.S. 181 (2023).

56   Eugene Volokh, "Discard [Library] Books … That Reflect Gender, Family, Ethnic, or Racial Bias," *The Volokh Conspiracy*, September 19, 2024, https://reason.com/volokh/2024/09/19/discard-library-books-that-reflect-gender-family-ethnic-or-racial-bias/.

57   Ibid.

58   *Little v. Llano County*, No. 23-50224 (5th Cir. May 23, 2025), 84.

59   Ibid., 88.

60   *Island Trees v. Pico*, 457 U.S. 853, 881.

61   *Burwell v. Hobby Lobby Stores, Inc.*, 573 U.S. 682 (2014).

62   *Kennedy v. Bremerton School District*, 597 U.S. 507 (2022).

63   *Masterpiece Cakeshop v. Colorado Civil Rights Commission*, 584 U.S. 617 (2018).

64   *Little v. Llano County*, No. 23-50224 (5th Cir. May 23, 2025), 5.

65   EveryLibrary, "Rejecting Government Speech Doctrine in Public Libraries in Little v. Llano County," May 27, 2025, https://www.everylibrary.org/rejecting_government_speech_doctrine_public_libraries.

66   Aycock, "Desperately Seeking Sources."

Appendix

Syllabus

BOARD OF EDUCATION, ISLAND TREES UNION
FREE SCHOOL DISTRICT NO. 26, ET AL. *v.* PICO,

BY HIS NEXT FRIEND PICO, ET AL.

CERTIORARI TO THE UNITED STATES COURT OF APPEALS

FOR THE SECOND CIRCUIT

No. 80–2043. Argued March 2, 1982—Decided June 25, 1982

Petitioner Board of Education, rejecting recommendations of a committee of parents and school staff that it had appointed, ordered that certain books, which the Board characterized as "anti-American, anti-Christian, anti-Sem[i]tic, and just plain filthy," be removed from high school and junior high school libraries. Respondent students then brought this action for declaratory and injunctive relief under 42 U. S. C. § 1983 against the Board and petitioner Board members, alleging that the Board's actions had denied respondents their rights under the First Amendment. The District Court granted summary judgment in petitioners' favor. The Court of Appeals reversed and remanded for a trial on the merits of respondents' allegations.

Held: The judgment is affirmed.

638 F. 2d 404, affirmed.

JUSTICE BRENNAN, joined by JUSTICE MARSHALL and JUSTICE STEVENS, concluded:

1 The First Amendment imposes limitations upon a local school board's exercise of its discretion to remove books from high school and junior high school libraries; pp. 863–872.

   a Local school boards have broad discretion in the management of school affairs, but such discretion must be exercised in a manner that comports with the transcendent imperatives of the First Amendment.

Students do not "shed their constitutional rights to freedom of speech or expression at the schoolhouse gate," *Tinker* v. *Des Moines School Dist.*, 393 U. S. 503, 506, and such rights may be directly and sharply implicated by the removal of books from the shelves of a school library. While students' First Amendment rights must be construed "in light of the special characteristics of the school environment," *ibid.*, the special characteristics of the school *library* make that environment especially appropriate for the recognition of such rights; pp. 863–869.

b While petitioners might rightfully claim absolute discretion in matters of *curriculum* by reliance upon their duty to inculcate community values in schools, petitioners' reliance upon that duty is misplaced where they attempt to extend their claim of absolute discretion beyond the compulsory environment of the classroom into the school library and the regime of voluntary inquiry that there holds sway; p. 869.

c Petitioners possess significant discretion to determine the content of their school libraries, but that discretion may not be exercised in a narrowly partisan or political manner. Whether petitioners' removal of books from the libraries denied respondents their First Amendment rights depends upon the motivation behind petitioners' actions. Local school boards may not remove books from school libraries simply because they dislike the ideas contained in those books and seek by their removal to "prescribe what shall be orthodox in politics, nationalism, religion, or other matters of opinion." *West Virginia Board of Education* v. *Barnette*, 319 U. S. 624, 642. If such an intention was the decisive factor in petitioners' decision, then petitioners have exercised their discretion in violation of the Constitution; pp. 869–872.

2 The evidentiary materials before the District Court must be construed favorably to respondents, given the procedural posture of this case. When so construed, those evidentiary materials raise a genuine issue of material fact as to whether petitioners exceeded constitutional limitations in exercising their discretion to remove the books at issue from their school libraries. Respondents' allegations, and some of the evidentiary materials before the District Court, also fail to exclude the possibility that petitioners' removal procedures were highly irregular and ad hoc— the antithesis of those procedures that might tend to allay suspicions regarding petitioners' motivation; pp. 872–875.

JUSTICE BLACKMUN concluded that a proper balance between the limited constitutional restriction imposed on school officials by the First Amendment and the broad state authority to regulate education, would be struck by holding that school officials may not remove books from school libraries for the *purpose* of restricting access to the political ideas or social perspectives discussed in the books, when that action is motivated simply by the officials' disapproval of the ideas involved; pp. 879–882.

JUSTICE WHITE, while agreeing that there should be a trial to resolve the factual issues, concluded that there is no necessity at this point for discussing the extent to which the First Amendment limits the school board's discretion to remove books from the school libraries; pp. 883–884.

BRENNAN, J., announced the judgment of the Court and delivered an opinion, in which MARSHALL and STEVENS, JJ. Joined and in all but Part II–A(1) of which BLACKMUN, J., joined. BLACKMUN, J., filed an opinion concurring in part and concurring in the judgment, *post*, p. 875. WHITE, J., filed an opinion concurring in the judgment, *post*, p. 883. BURGER, C. J., filed a dissenting opinion, in which POWELL, REHNQUIST, and O'CONNOR, JJ., joined, *post*, p. 885. POWELL, J., filed a dissenting opinion, *post*, p. 893. REHNQUIST, J., filed a dissenting opinion, in which BURGER, C. J., and POWELL, J., joined, *post*, p. 904. O'CONNOR, J., filed a dissenting opinion, *post*, p. 921.

George W. Lipp, Jr., argued the cause for petitioners. With him on the briefs was *David S. J. Rubin*.

Alan H. Levine argued the cause for respondents. With him on the brief were *Steven R. Shapiro, Burt Neubome, Alan Azzara, Bruce J. Ennis, Jr.*, and *Charles S. Sims*.[1]

JUSTICE BRENNAN announced the judgment of the Court and delivered an opinion, in which JUSTICE MARSHALL and JUSTICE STEVENS joined, and in which JUSTICE BLACKMUN joined except for Part II–A–(1).

The principal question presented is whether the First Amendment[2] imposes limitations upon the exercise by a local school board of its discretion to remove library books from high school and junior high school libraries.

I

Petitioners are the Board of Education of the Island Trees Union Free School District No. 26, in New York, and Richard Ahrens, Frank Martin, Christina Fasulo, Patrick Hughes, Richard Melchers, Richard Michaels, and Louis Nessim. When this suit was brought, Ahrens was the President of the Board, Martin was the Vice President, and the remaining petitioners were Board members. The Board is a state agency charged with responsibility for the operation and administration of the public schools within the Island Trees School District, including the Island Trees High School and Island Trees Memorial Junior High School. Respondents are Steven Pico, Jacqueline Gold, Glenn Yarris, Russell Rieger, and Paul Sochinski. When this suit was brought, Pico, Gold, Yarris, and Rieger were students at the High School, and Sochinski was a student at the Junior High School.

In September 1975, petitioners Ahrens, Martin, and Hughes attended a conference sponsored by Parents of New York United (PONYU), a politically conservative organization of parents concerned about education legislation in the State of New York. At the conference, these petitioners obtained lists of books described by Ahrens as "objectionable," App. 22, and by Martin as "improper fare for school students," id., at 101.[3] It was later determined that the High School library contained nine of the listed books, and that another listed book was in the Junior High School library.[4] In February 1976, at a meeting with the Superintendent of Schools and the Principals of the High School and Junior High School, the Board gave an "unofficial direction" that the listed books be removed from the library shelves and delivered to the Board's offices, so that Board members could read them.[5] When this directive was carried out, it became publicized, and the Board issued a press release justifying its action. It characterized the removed books as "anti-American, anti-Christian, anti-Sem[i]tic, and just plain filthy," and concluded that "[i]t is our duty, our moral obligation, to protect the children in our schools from this moral danger as surely as from physical and medical dangers." 474 F. Supp. 387, 390 (EDNY 1979).

A short time later, the Board appointed a "Book Review Committee," consisting of four Island Trees parents and four members of the Island Trees schools staff, to read the listed books and to recommend to the Board whether the books should be retained, taking into account the books' "educational suitability," "good taste," "relevance," and "appropriateness to age and grade level." In July, the Committee made its final report to the Board, recommending that five of the listed books be retained[6] and that two others be removed from the school libraries.[7] As for the remaining four books, the Committee could not agree on two,[8] took no position on one,[9] and recommended that the last book be made available to students only with parental approval.[10] The Board substantially rejected the Committee's report later that month, deciding that only one book should be returned to the High School library without restriction,[11] that another should be made available subject to parental approval,[12] but that the remaining nine books should "be removed from elementary and secondary libraries and [from] use in the curriculum." Id., at 391.[13] The Board gave no reasons for rejecting the recommendations of the Committee that it had appointed.

Respondents reacted to the Board's decision by bringing the present action under 42 U. S. C. § 1983 in the United States District Court for the Eastern District of New York. They alleged that petitioners had

"ordered the removal of the books from school libraries and proscribed their use in the curriculum because particular passages in the books offended their social, political and moral tastes and not because the books, taken as a whole, were lacking in educational value." App. 4.

Respondents claimed that the Board's actions denied them their rights under the First Amendment. They asked the court for a declaration that the Board's actions were unconstitutional, and for preliminary and permanent injunctive relief ordering the Board to return the nine books to the school libraries and to refrain from interfering with the use of those books in the schools' curricula. *Id.*, at 5–6.

The District Court granted summary judgment in favor of petitioners. 474 F. Supp. 387 (1979). In the court's view, "the parties substantially agree[d] about the motivation behind the board's actions," *id.*, at 391—namely, that

"the board acted not on religious principles but on its conservative educational philosophy, and on its belief that the nine books removed from the school library and curriculum were irrelevant, vulgar, immoral, and in bad taste, making them educationally unsuitable for the district's junior and senior high school students." *Id.*, at 392.

With this factual premise as its background, the court rejected respondents' contention that their First Amendment rights had been infringed by the Board's actions. Noting that statutes, history, and precedent had vested local school boards with a broad discretion to formulate educational policy,[14] the court concluded that it should not intervene in " 'the daily operations of school systems' " unless " 'basic constitutional values' " were " 'sharply implicate[d],' "[15] and determined that the conditions for such intervention did not exist in the present case. Acknowledging that the "removal [of the books] … clearly was content-based," the court nevertheless found no constitutional violation of the requisite magnitude:

"The board has restricted access only to certain books which the board believed to be, in essence, vulgar. While removal of such books from a school library may … reflect a misguided educational philosophy, it does not constitute a sharp and direct infringement of any first amendment right." *Id.*, at 397.

A three-judge panel of the United States Court of Appeals for the Second Circuit reversed the judgment of the District Court, and remanded the action for a trial on respondents' allegations. 638 F. 2d 404 (1980). Each judge on the panel filed a separate opinion. Delivering the judgment of the court, Judge Sifton treated the case as involving "an unusual and irregular intervention in the school libraries' operations by persons not routinely concerned with such matters," and concluded that petitioners were obliged to demonstrate a reasonable basis for interfering with respondents' First Amendment rights. *Id.*, at 414–415. He then determined that, at least at the summary judgment stage, petitioners had not offered sufficient justification for their action,[16] and concluded that respondents "should have … been offered an opportunity to persuade a finder of fact that the ostensible justifications for [petitioners'] actions ... were simply pretexts for the suppression of free speech." *Id.*, at 417.[17] Judge Newman concurred in the result. *Id.*, at 432–438. He viewed the case as turning on the contested factual issue of whether petitioners' removal decision was motivated by a justifiable desire to remove books containing vulgarities and sexual explicitness, or rather by an impermissible desire to suppress ideas. *Id.*, at 436–437.[18] We granted certiorari, 454 U. S. 891 (1981).

II

We emphasize at the outset the limited nature of the substantive question presented by the case before us. Our precedents have long recognized certain constitutional limits upon the power of the State to control even the curriculum and classroom. For example, *Meyer* v. *Nebraska*, 262 U. S. 390 (1923), struck down a state law that forbade the teaching of modern foreign languages in public and private schools, and *Epperson* v. *Arkansas*, 393 U. S. 97 (1968), declared unconstitutional a state law that prohibited the teaching of the Darwinian theory of evolution in any state-supported school. But the current action does not require us to re-enter this difficult terrain, which *Meyer* and *Epperson* traversed without apparent misgiving. For as this case is presented to us, it does not involve textbooks, or indeed any books that Island Trees students would be required to read.[19] Respondents do not seek in this Court to impose limitations upon their school Board's discretion to prescribe the curricula of the Island Trees schools. On the contrary, the only books at issue in this case are *library* books, books that by their nature are optional rather than required reading. Our adjudication of the present case thus does not intrude into the classroom, or into the compulsory courses taught there. Furthermore, even as to library books, the action before us does not involve the *acquisition* of books. Respondents have not sought to compel their school Board to add to the school library shelves any books that students desire to read. Rather, the only action challenged in this case is the *removal* from school libraries of books originally placed there by the school authorities, or without objection from them.

The substantive question before us is still further constrained by the procedural posture of this case. Petitioners were granted summary judgment by the District Court. The Court of Appeals reversed that judgment, and remanded the action for a trial on the merits of respondents' claims. We can reverse the judgment of the Court of Appeals, and grant petitioners' request for reinstatement of the summary judgment in their favor, only if we determine that "there is no genuine issue as to any material fact," and that petitioners are "entitled to a judgment as a matter of law." Fed. Rule Civ. Proc. 56(c). In making our determination, any doubt as to the existence of a genuine issue of material fact must be resolved against petitioners as the moving party. *Adickes* v. *S. H. Kress & Co.*, 398 U. S. 144, 157–159 (1970). Furthermore, "[o]n summary judgment the inferences to be drawn from the underlying facts contained in [the affidavits, attached exhibits, and depositions submitted below] must be viewed in the light most favorable to the party opposing the motion." *United States* v. *Diebold, Inc.*, 369 U. S. 654, 655 (1962).

In sum, the issue before us in this case is a narrow one, both substantively and procedurally. It may best be restated as two distinct questions. First, does the First Amendment impose *any* limitations upon the discretion of petitioners to remove library books from the Island Trees High School and Junior High School? Second, if so, do the affidavits and other evidentiary materials before the District Court, construed most favorably to respondents, raise a genuine issue of fact whether petitioners might have exceeded those limitations? If we answer either of these questions in the negative, then we must reverse the judgment of the Court of Appeals and reinstate the District Court's summary judgment for petitioners. If we answer both questions in the affirmative, then we must affirm the judgment below. We examine these questions in turn.

A

(1)

The Court has long recognized that local school boards have broad discretion in the management of school affairs. See, *e. g., Meyer* v. *Nebraska, supra*, at 402; *Pierce* v. *Society of Sisters*, 268 U. S. 510, 534 (1925). *Epperson* v. *Arkansas, supra*, at 104, reaffirmed that, by and large, "public education in our Nation is committed to the control of state and local authorities," and that federal courts should not ordinarily "intervene in the resolution of conflicts which arise in the daily operation of school systems." *Tinker* v. *Des Moines School Dist.*, 393 U. S. 503, 507 (1969), noted that we have "repeatedly emphasized … the comprehensive authority of the States and of school officials … to prescribe and control conduct in the schools." We have also acknowledged that public schools are vitally important "in the preparation of individuals for participation as citizens," and as vehicles for "inculcating fundamental values necessary to the maintenance of a democratic political system." *Ambach* v. *Norwich*, 441 U. S. 68, 76–77 (1979). We are therefore in full agreement with petitioners that local school boards must be permitted "to establish and apply their curriculum in such a way as to transmit community values," and that "there is a legitimate and substantial community interest in promoting respect for authority and traditional values be they social, moral, or political." Brief for Petitioners 10.[20]

At the same time, however, we have necessarily recognized that the discretion of the States and local school boards in matters of education must be exercised in a manner that comports with the transcendent imperatives of the First Amendment. In *West Virginia Board of Education* v. *Barnette*, 319 U. S. 624 (1943), we held that under the First Amendment a student in a public school could not be compelled to salute the flag. We reasoned:

> "Boards of Education … have, of course, important, delicate, and highly discretionary functions, but none that they may not perform within the limits of the Bill of Rights. That they are educating the young for citizenship is reason for scrupulous protection of Constitutional freedoms of the individual, if we are not to strangle the free mind at its source and teach youth to discount important principles of our government as mere platitudes." *Id.*, at 637.

Later cases have consistently followed this rationale. Thus, *Epperson* v. *Arkansas* invalidated a State's anti-evolution statute as violative of the Establishment Clause, and reaffirmed the duty of federal courts "to apply the First Amendment's mandate in our educational system where essential to safeguard the fundamental values of freedom of speech and inquiry." 393 U. S., at 104. And *Tinker* v. *Des Moines School Dist.*, *supra*, held that a local school board had infringed the free speech rights of high school and junior high school students by suspending them from school for wearing black armbands in class as a protest against the Government's policy in Vietnam; we stated there that the "comprehensive authority … of school officials" must be exercised "consistent with fundamental constitutional safeguards." 393 U. S., at 507. In sum, students do not "shed their constitutional rights to freedom of speech or expression at the schoolhouse gate," *id.*, at 506, and therefore local school boards must discharge their "important, delicate, and highly discretionary functions" within the limits and constraints of the First Amendment.

The nature of students' First Amendment rights in the context of this case requires further examination. *West Virginia Board of Education* v. *Barnette*, *supra*, is instructive. There, the Court held that students' liberty of conscience could not be infringed in the name of "national unity" or "patriotism." 319 U. S., at 640–641. We explained that

> "the action of the local authorities in compelling the flag salute and pledge transcends constitutional limitations on their power and invades the sphere of intellect and spirit which it is the purpose of the First Amendment to our Constitution to reserve from all official control." *Id.*, at 642.

Similarly, *Tinker v. Des Moines School Dist., supra,* held that students' rights to freedom of expression of their political views could not be abridged by reliance upon an "undifferentiated fear or apprehension of disturbance" arising from such expression:

"Any departure from absolute regimentation may cause trouble. Any variation from the majority's opinion may inspire fear. Any word spoken, in class, in the lunchroom, or on the campus, that deviates from the views of another person may start an argument or cause a disturbance. But our Constitution says we must take this risk, *Terminiello v. Chicago,* 337 U. S. 1 (1949); and our history says that it is this sort of hazardous freedom—this kind of openness—that is the basis of our national strength and of the independence and vigor of Americans who grow up and live in this ... often disputatious society." 393 U. S., at 508–509.

In short, "First Amendment rights, applied in light of the special characteristics of the school environment, are available to ... students." *Id.,* at 506.

Of course, courts should not "intervene in the resolution of conflicts which arise in the daily operation of school systems" unless "basic constitutional values" are "directly and sharply implicate[d]" in those conflicts. *Epperson v. Arkansas,* 393 U. S., at 104. But we think that the First Amendment rights of students may be directly and sharply implicated by the removal of books from the shelves of a school library. Our precedents have focused "not only on the role of the First Amendment in fostering individual self-expression but also on its role in affording the public access to discussion, debate, and the dissemination of information and ideas." *First National Bank of Boston v. Bellotti,* 435 U. S. 765, 783 (1978). And we have recognized that "the State may not, consistently with the spirit of the First Amendment, contract the spectrum of available knowledge." *Griswold v. Connecticut,* 381 U. S. 479, 482 (1965). In keeping with this principle, we have held that in a variety of contexts "the Constitution protects the right to receive information and ideas." *Stanley v. Georgia,* 394 U. S. 557, 564 (1969); see *Kleindienst v. Mandel,* 408 U. S. 753, 762–763 (1972) (citing cases). This right is an inherent corollary of the rights of free speech and press that are explicitly guaranteed by the Constitution, in two senses. First, the right to receive ideas follows ineluctably from the *sender's* First Amendment right to send them: "The right of freedom of speech and press ... embraces the right to distribute literature, and necessarily protects the right to receive it." *Martin v. Struthers,* 319 U. S. 141, 143 (1943) (citation omitted). "The dissemination of ideas can accomplish nothing if otherwise willing addressees are not free to receive and consider them. It would be a barren marketplace of ideas that had only sellers and no buyers." *Lamont v. Postmaster General,* 381 U. S. 301, 308 (1965) (BRENNAN, J., concurring).

More importantly, the right to receive ideas is a necessary predicate to the *recipient's* meaningful exercise of his own rights of speech, press, and political freedom. Madison admonished us:

"A popular Government, without popular information, or the means of acquiring it, is but a Prologue to a Farce or a Tragedy; or, perhaps both. Knowledge will forever govern ignorance: And a people who mean to be their own Governors, must arm themselves with the power which knowledge gives." 9 Writings of James Madison 103 (G. Hunt ed. 1910).[21]

As we recognized in *Tinker,* students too are beneficiaries of this principle:

"In our system, students may not be regarded as closed-circuit recipients of only that which the State chooses to communicate …. [S]chool officials cannot suppress 'expressions of feeling with which they do not wish to contend.' " 393 U. S., at 511 (quoting *Burnside* v. *Byars,* 363 F. 2d 744, 749 (CA5 1966)).

In sum, just as access to ideas makes it possible for citizens generally to exercise their rights of free speech and press in a meaningful manner, such access prepares students for active and effective participation in the pluralistic, often contentious society in which they will soon be adult members. Of course, all First Amendment rights accorded to students must be construed "in light of the special characteristics of the school environment." *Tinker* v. *Des Moines School Dist.,* 393 U. S., at 506. But the special characteristics of the school *library* make that environment especially appropriate for the recognition of the First Amendment rights of students.

A school library, no less than any other public library, is "a place dedicated to quiet, to knowledge, and to beauty." *Brown* v. *Louisiana,* 383 U. S. 131, 142 (1966) (opinion of Fortas, J.). *Keyishian* v. *Board of Regents,* 385 U. S. 589 (1967), observed that " 'students must always remain free to inquire, to study and to evaluate, to gain new maturity and understanding.' "[22] The school library is the principal locus of such freedom. As one District Court has well put it, in the school library

"a student can literally explore the unknown, and discover areas of interest and thought not covered by the prescribed curriculum …. Th[e] student learns that a library is a place to test or expand upon ideas presented to him, in or out of the classroom." *Right to Read Defense Committee* v. *School Committee,* 454 F. Supp. 703, 715

(Mass. 1978).

Petitioners emphasize the inculcative function of secondary education, and argue that they must be allowed *unfettered* discretion to "transmit community values" through the Island Trees schools. But that sweeping claim overlooks the unique role of the school library. It appears from the record that use of the Island Trees school libraries is completely voluntary on the part of students. Their selection of books from these libraries is entirely a matter of free choice; the libraries afford them an opportunity at self-education and individual enrichment that is wholly optional. Petitioners might well defend their claim of absolute discretion in matters of *curriculum* by reliance upon their duty to inculcate community values. But we think that petitioners' reliance upon that duty is misplaced where, as here, they attempt to extend their claim of absolute discretion beyond the compulsory environment of the classroom, into the school library and the regime of voluntary inquiry that there holds sway.

(2)

In rejecting petitioners' claim of absolute discretion to remove books from their school libraries, we do not deny that local school boards have a substantial legitimate role to play in the determination of school library content. We thus must turn to the question of the extent to which the First Amendment places limitations upon the discretion of petitioners to remove books from their libraries. In this inquiry, we enjoy the guidance of several precedents. *West Virginia Board of Education* v. *Barnette* stated:

> "If there is any fixed star in our constitutional constellation, it is that no official, high or petty, can prescribe what shall be orthodox in politics, nationalism, religion, or other matters of opinion .... If there are any circumstances which permit an exception, they do not now occur to us." 319 U. S., at 642.

This doctrine has been reaffirmed in later cases involving education. For example, *Keyishian* v. *Board of Regents, supra*, at 603, noted that "the First Amendment ... does not tolerate laws that cast a pall of orthodoxy over the classroom;" see also *Epperson* v. *Arkansas*, 393 U. S., at 104–105. And *Mt. Healthy City Board of Ed.* v. *Doyle*, 429 U. S. 274 (1977), recognized First Amendment limitations upon the discretion of a local school board to refuse to rehire a nontenured teacher. The school board in *Mt. Healthy* had declined to renew respondent Doyle's employment contract, in part because he had exercised his First Amendment rights. Although Doyle did not have tenure, and thus "could have been discharged for no reason whatever," *Mt. Healthy* held that he could "nonetheless establish a claim to reinstatement if the decision not to rehire him was made by reason of his exercise of constitutionally protected First Amendment freedoms." *Id.*, at 283–284. We held further that once Doyle had shown "that his conduct was constitutionally protected, and that this conduct was a 'substantial factor' ... in the Board's decision not to rehire him," the school board was obliged to show "by a preponderance of the evidence that it would have reached the same decision as to respondent's reemployment even in the absence of the protected conduct." *Id.*, at 287.

With respect to the present case, the message of these precedents is clear. Petitioners rightly possess significant discretion to determine the content of their school libraries. But that discretion may not be exercised in a narrowly partisan or political manner. If a Democratic school board, motivated by party affiliation, ordered the removal of all books written by or in favor of Republicans, few would doubt that the order violated the constitutional rights of the students denied access to those books. The same conclusion would surely apply if an all-white school board, motivated by racial animus, decided to remove all books authored by blacks or advocating racial equality and integration. Our Constitution does not permit the official suppression of *ideas*. Thus, whether petitioners' removal of books from their school libraries denied respondents their First Amendment rights depends upon the motivation behind petitioners' actions. If petitioners *intended* by their removal decision to deny respondents access to ideas with which petitioners disagreed, and if this intent was the decisive factor in petitioners' decision,[23] then petitioners have exercised their discretion in violation of the Constitution. To permit such intentions to control official actions would be to encourage the precise sort of officially prescribed orthodoxy unequivocally condemned in *Barnette*. On the other hand, respondents implicitly concede that an unconstitutional motivation would *not* be demonstrated if it were shown that petitioners had decided to remove the books at issue because those books were pervasively vulgar. Tr. of Oral Arg. 36. And again, respondents concede that if it were demonstrated that the removal decision was based solely upon the "educational suitability" of the books in question, then their removal would be "perfectly permissible." *Id.*, at 53. In other words, in respondents' view such motivations, if decisive of petitioners' actions, would not carry the danger of an official suppression of ideas, and thus would not violate respondents' First Amendment rights.

As noted earlier, nothing in our decision today affects in any way the discretion of a local school board to choose books to *add* to the libraries of their schools. Because we are concerned in this case with the suppression of ideas, our holding today affects only the discretion to *remove* books. In brief, we hold that local school boards may not remove books from school library shelves simply because they dislike the ideas contained in those books and seek by their removal to "prescribe what shall be orthodox in politics, nationalism, religion, or other matters of opinion." *West Virginia Board of Education* v. *Barnette*, 319 U. S., at 642. Such purposes stand inescapably condemned by our precedents.

B

We now turn to the remaining question presented by this case: Do the evidentiary materials that were before the District Court, when construed most favorably to respondents, raise a genuine issue of material fact whether petitioners exceeded constitutional limitations in exercising their discretion to remove the books from the school libraries? We conclude that the materials do raise such a question, which forecloses summary judgment in favor of petitioners.

Before the District Court, respondents claimed that petitioners' decision to remove the books "was based on [their] personal values, morals and tastes." App. 139. Respondents also claimed that petitioners objected to the books in part because excerpts from them were "anti-American." *Id.*, at 140. The accuracy of these claims was partially conceded by petitioners,[24] and petitioners' own affidavits lent further support to respondents' claims.[25] In addition, the record developed in the District Court shows that when petitioners offered their first public explanation for the removal of the books, they relied in part on the assertion that the removed books were "anti-American," and "offensive to ... Americans in general." 474 F. Supp., at 390.[26] Furthermore, while the Book Review Committee appointed by petitioners was instructed to make its recommendations based upon criteria that appear on their face to be permissible—the books' "educational suitability," "good taste," "relevance," and "appropriateness to age and grade level," App. 67—the Committee's recommendations that five of the books be retained and that only two be removed were essentially rejected by petitioners, without any statement of reasons for doing so. Finally, while petitioners originally defended their removal decision with the explanation that "these books contain obscenities, blasphemies, brutality, and perversion beyond description," 474 F. Supp., at 390, one of the books, A Reader for Writers, was removed even though it contained no such language. 638 F. 2d, at 428, n. 6 (Mansfield, J., dissenting).

Standing alone, this evidence respecting the substantive motivations behind petitioners' removal decision would not be decisive. This would be a very different case if the record demonstrated that petitioners had employed established, regular, and facially unbiased procedures for the review of controversial materials. But the actual record in the case before us suggests the exact opposite. Petitioners' removal procedures were vigorously challenged below by respondents, and the evidence on this issue sheds further light on the issue of petitioners' motivations.[27] Respondents alleged that in making their removal decision petitioners ignored "the advice of literary experts," the views of "librarians and teachers within the Island Trees School system," the advice of the Superintendent of Schools, and the guidance of publications that rate books for junior and senior high school students. App. 128–129. Respondents also claimed that petitioners' decision was based solely on the fact that the books were named on the PON YU list received by petitioners Ahrens, Martin, and Hughes, and that petitioners "did not undertake an independent review of other books in the [school] libraries." *Id.*, at 129–130. Evidence before the District Court lends support to these claims. The record shows that immediately after petitioners first ordered the books removed from the library shelves, the Superintendent of Schools reminded them that "we already have a policy ... designed expressly to handle such problems," and recommended that the removal decision be approached through this established channel. See n. 4, *supra*. But the Board disregarded the Superintendent's advice, and instead resorted to the extraordinary procedure of appointing a Book Review Committee—the advice of which was later rejected without explanation. In sum, respondents' allegations and some of the evidentiary materials presented below do not rule out the possibility that petitioners' removal procedures were highly irregular and ad hoc—the antithesis of those procedures that might tend to allay suspicions regarding petitioners' motivations.

Construing these claims, affidavit statements, and other evidentiary materials in a manner favorable to respondents, we cannot conclude that petitioners were "entitled to a judgment as a matter of law." The evidence plainly does not foreclose the possibility that petitioners' decision to remove the books rested decisively upon disagreement with constitutionally protected ideas in those books, or upon a desire on petitioners' part to impose upon the students of the Island Trees High School and Junior High School a political orthodoxy to which petitioners and their constituents adhered. Of course, some of the evidence before the District Court might lead a finder of fact to accept the petitioners' claim that their removal decision was based upon constitutionally valid concerns. But that evidence at most creates a genuine issue of material fact on the critical question of the credibility of petitioners' justifications for their decision: On that issue, it simply cannot be said that there is no genuine issue as to any material fact.

The mandate shall issue forthwith.

Affirmed.

JUSTICE BLACKMUN, concurring in part and concurring in the judgment.

While I agree with much in today's plurality opinion, and while I accept the standard laid down by the plurality to guide proceedings on remand, I write separately because I have a somewhat different perspective on the nature of the First Amendment right involved.

I

To my mind, this case presents a particularly complex problem because it involves two competing principles of constitutional stature. On the one hand, as the dissenting opinions demonstrate, and as we all can agree, the Court has acknowledged the importance of the public schools "in the preparation of individuals for participation as citizens, and in the preservation of the values on which our society rests." *Ambach* v. *Norwich,* 441 U. S. 68, 76 (1979). See, also, *ante,* at 863–864 (plurality opinion). Because of the essential socializing function of schools, local education officials may attempt "to promote civic virtues," *Ambach* v. *Norwich,* 441 U. S., at 80, and to "awake[n] the child to cultural values." *Brown* v. *Board of Education,* 347 U. S. 483, 493 (1954). Indeed, the Constitution presupposes the existence of an informed citizenry prepared to participate in governmental affairs, and these democratic principles obviously are constitutionally incorporated into the structure of our government. It therefore seems entirely appropriate that the State use "public schools [to] … inculcat[e] fundamental values necessary to the maintenance of a democratic political system." *Ambach* v. *Norwich,* 441 U. S., at 77.

On the other hand, as the plurality demonstrates, it is beyond dispute that schools and school boards must operate within the confines of the First Amendment. In a variety of academic settings, the Court therefore has acknowledged the force of the principle that schools, like other enterprises operated by the State, may not be run in such a manner as to "prescribe what shall be orthodox in politics, nationalism, religion, or other matters of opinion." *West Virginia Board of Education* v. *Barnette,* 319 U. S. 624, 642 (1943). While none of these cases define the limits of a school board's authority to choose a curriculum and academic materials, they are based on the general proposition that "state-operated schools may not be enclaves of totalitarianism …. In our system, students may not be regarded as closed-circuit recipients of only that which the State chooses to communicate." *Tinker* v. *Des Moines School Dist.,* 393 U. S. 503, 511 (1969).

The Court in *Tinker* thus rejected the view that "a State might so conduct its schools as to 'foster a homogeneous people.'" *Id.,* at 511, quoting *Meyer* v. *Nebraska,* 262 U. S. 390, 402 (1923). Similarly, *Keyishian* v. *Board of Regents,* 385 U. S. 589 (1967)—a case that involved the State's attempt to remove "subversives" from academic positions at its universities, but that addressed itself more broadly to public education in general—held that "[t]he classroom is peculiarly the 'marketplace of ideas'" the First Amendment therefore "does not tolerate laws that cast a pall of orthodoxy over the classroom." *Id.,* at 603. And *Barnette* is most clearly applicable here: its holding was based squarely on the view that "[f]ree public education, if faithful to the ideal of secular instruction and political neutrality, will not be partisan or enemy of any class, creed, party, or faction." 319 U. S., at 637. The Court therefore made it clear that imposition of "ideological discipline" was not a proper undertaking for school authorities. *Ibid.*

In combination with more generally applicable First Amendment rules, most particularly the central proscription of content-based regulations of speech, see *Police Department of Chicago* v. *Mosley,* 408 U. S. 92 (1972), the cases outlined above yield a general principle: the State may not suppress exposure to ideas— for the sole *purpose* of suppressing exposure to those ideas—absent sufficiently compelling reasons. Because the school board must perform all its functions "within the limits of the Bill of Rights," *Barnette*, 319 U. S., at 637, this principle necessarily applies in at least a limited way to public education. Surely this is true in an extreme case: as the plurality notes, it is difficult to see how a school board, consistent with the First Amendment, could refuse for political reasons to buy books written by Democrats or by Negroes, or books that are "anti-American" in the broadest sense of that term. Indeed, JUSTICE REHNQUIST appears "cheerfully [to] concede" this point. *Post,* at 907 (dissenting opinion).

In my view, then, the principle involved here is both narrower and more basic than the "right to receive information" identified by the plurality. I do not suggest that the State has any affirmative obligation to provide students with information or ideas, something that may well be associated with a "right to receive." See *post,* at 887 (BURGER, C. J., dissenting); *post,* at 915–918 (REHNQUIST, J., dissenting). And I do not believe, as the plurality suggests, that the right at issue here is somehow associated with the peculiar nature of the school library, see *ante,* at 868–869; if schools may be used to inculcate ideas, surely libraries may play a role in that process.[28] Instead, I suggest that certain forms of state discrimination *between* ideas are improper. In particular, our precedents command the conclusion that the State may not act to deny access to an idea simply because state officials disapprove of that idea for partisan or political reasons.[29]

Certainly, the unique environment of the school places substantial limits on the extent to which official decisions may be restrained by First Amendment values. But that environment also makes it particularly important that *some* limits be imposed. The school is designed to, and inevitably will, inculcate ways of thought and outlooks; if educators intentionally may eliminate all diversity of thought, the school will "strangle the free mind at its source and teach youth to discount important principles of our government as mere platitudes." *Barnette,* 319 U. S., at 637. As I see it, then, the question in this case is how to make the delicate accommodation between the limited constitutional restriction that I think is imposed by the First Amendment, and the necessarily broad state authority to regulate education. In starker terms, we must reconcile the schools' "inculcative" function with the First Amendment's bar on "prescriptions of orthodoxy."

II

In my view, we strike a proper balance here by holding that school officials may not remove books for the *purpose* of restricting access to the political ideas or social perspectives discussed in them, when that action is motivated simply by the officials' disapproval of the ideas involved. It does not seem radical to suggest that state action calculated to suppress novel ideas or concepts is fundamentally antithetical to the values of the First Amendment. At a minimum, allowing a school board to engage in such conduct hardly teaches children to respect the diversity of ideas that is fundamental to the American system. In this context, then, the school board must "be able to show that its action was caused by something more than a mere desire to avoid the discomfort and unpleasantness that always accompany an unpopular viewpoint," *Tinker* v. *Des Moines School Dist.*, 393 U. S., at 509, and that the board had something in mind in addition to the suppression of partisan or political views it did not share.

As I view it, this is a narrow principle. School officials must be able to choose one book over another, without outside interference, when the first book is deemed more relevant to the curriculum, or better written, or when one of a host of other politically neutral reasons is present. These decisions obviously will not implicate First Amendment values. And even absent space or financial limitations, First Amendment principles would allow a school board to refuse to make a book available to students because it contains offensive language, cf. *FCC* v. *Pacifica Foundation,* 438 U. S. 726, 757 (1978) (POWELL, J., concurring), or because it is psychologically or intellectually inappropriate for the age group, or even, perhaps, because the ideas it advances are "manifestly inimical to the public welfare." *Pierce* v. *Society of Sisters,* 268 U. S. 510, 534 (1925). And, of course, school officials may choose one book over another because they believe that one subject is more important, or is more deserving of emphasis.

As is evident from this discussion, I do not share JUSTICE REHNQUIST's view that the notion of "suppression of ideas" is not a useful analytical concept. See *post,* at 918–920 (dissenting opinion). Indeed, JUSTICE REHNQUIST's discussion itself demonstrates that "access to ideas" has been given meaningful application in a variety of contexts. See *post,* at 910–920, 914 ("[education consists of the selective presentation and explanation of ideas"). And I believe that tying the First Amendment right to the *purposeful* suppression of ideas makes the concept more manageable than JUSTICE REHNQUIST acknowledges. Most people would recognize that refusing to allow discussion of current events in Latin class is a policy designed to "inculcate" Latin, not to suppress ideas. Similarly, removing a learned treatise criticizing American foreign policy from an elementary school library because the students would not understand it is an action unrelated to the *purpose* of suppressing ideas. In my view, however, removing the same treatise because it is "anti-American" raises a far more difficult issue.

It is not a sufficient answer to this problem that a State operates a school in its role as "educator," rather than its role as "sovereign," see *post,* at 908–910 (REHNQUIST, J., dissenting), for the First Amendment has application to all the State's activities. While the State may act as "property owner" when it prevents certain types of expressive activity from taking place on public lands, for example, see *post*, at 908–909, few would suggest that the State may base such restrictions on the content of the speaker's message, or may take its action for the purpose of suppressing access to the ideas involved. See *Police Department of Chicago* v. *Mosley*, 408 U. S., at 96. And while it is not clear to me from JUSTICE REHNQUIST'S discussion whether a State operates its public libraries in its "role as sovereign," surely difficult constitutional problems would arise if a State chose to exclude "anti-American" books from its public libraries—even if those books remained available at local bookstores.

Concededly, a tension exists between the properly inculcative purposes of public education and any limitation on the school board's absolute discretion to choose academic materials. But that tension demonstrates only that the problem here is a difficult one, not that the problem should be resolved by choosing one principle over another. As the Court has recognized, school officials must have the authority to make educationally appropriate choices in designing a curriculum: "the State may 'require teaching by instruction and study of all in our history and in the structure and organization of our government, including the guaranties of civil liberty, which tend to inspire patriotism and love of country.' " *Barnette*, 319 U. S., at 631, quoting *Minersville School District* v. *Gobitis*, 310 U. S. 586, 604 (1940) (Stone, J., dissenting). Thus school officials may seek to instill certain values "by persuasion and example," 319 U. S., at 640, or by choice of emphasis. That sort of positive educational action, however, is the converse of an intentional attempt to shield students from certain ideas that officials find politically distasteful. Arguing that the majority in the community rejects the ideas involved, *see post*, at 889, 891–892 (BURGER, C. J., dissenting), does not refute this principle: "The very purpose of a Bill of Rights was to withdraw certain subjects from the vicissitudes of political controversy, to place them beyond the reach of majorities and officials...." *Barnette*, 319 U. S., at 638.

As THE CHIEF JUSTICE notes, the principle involved here may be difficult to apply in an individual case. See *post*, at 889 (dissenting opinion). But on a record as sparse as the one before us, the plurality can hardly be faulted for failing to explore every possible ramification of its decision. And while the absence of a record "underscore[s] the views of those of us who originally felt that the cas[e] should not be taken," *Ferguson* v. *Moore-McCormack Lines, Inc.*, 352 U. S. 521, 559 (1957) (opinion of Harlan, J.), the case is here, and must be decided.

Because I believe that the plurality has derived a standard similar to the one compelled by my analysis, I join all but Part II–A(1) of the plurality opinion.

JUSTICE WHITE, concurring in the judgment.

The District Court found that the books were removed from the school library because the school board believed them "to be, in essence, vulgar." 474 F. Supp. 387, 397 (EDNY 1979). Both Court of Appeals judges in the majority concluded, however, that there was a material issue of fact that precluded the summary judgment sought by the petitioners. The unresolved factual issue, as I understand it, is the reason or reasons underlying the school board's removal of the books. I am not inclined to disagree with the Court of Appeals on such a fact-bound issue and hence concur in the judgment of affirmance. Presumably, this will result in a trial and the making of a full record and findings on the critical issues.

The plurality seems compelled to go further and issue a dissertation on the extent to which the First Amendment limits the discretion of the school board to remove books from the school library. I see no necessity for doing so at this point. When findings of fact and conclusions of law are made by the District Court, that may end the case. If, for example, the District Court concludes after a trial that the books were removed for their vulgarity, there may be no appeal. In any event, if there is an appeal, if there is dissatisfaction with the subsequent Court of Appeals' judgment, and if certiorari is sought and granted, there will be time enough to address the First Amendment issues that may then be presented.

I thus prefer the course taken by the Court in *Kennedy* v. *Silas Mason Co.*, 334 U. S. 249 (1948), a suit involving overtime compensation under the Fair Labor Standards Act. Summary judgment had been granted by the District Court and affirmed by the Court of Appeals. This Court reversed, holding that summary judgment was improvidently granted, and remanded for trial so that a proper record could be made. The Court expressly abjured issuing its advice on the legal issues involved. Writing for the Court, Justice Jackson stated:

"We consider it the part of good judicial administration to withhold decision of the ultimate questions involved in this case until this or another record shall present a more solid basis of findings based on litigation or on a comprehensive statement of agreed facts. While we might be able, on the present record, to reach a conclusion that would decide the case, it might well be found later to be lacking in the thoroughness that should precede judgment of this importance and which it is the purpose of the judicial process to provide.

"Without intimating any conclusion on the merits, we vacate the judgments below and remand the case to the District Court for reconsideration and amplification of the record in the light of this opinion and of present contentions." *Id.*, at 257.

We took a similar course in a unanimous *per curiam* opinion in *Dombrowski* v. *Eastland*, 387 U. S. 82 (1967). There we overturned a summary judgment since it was necessary to resolve a factual dispute about collaboration between one of the respondents and a state legislative committee. We remanded, saying: "In the absence of the factual refinement which can occur only as a result of trial, we need not and, indeed, could not express judgment as to the legal consequences of such collaboration, if it occurred." *Id.*, at 84.

The *Silas Mason* case turned on issues of statutory construction. It is even more important that we take a similar course in cases like *Dombrowski*, which involved Speech or Debate Clause immunity, and in this one, which poses difficult First Amendment issues in a largely uncharted field. We should not decide constitutional questions until it is necessary to do so, or at least until there is a better reason to address them than are evident here. I therefore concur in the judgment of affirmance.

CHIEF JUSTICE BURGER, with whom JUSTICE POWELL, JUSTICE REHNQUIST, and JUSTICE O'CONNOR join, dissenting.

The First Amendment, as with other parts of the Constitution, must deal with new problems in a changing world. In an attempt to deal with a problem in an area traditionally left to the states, a plurality of the Court, in a lavish expansion going beyond any prior holding under the First Amendment, expresses its view that a school board's decision concerning what books are to be in the school library is subject to federal-court review.[30] Were this to become the law, this Court would come perilously close to becoming a "super censor" of school board library decisions. Stripped to its essentials, the issue comes down to two important propositions: *first,* whether local schools are to be administered by elected school boards, or by federal judges and teenage pupils; and *second,* whether the values of morality, good taste, and relevance to education are valid reasons for school board decisions concerning the contents of a school library. In an attempt to place this case within the protection of the First Amendment, the plurality suggests a new "right" that, when shorn of the plurality's rhetoric, allows this Court to impose its own views about what books must be made available to students.[31]

I

A

I agree with the fundamental proposition that "students do not 'shed their constitutional rights to freedom of speech or expression at the schoolhouse gate.'" *Ante,* at 865. For example, the Court has held that a school board cannot compel a student to participate in a flag salute ceremony, *West Virginia Bd. of Education* v. *Barnette,* 319 U. S. 624 (1943), or *prohibit* a student from expressing certain views, so long as that expression does not disrupt the educational process. *Tinker* v. *Des Moines School Dist.,* 393 U. S. 503 (1969). Here, however, no restraints of any kind are placed on the students. They are free to read the books in question, which are available at public libraries and bookstores; they are free to discuss them in the classroom or elsewhere. Despite this absence of any direct external control on the students' ability to express themselves, the plurality suggests that there is a new First Amendment "entitlement" to have access to particular books in a school library.

The plurality cites *Meyer* v. *Nebraska*, 262 U. S. 390 (1923), which struck down a state law that restricted the teaching of modern foreign languages in public and private schools, and *Epperson* v. *Arkansas*, 393 U. S. 97 (1968), which declared unconstitutional under the Establishment Clause a law banning the teaching of Darwinian evolution, to establish the validity of federal-court interference with the functioning of schools. The plurality finds it unnecessary "to re-enter this difficult terrain," *ante*, at 861, yet in the next breath relies on these very cases and others to establish the previously unheard of "right" of access to particular books in the public school library.[32] The apparent underlying basis of the plurality's view seems to be that students have an enforceable "right" to receive the information and ideas that are contained in junior and senior high school library books. *Ante*, at 866. This "right" purportedly follows "ineluctably" from the sender's First Amendment right to freedom of speech and as a "necessary predicate" to the recipient's meaningful exercise of his own rights of speech, press, and political freedom. *Ante*, at 866–867. No such right, however, has previously been recognized.

It is true that where there is a willing distributor of materials, the government may not impose unreasonable obstacles to dissemination by the third party. *Virginia Pharmacy Board* v. *Virginia Citizens Consumer Council, Inc.*, 425 U. S. 748 (1976). And where the speaker desires to express certain ideas, the government may not impose unreasonable restraints. *Tinker* v. *Des Moines School Dist.*, *supra*. It does not follow, however, that a school board must affirmatively aid the speaker in his communication with the recipient. In short, the plurality suggests today that if a writer has something to say, the government through its schools must be the courier. None of the cases cited by the plurality establish this broad-based proposition.

First, the plurality argues that the right to receive ideas is derived in part from the sender's First Amendment rights to send them. Yet we have previously held that a sender's rights are not absolute. *Rowan* v. *Post Office Dept.*, 397 U. S. 728 (1970).[33] Never before today has the Court indicated that the government has an *obligation* to aid a speaker or author in reaching an audience.

Second, the plurality concludes that "the right to receive ideas is a necessary predicate to the *recipient's* meaningful exercise of his own rights of speech, press, and political freedom." *Ante*, at 867 (emphasis in original). However, the "right to receive information and ideas," *Stanley* v. *Georgia*, 394 U. S. 557, 564 (1969), cited *ante*, at 867, does not carry with it the concomitant right to have those ideas affirmatively provided at a particular place by the government. The plurality cites James Madison to emphasize the importance of having an informed citizenry. *Ibid.* We all agree with Madison, of course, that knowledge is necessary for effective government. Madison's view, however, does not establish a *right* to have particular books retained on the school library shelves if the school board decides that they are inappropriate or irrelevant to the school's mission. Indeed, if the need to have an informed citizenry creates a "right," why is the government not also required to provide ready access to a variety of information? This same need would support a constitutional "right" of the people to have public libraries as part of a new constitutional "right" to continuing adult education.

The plurality also cites *Tinker, supra,* to establish that the recipient's right to free speech encompasses a right to have particular books retained on the school library shelf. *Ante,* at 868. But the cited passage of *Tinker* notes only that school officials may not *prohibit* a student from expressing his or her view on a subject unless that expression interferes with the legitimate operations of the school. The government does not "contract the spectrum of available knowledge." *Griswold* v. *Connecticut,* 381 U. S. 479, 482 (1965), cited *ante,* at 866, by choosing not to retain certain books on the school library shelf; it simply chooses not to be the conduit for that particular information. In short, even assuming the desirability of the policy expressed by the plurality, there is not a hint in the First Amendment, or in any holding of this Court, of a "right" to have the government provide continuing access to certain books.

B

Whatever role the government might play as a conduit of information, schools in particular ought not be made a slavish courier of the material of third parties. The plurality pays homage to the ancient verity that in the administration of the public schools " 'there is a legitimate and substantial community interest in promoting respect for authority and traditional values be they social, moral, or political.' " *Ante,* at 864. If, as we have held, schools may legitimately be used as vehicles for "inculcating fundamental values necessary to the maintenance of a democratic political system," *Ambach* v. *Norwich,* 441 U. S. 68, 77 (1979), school authorities must have broad discretion to fulfill that obligation. Presumably all activity within a primary or secondary school involves the conveyance of information and at least an implied approval of the worth of that information. How are "fundamental values" to be inculcated except by having school boards make content-based decisions about the appropriateness of retaining materials in the school library and curriculum. In order to fulfill its function, an elected school board *must* express its views on the subjects which are taught to its students. In doing so those elected officials express the views of their community; they may err, of course, and the voters may remove them. It is a startling erosion of the very idea of democratic government to have this Court arrogate to itself the power the plurality asserts today.

The plurality concludes that under the Constitution school boards cannot choose to retain or dispense with books if their discretion is exercised in a "narrowly partisan or political manner." *Ante,* at 870. The plurality concedes that permissible factors are whether the books are "pervasively vulgar," *ante,* at 871, or educationally unsuitable. *Ibid.* "Educational suitability," however, is a standardless phrase. This conclusion will undoubtedly be drawn in many—if not most—instances because of the decisionmaker's content-based judgment that the ideas contained in the book or the idea expressed from the author's method of communication are inappropriate for teenage pupils.

The plurality also tells us that a book may be removed from a school library if it is "pervasively vulgar." But why must the vulgarity be "pervasive" to be offensive? Vulgarity might be concentrated in a single poem or a single chapter or a single page, yet still be inappropriate. Or a school board might reasonably conclude that even "random" vulgarity is inappropriate for teenage school students. A school board might also reasonably conclude that the school board's retention of such books gives those volumes an implicit endorsement. Cf. *FCC* v. *Pacifica Foundation,* 438 U. S. 726 (1978).

Further, there is no guidance whatsoever as to what constitutes "political" factors. This Court has previously recognized that public education involves an area of broad public policy and " 'go[es] to the heart of representative government.' " *Ambach* v. *Norwich, supra,* at 74. As such, virtually all educational decisions necessarily involve "political" determinations.

What the plurality views as valid reasons for removing a book at their core involve partisan judgments. Ultimately, the federal courts will be the judge of whether the motivation for book removal was "valid" or "reasonable." Undoubtedly, the validity of many book removals will ultimately turn on a judge's evaluation of the books. Discretion must be used, and the appropriate body to exercise that discretion is the local elected school board, not judges.[34]

We can all agree that as a matter of *educational policy,* students should have wide access to information and ideas. But the people elect school boards, who in turn select administrators, who select the teachers, and these are the individuals best able to determine the substance of that policy. The plurality fails to recognize the fact that local control of education involves democracy in a microcosm. In most public schools in the United States, the *parents* have a large voice in running the school.[35] Through participation in the election of school board members, the parents influence, if not control, the direction of their children's education. A school board is not a giant bureaucracy far removed from accountability for its actions; it is truly "of the people and by the people." A school board reflects its constituency in a very real sense and thus could not long exercise unchecked discretion in its choice to acquire or remove books. If the parents disagree with the educational decisions of the school board, they can take steps to remove the board members from office. Finally, even if parents and students cannot convince the school board that book removal is inappropriate, they have alternative sources to the same end. Books may be acquired from bookstores, public libraries, or other alternative sources unconnected with the unique environment of the local public schools.[36]

II

No amount of "limiting" language could rein in the sweeping "right" the plurality would create. The plurality distinguishes library books from textbooks because library books "by their nature are optional rather than required reading." *Ante,* at 862. It is not clear, however, why this distinction requires *greater* scrutiny before "optional" reading materials may be removed. It would appear that required reading and textbooks have a greater likelihood of imposing a " 'pall of orthodoxy' " over the educational process than do optional reading. *Ante,* at 870. In essence, the plurality's view transforms the availability of this "optional" reading into a "right" to have this "optional" reading maintained at the demand of teenagers.

The plurality also limits the new right by finding it applicable only to the *removal* of books once acquired. Yet if the First Amendment commands that certain books cannot be *removed,* does it not equally require that the same books be *acquired*? Why does the coincidence of timing become the basis of a constitutional holding? According to the plurality, the evil to be avoided is the "official suppression of ideas." *Ante,* at 871. It does not follow that the decision to *remove* a book is less "official suppression" than the decision not to acquire a book desired by someone.[37] Similarly, a decision to eliminate certain material from the curriculum, history, for example, would carry an equal—probably greater—prospect of "official suppression." Would the decision be subject to our review?

III

Through the use of bits and pieces of prior opinions unrelated to the issue of this case, the plurality demeans our function of constitutional adjudication. Today the plurality suggests that the *Constitution* distinguishes between school libraries and school classrooms, between *removing* unwanted books and *acquiring* books. Even more extreme, the plurality concludes that the Constitution *requires* school boards to justify to its teenage pupils the decision to remove a particular book from a school library. I categorically reject this notion that the Constitution dictates that judges, rather than parents, teachers, and local school boards, must determine how the standards of morality and vulgarity are to be treated in the classroom.

JUSTICE POWELL, dissenting.

The plurality opinion today rejects a basic concept of public school education in our country: that the States and locally elected school boards should have the responsibility for determining the educational policy of the public schools. After today's decision any junior high school student, by instituting a suit against a school board or teacher, may invite a judge to overrule an educational decision by the official body designated by the people to operate the schools.

I

School boards are uniquely local and democratic institutions. Unlike the governing bodies of cities and counties, school boards have only one responsibility: the education of the youth of our country during their most formative and impressionable years. Apart from health, no subject is closer to the hearts of parents than their children's education during those years. For these reasons, the governance of elementary and secondary education traditionally has been placed in the hands of a local board, responsible locally to the parents and citizens of school districts. Through parent-teacher associations (PTA's), and even less formal arrangements that vary with schools, parents are informed and often may influence decisions of the board. Frequently, parents know the teachers and visit classes. It is fair to say that no single agency of government at any level is closer to the people whom it serves than the typical school board.

I therefore view today's decision with genuine dismay. Whatever the final outcome of this suit and suits like it, the resolution of educational policy decisions through litigation, and the exposure of school board members to liability for such decisions, can be expected to corrode the school board's authority and effectiveness. As is evident from the generality of the plurality's "standard" for judicial review, the decision as to the educational worth of a book is a highly subjective one. Judges rarely are as competent as school authorities to make this decision; nor are judges responsive to the parents and people of the school district.[38]

The new constitutional right, announced by the plurality, is described as a "right to receive ideas" in a school. *Ante,* at 867. As the dissenting opinions of THE CHIEF JUSTICE and JUSTICE REHNQUIST so powerfully demonstrate, however, this newfound right finds no support in the First Amendment precedents of this Court. And even apart from the inappropriateness of judicial oversight of educational policy, the new constitutional right is framed in terms that approach a meaningless generalization. It affords little guidance to courts, if they—as the plurality now authorizes them—are to oversee the inculcation of ideas. The plurality does announce the following standard: A school board's "discretion may not be exercised in a narrowly partisan or political manner." *Ante,* at 870. But this is a standardless standard that affords no more than subjective guidance to school boards, their counsel, and to courts that now will be required to decide whether a particular decision was made in a "narrowly partisan or political manner." Even the "chancellor's foot" standard in ancient equity jurisdiction was never this fuzzy.

As JUSTICE REHNQUIST tellingly observes, how does one limit—on a principled basis—today's new constitutional right? If a 14-year-old child may challenge a school board's decision to remove a book from the library, upon what theory is a court to prevent a like challenge to a school board's decision not to purchase that identical book? And at the even more "sensitive" level of "receiving ideas," does today's decision entitle student oversight of which courses may be added or removed from the curriculum, or even of what a particular teacher elects to teach or not teach in the classroom? Is not the "right to receive ideas" as much—or indeed even more—implicated in these educational questions?[39]

II

The plurality's reasoning is marked by contradiction. It purports to acknowledge the traditional role of school boards and parents in deciding what should be taught in the schools. It states the truism that the schools are "vitally important 'in the preparation of individuals for participation as citizens,' and as vehicles for 'inculcating fundamental values necessary to the maintenance of a democratic political system.'" *Ante,* at 864. Yet when a school board, as in this case, takes its responsibilities seriously and seeks to decide what the fundamental values are that should be imparted, the plurality finds a constitutional violation.

Just this Term the Court held, in an opinion I joined, that the children of illegal aliens must be permitted to attend the public schools. See *Plyler* v. *Doe, ante,* p. 202. Quoting from earlier opinions, the Court noted that the "'public schoo[l is] a most vital civic institution for the preservation of democratic system of government'" and that the public schools are "the primary vehicle for transmitting 'the values on which our society rests.'" *Ante,* at 221. By denying to illegal aliens the opportunity "to absorb the values and skills upon which our social order rests" the law under review placed a lifelong disability upon these illegal alien children. *Ibid.*

Today the plurality drains much of the content from these apt phrases. A school board's attempt to instill in its students the ideas and values on which a democratic system depends is viewed as an impermissible suppression of other ideas and values on which other systems of government and other societies thrive. Books may not be removed because they are indecent; extol violence, intolerance, and racism; or degrade the dignity of the individual. Human history, not the least that of the 20th century, records the power and political life of these very ideas. But they are not our ideas or values. Although I would leave this educational decision to the duly constituted board, I certainly would not *require* a school board to promote ideas and values repugnant to a democratic society or to teach such values to *children.*

In different contexts and in different times, the destruction of written materials has been the symbol of despotism and intolerance. But the removal of nine vulgar or racist books from a high school library by a concerned local school board does not raise this specter. For me, today's decision symbolizes a debilitating encroachment upon the institutions of a free people.

Attached as an Appendix hereto is Judge Mansfield's summary of excerpts from the books at issue in this case.

APPENDIX TO OPINION OF POWELL, J., DISSENTING

"The excerpts which led the Board to look into the educational suitability of the books in question are set out (with minor corrections after comparison with the text of the books themselves) below. The pagination and the underlinings are retained from the original report used by the board. In newer editions of some of the books, the quotes appear at different pages.

"1) *SOUL ON ICE* by Eldridge Cleaver
PAGE QUOTE

157–158 ' … There are white men who will pay you to fuck their wives. They approach you and say, "How would you like to fuck a white woman?" "What is this?" you ask. "On the up-and-up," he assures you. "It's all right. She's my wife. She needs black rod, is all. She has to have it. It's like a medicine or drug to her. She has to have it. I'll pay you. It's all on the level, no trick involved. Interested?" You go with him and he drives you to their home. The three of you go into the bedroom. There is a certain type who will leave you and his wife alone and tell you to pile her real good. After it is all over, he will pay you and drive you to wherever you want to go. Then there are some who like to peep at you through a keyhole and watch you have his woman, or peep at you through a window, or lie under the bed and listen to the creaking of the bed as you work out. There is another type who likes to masturbate while he stands beside the bed and watches you pile her. There is the type who likes to eat his woman up after you get through piling her. And there is the type who only wants you to pile her for a little while, just long enough to thaw her out and kick her motor over and arouse her to heat, then he wants you to jump off real quick and he will jump onto her and together they can make it from there by themselves.'

"2) *A HERO AIN'T NOTHING BUT A SANDWICH* by Alice Childress
PAGE QUOTE

10 'Hell, no! *Fuck the society.*'

64–65 'The hell with the junkie, the wino, the capitalist, the welfare checks, the world … yeah, and *fuck* you too!'

75–76 'They can have back the spread and curtains, I'm too old for them *fuckin* bunnies anyway.'

"3) *THE FIXER* by Bernard Malamud
PAGE QUOTE

52 'What do you think goes on in the wagon at night: Are the drivers on their knees *fucking their mothers?*'

90 '*Fuck yourself,* said the blinker, etc.'

92 'Who else would do anything like that but a *mother-fucking* Zhid?'

146 'No more noise out of you or I'll shoot your *Jew cock off.*'

189 'Also there's a lot of *fucking in the Old Testament,* so how is that religious?'

192 'You better *go fuck yourself,* Bok, said Kogin, I'm onto your Jew tricks.'

215 'Ding-dong giddyap. A *Jew's cock's* in the devil's hock.'

216 'You *cocksucker* Zhid, I ought make you lick it up off the floor.'

"4) *GO ASK ALICE* by Anonymous
PAGE QUOTE

31 'I wonder if sex without acid could be so exciting, so wonderful, so indescribable. I always thought it just took a minute, or that it would be like dogs mating.'

47 'Chris and I walked into Richie and Ted's apartment to find the bastards stoned and making love to each other … low class queer.'

81 'shitty, goddamned, pissing, ass, goddamned beJesus, screwing life's, ass, shit. Doris was ten and had *humped* with who knows how many men in between … her current stepfather started having sex with her but good … *sonofabitch balling her*'

83 'but now when I face a girl its like facing a boy. I get all excited and turned on. *I want to screw with the girl* ….'

84 'I'd rather screw with a guy … sometimes I want one of the girls to kiss me. I want her to touch me, to have her sleep under me.'

84 'Another day, another *blow job* … If I don't give *Big Ass a blow* he'll cut off my supply … and LittleJacon is yelling, "Mama, *Daddy can't come now. He's humping Carla.*"

85 'Shit, goddamn, goddamn prick, son-of-a-bitch, ass, pissed, bastard, goddamn, bullshit

94 'I hope you have a *nice orgasm with your dog tonight.*'

110 'You *fucking* Miss Polly pure

117 'Then he said that all I needed was a *good fuck.*'

146 'It might be great because I'm practically a virgin in the sense that I've never had sex except when I've been stoned ….'

"5) *SLAUGHTERHOUSE FIVE* by Kurt Vonnegut, Jr. *PAGE QUOTE*

29 'Get out of the road, you dumb *motherfucker.*' The last word was still a novelty in the speech of white people in 1944. It was fresh and astonishing to Billy, who had never *fucked* anybody … '

32 'You stake a guy out on an anthill in the desert-see? He's facing upward, and you put *honey* all over his *balls and pecker,* and you cut off his eyelids so he has to stare at the sun till he dies.'

34 'He had a prophylactic kit containing two tough condoms 'For the prevention of disease only!' … He had a dirty picture of a *woman* attempting *sexual intercourse with a Shetland pony.*'

94 & 95 'But the Gospels actually taught this: Before you kill somebody, make absolutely sure he isn't well connected … The flaw in the Christ stories, said the visitor from outer space, was that Christ who didn't look like much, was actually the son of the Most Powerful Being in the Universe. Readers understood that, so, when they came to the crucifixion, they naturally thought … Oh boy-they sure picked the wrong guy to lynch this time! And that thought had a brother: There are right people to lynch. People not well connected …. The visitor from outer space made a gift to Earth of a new Gospel. In it, Jesus really WAS a nobody, and a pain in the neck to a lot of people with better connections then he had …. So the people amused themselves one day by nailing him to a cross and planting the cross in the ground. There couldn't possibly be any repercussions, the lynchers thought … since the new Gospel hammered home again and again what a nobody Jesus was. And then just before the nobody died …. The voice of God came crashing down. He told the people that he was adopting the bum as his son … God said this: *From this moment on, He will punish horribly anybody who torments a bum who has no connections.*'

99 'They told him that there could be no Earthling babies without male homosexuals. There could be babies without female homosexuals.'

120 'Why don't you go *fuck* yourself? Don't think I haven't tried … he was going to have revenge, and that revenge was sweet … It's the sweetest thing there is, said Lazzaro. People *fuck* with me, he said, and *Jesus Christ* are they ever fucking sorry.'

122 'And he'll pull out a gun and *shoot his pecker off.* The stranger'll let him think a couple of seconds about who Paul Lazzaro is and what life's gonna be like without a *pecker.* Then he'll shoot him once in the guts and walk away …. He died on account

of this silly *cocksucker* here. So I promised him I'd have this silly *cocksucker* shot after the war.'

134 'In my prison cell I sit … With my *britches full of shit*, And my *balls are bouncing* gently on the floor. And I see the bloody snag when she bit me in the bag … Oh, I'll never fuck *a Polack* any more.'

173 'And the peckers of the young men would still be *semierect*, and their *muscles* would be *bulging like cannonballs*.'

175 'They didn't have *hard-ons* … Everybody else did.'

177 'The magazine, which was published for *lonesome men to jerk off to*.'

178 'and one critic said …. 'To describe *blow-jobs* artistically.''

"6) *THE BEST SHORT STORIES BY NEGRO WRITERS* Ed. *by Langston Hughes* PAGE QUOTE

176 'like bat's shit and camel piss,'

228 'that no-count bitch of a daughter of yours is up there up North making a whore of herself.'

237 'they made her get out and stand in front of the headlights of the car and pull down her pants and raise her dress—they said that was the only way they could be sure. And you can imagine what they said and what they did—'

303 'You need some pussy. Come on, let's go up to the whore house on the hill.' 'Oh, these bastards, these bastards, this God damned Army and the bastards in it. The sons of bitches!'

436 'he produced a brown rag doll, looked at her again, then grabbed the doll by its legs and tore it part way up the middle. Then he jammed his finger into the rip between the doll's legs. The other men laughed ….'

444 'The pimps, hustlers, lesbians, and others trying to misuse me.'

462 'But she had straight firm legs and her breasts were small and upright. No doubt if she'd had children her breasts would be hanging like little empty purses.'

464 'She first became aware of the warm tense nipples on her breasts. Her hands went up gently to clam them.' 'In profile, his penis hung like a stout tassle. She could even tell that he was circumcised.'

406 'Cadillac Bill was busy following Luheaster around, rubbing her stomach and saying, "Magic Stomach, Magic Stomach, bring me a little baby Cadillac." ' 'One of the girls went upstairs with Red Top and stayed for about forty five minutes.'

"7) *BLACK BOY* by Richard Wright PAGE QUOTE

70–71 'We black children—seven or eight or nine years of age—used to run to the Jew's store and shout:

... Bloody Christ Killers
Never trust a Jew
Bloody Christ Killers
What won't a Jew do ...
Red, white and blue
Your pa was a Jew
Your ma a dirty dago
What the hell is you?'
265 'Crush that nigger's nuts, nigger!' 'Hit that nigger!' 'Aw, fight, you goddam niggers!' 'Sock 'im, in his f-k-g-piece!' 'Make 'im bleed!'

"8) *LAUGHING BOY* by Oliver LaFarge
PAGE QUOTE

38 'I'll tell you, she is all bad; for two bits she will do the worst thing.'
258–9 'I was frightened when he wanted me to lie with him, but he made me feel all right. He knew all about how to make women forget themselves, that man.'

"9) *THE NAKED APE* by Desmond Morris
PAGE QUOTE

73–74 'Also, the frontal approach provides the maximum possibility for stimulation of the female's clitoris during the pelvic thrusting of the male. It is true that it will be passively, stimulated by the pulling effect of the male's thrusts, regardless of his body position in relation to the female, but in a face-to-face mating there will in addition be the direct rhythmic pressure of the male's pubic region on to the clitoral area, and this will considerably heighten the stimulation ... ' 'So it seems plausible to consider that face-to-face copulation is basic to our species. There are, of course, a number of variations that do not eliminate the frontal element: male above, female above, side by side, squatting, standing, and so on, but the most efficient and commonly used one is with both partners horizontal, the male above the female ....'
80 ' ... This broadening of the penis results in the female's external genitals being subjected to much more pulling and pushing during the performance of pelvic thrusts. With each inward thrust of the penis, the clitoral region is pulled downwards and then with each withdrawal, it moves up again. Add to this the rhythmic pressure being exerted on the clitoris region by the pubic region of the frontally copulating male, and you have a repeated massaging of the clitoris that— were she a male—would virtually be masturbatory.'
94–99 ' ... If either males or females cannot for some reason obtain sexual access to their opposite numbers, they will find sexual outlets in other ways. They may use other members of their own sex, or they may even use members of other species, or they may masturbate ....'

"10) *READER FOR WRITERS ... "*

638 F. 2d 404, 419–422, n. 1 (CA2 1980) (Mansfield, J., dissenting).

JUSTICE REHNQUIST, with whom THE CHIEF JUSTICE and JUSTICE POWELL join, dissenting.

Addressing only those aspects of the constitutional question which must be decided to determine whether or not the District Court was correct in granting summary judgment, I conclude that it was. I agree fully with the views expressed by THE CHIEF JUSTICE, and concur in his opinion. I disagree with JUSTICE BRENNAN's opinion because it is largely hypothetical in character, failing to take account of the facts as admitted by the parties pursuant to local rules of the District Court for the Eastern District of New York, and because it is analytically unsound and internally inconsistent.[40]

I

A

JUSTICE BRENNAN's opinion deals far more sparsely with the procedural posture of this case than it does with the constitutional issues which it conceives to arise under the First Amendment. It first launches into a confusing, discursive exegesis on these constitutional issues as applied to junior high school and high school libraries, *ante,* at 863–872, and only thereafter does it discuss the state of the record before the Court. *Ante,* at 872–875. Because the record facts should always establish the limits of the Court's constitutional analysis, and are particularly relevant in cases where the trial court has granted summary judgment, I think that JUSTICE BRENNAN's approach violates our "long ... considered practice not to decide abstract, hypothetical or contingent questions, or to decide any constitutional question in advance of the necessity for its decision." *Alabama State Federation of Labor* v. *McAdory,* 325 U. S. 450, 461 (1945) (citations omitted).

When JUSTICE BRENNAN finally does address the state of the record, he refers to snippets and excerpts of the relevant facts to explain why a grant of summary judgment was improper. But he totally ignores the effect of Rule 9(g) of the local rules of the District Court, under which the parties set forth their version of the disputed facts in this case.[41] Since summary judgment was entered against respondents, they are entitled to have their version of the facts, as embodied in their Rule 9(g) statement, accepted for purposes of our review. Since the parties themselves are presumably the best judges of the extent of the factual dispute between them, however, respondents certainly are not entitled to any more favorable version of the facts than that contained in their own Rule 9(g) statement. JUSTICE BRENNAN's combing through the record of affidavits, school bulletins, and the like for bits and snatches of dispute is therefore entirely beside the point at this stage of the case.

Considering only the respondents' description of the factual aspects of petitioners' motivation, JUSTICE BRENNAN's apparent concern that the Board's action may have been a sinister political plot "to suppress ideas" may be laid to rest. The members of the Board, in deciding to remove these books, were undoubtedly influenced by their own "personal values, morals, and tastes,"[42] just as any member of a school board is apt to be so influenced in making decisions as to whether a book is educationally suitable. Respondents essentially conceded that some excerpts of the removed books "contained profanities, some were sexually explicit, some were ungrammatical, some were anti-American, and some were offensive to racial, religious or ethnic groups."[43]

Respondents also agreed that, "[although the books them-selves were excluded from use in the schools in any way, [petitioners] have not precluded discussion about the themes of the books or the books themselves." App. 140. JUSTICE BRENNAN's concern with the "suppression of ideas" thus seems entirely unwarranted on this state of the record, and his creation of constitutional rules to cover such eventualities is entirely gratuitous. Though for reasons stated in Part II of this opinion I entirely disagree with JUSTICE BRENNAN's treatment of the constitutional issue, I also disagree with his opinion for the entirely separate reason that it is not remotely tailored to the facts presented by this case.

In the course of his discussion, JUSTICE BRENNAN states:

> "Petitioners rightly possess significant discretion to determine the content of their school libraries. But that discretion may not be exercised in a narrowly partisan or political manner. If a Democratic school board, motivated by party affiliation, ordered the removal of all books written by or in favor of Republicans, few would doubt that the order violated the constitutional rights of the students .... The same conclusion would surely apply if an all-white school board, motivated by racial animus, decided to remove all books authored by blacks or advocating racial equality and integration. Our Constitution does not permit the official suppression of *ideas*" Ante, at 870–871
>
> (emphasis in original).

I can cheerfully concede all of this, but as in so many other cases the extreme examples are seldom the ones that arise in the real world of constitutional litigation. In *this case* the facts taken most favorably to respondents suggest that nothing of this sort happened. The nine books removed undoubtedly did contain "ideas," but in the light of the excerpts from them found in the dissenting opinion of Judge Mansfield in the Court of Appeals, it is apparent that eight of them contained demonstrable amounts of vulgarity and profanity, see 638 F. 2d 404, 419–422, n. 1 (CA2 1980), and the ninth contained nothing that could be considered partisan or political, see *id.*, at 428, n. 6. As already demonstrated, respondents admitted as much. Petitioners did not, for the reasons stated hereafter, run afoul of the First and Fourteenth Amendments by removing these particular books from the library in the manner in which they did. I would save for another day—feeling quite confident that that day will not arrive—the extreme examples posed in JUSTICE BRENNAN's opinion.

B

Considerable light is shed on the correct resolution of the constitutional question in this case by examining the role played by petitioners. Had petitioners been the members of a town council, I suppose all would agree that, absent a good deal more than is present in this record, they could not have prohibited the sale of these books by private booksellers within the municipality. But we have also recognized that the government may act in other capacities than as sovereign, and when it does, the First Amendment may speak with a different voice:

> "[I]t cannot be gainsaid that the State has interests as an employer in regulating the speech of its employees that differ significantly from those it possesses in connection with regulation of the speech of the citizenry in general. The problem in any case is to arrive at a balance between the interests of the teacher, as a citizen, in commenting upon matters of concern and the interest of the State, as an employer, in promoting the efficiency of the public services it performs through its employees." *Pickering* v. *Board of Education*, 391 U. S. 563, 568
> (1968).

By the same token, expressive conduct which may not be prohibited by the State as sovereign may be proscribed by the State as property owner: "The State, no less than a private owner of property, has power to preserve the property under its control for the use to which it is lawfully dedicated." *Adderley* v. *Florida*, 385 U. S. 39, 47 (1966) (upholding state prohibition of expressive conduct on certain state property).

With these differentiated roles of government in mind, it is helpful to assess the role of government as educator, as compared with the role of government as sovereign. When it acts as an educator, at least at the elementary and secondary school level, the government is engaged in inculcating social values and knowledge in relatively impressionable young people. Obviously there are innumerable decisions to be made as to what courses should be taught, what books should be purchased, or what teachers should be employed. In every one of these areas the members of a school board will act on the basis of their own personal or moral values, will attempt to mirror those of the community, or will abdicate the making of such decisions to so-called "experts."[44] In this connection I find myself entirely in agreement with the observation of the Court of Appeals for the Seventh Circuit in *Zykan* v. *Warsaw Community School Corp.*, 631 F. 2d 1300, 1305 (1980), that it is "permissible and appropriate for local boards to make educational decisions based upon their personal social, political and moral views." In the very course of administering the many-faceted operations of a school district, the mere decision to purchase some books will necessarily preclude the possibility of purchasing others. The decision to teach a particular subject may preclude the possibility of teaching another subject. A decision to replace a teacher because of ineffectiveness may by implication be seen as a disparagement of the subject matter taught. In each of these instances, however, the book or the exposure to the subject matter may be acquired elsewhere. The managers of the school district are not proscribing it as to the citizenry in general, but are simply determining that it will not be included in the curriculum or school library. In short, actions by the government as an educator do not raise the same First Amendment concerns as actions by the government as sovereign.

II

JUSTICE BRENNAN would hold that the First Amendment gives high school and junior high school students a "right to receive ideas" in the school. *Ante*, at 867. This right is a curious entitlement. It exists only in the library of the school, and only if the idea previously has been acquired by the school in book form. It provides no protection against a school board's decision not to acquire a particular book, even though that decision denies access to ideas as fully as removal of the book from the library, and it prohibits removal of previously acquired books only if the remover "dislike[s] the ideas contained in those books," even though removal for any other reason also denies the students access to the books. *Ante*, at 871–872.

But it is not the limitations which JUSTICE BRENNAN places on the right with which I disagree; they simply demonstrate his discomfort with the new doctrine which he fashions out of whole cloth. It is the very existence of a right to receive information, in the junior high school and high school setting, which I find wholly unsupported by our past decisions and inconsistent with the necessarily selective process of elementary and secondary education.

A

The right described by JUSTICE BRENNAN has never been recognized in the decisions of this Court and is not supported by their rationale. JUSTICE BRENNAN correctly observes that students do not "shed their constitutional rights to freedom of speech or expression at the schoolhouse gate." *Tinker* v. *Des Moines School District*, 393 U. S. 503, 506 (1969). But, as this language from *Tinker* suggests, our past decisions in this area have concerned freedom of speech and expression, not the right of access to particular ideas. We have held that students may not be prevented from symbolically expressing their political views by the wearing of black arm bands, *Tinker* v. *Des Moines School District, supra,* and that they may not be forced to participate in the symbolic expression of saluting the flag, *West Virginia Board of Education* v. *Barnette,* 319 U. S. 624 (1943). But these decisions scarcely control the case before us. Neither the District Court nor the Court of Appeals found that petitioners' removal of books from the school libraries infringed respondents' right to speak or otherwise express themselves.

Despite JUSTICE BRENNAN's suggestion to the contrary, this Court has never held that the First Amendment grants junior high school and high school students a right of access to certain information in school. It is true that the Court has recognized a limited version of that right in other settings, and JUSTICE BRENNAN quotes language from five such decisions and one of his own concurring opinions in order to demonstrate the viability of the right-to-receive doctrine. *Ante,* at 866–867. But not one of these cases concerned or even purported to discuss elementary or secondary educational institutions.[45] JUSTICE BRENNAN brushes over this significant omission in First Amendment law by citing *Tinker* v. *Des Moines School District* for the proposition that "students too are beneficiaries of this [right-to-receive] principle." *Ante,* at 868. But *Tinker* held no such thing. One may read *Tinker* in vain to find any recognition of a First Amendment right to receive information. *Tinker,* as already mentioned, was based entirely on the students' right to *express* their political views.

Nor does the right-to-receive doctrine recognized in our past decisions apply to schools by analogy. JUSTICE BRENNAN correctly characterizes the right of access to ideas as "an inherent corollary of the rights of free speech and press" which "follows ineluctably from the *sender's* First Amendment right to send them." *Ante,* at 867 (emphasis in original). But he then fails to recognize the predicate right to speak from which the students' right to receive must follow. It would be ludicrous, of course, to contend that all authors have a constitutional right to have their books placed in junior high school and high school libraries. And yet without such a right our prior precedents would not recognize the reciprocal right to receive information. JUSTICE BRENNAN disregards this inconsistency with our prior cases and fails to explain the constitutional or logical underpinnings of a right to hear ideas in a place where no speaker has the right to express them.

JUSTICE BRENNAN also correctly notes that the reciprocal nature of the right to receive information derives from the fact that it "is a necessary predicate to the *recipient's* meaningful exercise of his own rights of speech, press, and political freedom." *Ibid,* (emphasis in original). But the denial of access to ideas inhibits one's own acquisition of knowledge only when that denial is relatively complete. If the denied ideas are readily available from the same source in other accessible locations, the benefits to be gained from exposure to those ideas have not been foreclosed by the State. This fact is inherent in the right-to-receive cases relied on by JUSTICE BRENNAN, every one of which concerned the complete denial of access to the ideas sought.[46] Our past decisions are thus unlike this case, where the removed books are readily available to students and nonstudents alike at the corner bookstore or the public library.

B

There are even greater reasons for rejecting JUSTICE BRENNAN's analysis, however, than the significant fact that we have never adopted it in the past. "The importance of public schools in the preparation of individuals for participation as citizens, and in the preservation of the values on which our society rests, has long been recognized by our decisions." *Ambach v. Norwich,* 441 U. S. 68, 76 (1979). Public schools fulfill the vital role of teaching students the basic skills necessary to function in our society, and of "inculcating fundamental values necessary to the maintenance of a democratic political system." *Id.,* at 77. The idea that such students have a right of access, *in the school,* to information other than that thought by their educators to be necessary is contrary to the very nature of an inculcative education.

Education consists of the selective presentation and explanation of ideas. The effective acquisition of knowledge depends upon an orderly exposure to relevant information. Nowhere is this more true than in elementary and secondary schools, where, unlike the broad-ranging inquiry available to university students, the courses taught are those thought most relevant to the young students' individual development. Of necessity, elementary and secondary educators must separate the relevant from the irrelevant, the appropriate from the inappropriate. Determining what information *not* to present to the students is often as important as identifying relevant material. This winnowing process necessarily leaves much information to be discovered by students at another time or in another place, and is fundamentally inconsistent with any constitutionally required eclecticism in public education.

JUSTICE BRENNAN rejects this idea, claiming that it "overlooks the unique role of the school library." *Ante,* at 869. But the unique role referred to appears to be one of JUSTICE BRENNAN's own creation. No previous decision of this Court attaches unique First Amendment significance to the libraries of elementary and secondary schools. And in his paean of praise to such libraries as the "environment especially appropriate for the recognition of the First Amendment rights of students," *ante,* at 868, JUSTICE BRENNAN turns to language about *public* libraries from the three-Justice plurality in *Brown v. Louisiana,* 383 U. S. 131 (1966), and to language about universities and colleges from *Keyishian v. Board of Regents,* 385 U. S. 589 (1967).

Ante, at 868. Not only is his authority thus transparently thin, but also, and more importantly, his reasoning misapprehends the function of libraries in our public school system.

As already mentioned, elementary and secondary schools are inculcative in nature. The libraries of such schools serve as supplements to this inculcative role. Unlike university or public libraries, elementary and secondary school libraries are not designed for freewheeling inquiry; they are tailored, as the public school curriculum is tailored, to the teaching of basic skills and ideas. Thus, JUSTICE BRENNAN cannot rely upon the nature of school libraries to escape the fact that the First Amendment right to receive information simply has no application to the one public institution which, by its very nature, is a place for the selective conveyance of ideas.

After all else is said, however, the most obvious reason that petitioners' removal of the books did not violate respondents' right to receive information is the ready availability of the books elsewhere. Students are not denied books by their removal from a school library. The books may be borrowed from a public library, read at a university library, purchased at a bookstore, or loaned by a friend. The government as educator does not seek to reach beyond the confines of the school. Indeed, following the removal from the school library of the books at issue in this case, the local public library put all nine books on display for public inspection. Their contents were fully accessible to any inquisitive student.

C

JUSTICE BRENNAN's own discomfort with the idea that students have a right to receive information from their elementary or secondary schools is demonstrated by the artificial limitations which he places upon the right—limitations which are supported neither by logic nor authority and which are inconsistent with the right itself. The attempt to confine the right to the library is one such limitation, the fallacies of which have already been demonstrated.

As a second limitation, JUSTICE BRENNAN distinguishes the act of removing a previously acquired book from the act of refusing to acquire the book in the first place: "[N]othing in our decision today affects in any way the discretion of a local school board to choose books to *add* to the libraries of their schools. [O]ur holding today affects only the discretion to *remove* books." *Ante,* at 871–872 (emphasis in original). If JUSTICE BRENNAN truly has found a "right to receive ideas," *ante,* at 866–867, however, this distinction between acquisition and removal makes little sense. The failure of a library to acquire a book denies access to its contents just as effectively as does the removal of the book from the library's shelf. As a result of either action the book cannot be found in the "principal locus" of freedom discovered by JUSTICE BRENNAN. *Ante,* at 868.

The justification for this limiting distinction is said by JUSTICE BRENNAN to be his concern in this case with "the suppression of ideas." *Ante,* at 871. Whatever may be the analytical usefulness of this appealing sounding phrase, see Part II-D, *infra,* the suppression of ideas surely is not the identical twin of the denial of access to information. Not every official act which denies access to an idea can be characterized as a suppression of the idea. Thus unless the "right to receive information" and the prohibition against "suppression of ideas" are each a kind of Mother-Hubbard catch phrase for whatever First Amendment doctrines one wishes to cover, they would not appear to be interchangeable.

JUSTICE BRENNAN's reliance on the "suppression of ideas" to justify his distinction between acquisition and removal of books has additional logical pitfalls. Presumably the distinction is based upon the greater visibility and the greater sense of conscious decision thought to be involved in the removal of a book, as opposed to that involved in the refusal to acquire a book. But if "suppression of ideas" is to be the talisman, one would think that a school board's public announcement of its refusal to acquire certain books would have every bit as much impact on public attention as would an equally publicized decision to remove the books. And yet only the latter action would violate the First Amendment under JUSTICE BRENNAN's analysis.

The final limitation placed by JUSTICE BRENNAN upon his newly discovered right is a motive requirement: the First Amendment is violated only "[i]f petitioners *intended* by their removal decision to deny respondents access to ideas with Which petitioners disagreed." *Ante,* at 871 (emphasis in original). But bad motives and good motives alike deny access to the books removed. If JUSTICE BRENNAN truly recognizes a constitutional right to receive information, it is difficult to see why the reason for the denial makes any difference. Of course JUSTICE BRENNAN's view is that intent matters because the First Amendment does not tolerate an officially prescribed orthodoxy. *Ante,* at 870–872. But this reasoning mixes First Amendment apples and oranges. The right to receive information differs from the right to be free from an officially prescribed orthodoxy. Not every educational denial of access to information casts a pall of orthodoxy over the classroom.

It is difficult to tell from JUSTICE BRENNAN's opinion just what motives he would consider constitutionally impermissible. I had thought that the First Amendment proscribes content-based restrictions on the marketplace of ideas. See *Widmar* v. *Vincent,* 454 U. S. 263, 269–270 (1981). JUSTICE BRENNAN concludes, however, that a removal decision based solely upon the "educational suitability" of a book or upon its perceived vulgarity is "'perfectly permissible.'" *Ante,* at 871 (quoting Tr. of Oral Arg. 53). But such determinations are based as much on the content of the book as determinations that the book espouses pernicious political views.

Moreover, JUSTICE BRENNAN's motive test is difficult to square with his distinction between acquisition and removal. If a school board's removal of books might be motivated by a desire to promote favored political or religious views, there is no reason that its acquisition policy might not also be so motivated. And yet the "pall of orthodoxy" cast by a carefully executed book-acquisition program apparently would not violate the First Amendment under JUSTICE BRENNAN's view.

D

Intertwined as a basis for JUSTICE BRENNAN's opinion, along with the "right to receive information," is the statement that "[o]ur Constitution does not permit the official suppression of *ideas.*" *Ante,* at 871 (emphasis in original). There would be few champions, I suppose, of the idea that our Constitution *does* permit the official suppression of ideas; my difficulty is not with the admittedly appealing catchiness of the phrase, but with my doubt that it is really a useful analytical tool in solving difficult First Amendment problems. Since the phrase appears in the opinion "out of the blue," without any reference to previous First Amendment decisions of this Court, it would appear that the Court for years has managed to decide First Amendment cases without it.

I would think that prior cases decided under established First Amendment doctrine afford adequate guides in this area without resorting to a phrase which seeks to express "a complicated process of constitutional adjudication by a deceptive formula." *Kovacs* v. *Cooper,* 336 U. S. 77, 96 (1949) (Frankfurter, J., concurring). A school board which publicly adopts a policy forbidding the criticism of United States foreign policy by any student, any teacher, or any book on the library shelves is indulging in one kind of "suppression of ideas." A school board which adopts a policy that there shall be no discussion of current events in a class for high school sophomores devoted to second-year Latin "suppresses ideas" in quite a different context. A teacher who had a lesson plan consisting of 14 weeks of study of United States history from 1607 to the present time, but who because of a week's illness is forced to forgo the most recent 20 years of American history, may "suppress ideas" in still another way.

I think a far more satisfactory basis for addressing these kinds of questions is found in the Court's language in *Tinker* v. *Des Moines School District,* where we noted:

"[A] particular symbol—black armbands worn to exhibit opposition to this Nation's involvement in Vietnam—was singled out for prohibition. Clearly, the prohibition of expression of one particular opinion, at least without evidence that it is necessary to avoid material and substantial interference with school work or discipline, is not constitutionally permissible." 393 U. S., at 510–511.

In the case before us the petitioners may in one sense be said to have "suppressed" the "ideas" of vulgarity and profanity, but that is hardly an apt description of what was done. They ordered the removal of books containing vulgarity and profanity, but they did not attempt to preclude discussion about the themes of the books or the books themselves. App. 140. Such a decision, on respondents' version of the facts in this case, is sufficiently related to "educational suitability" to pass muster under the First Amendment.

E

The inconsistencies and illogic of the limitations placed by JUSTICE BRENNAN upon his notion of the right to receive ideas in school are not here emphasized in order to suggest that they should be eliminated. They are emphasized because they illustrate that the right itself is misplaced in the elementary and secondary school setting. Likewise, the criticism of JUSTICE BRENNAN's newly found prohibition against the "suppression of ideas" is by no means intended to suggest that the Constitution permits the suppression of ideas; it is rather to suggest that such a vague and imprecise phrase, while perhaps wholly consistent with the First Amendment, is simply too diaphanous to assist careful decision of cases such as this one.

I think the Court will far better serve the cause of First Amendment jurisprudence by candidly recognizing that the role of government as sovereign is subject to more stringent limitations than is the role of government as employer, property owner, or educator. It must also be recognized that the government as educator is subject to fewer strictures when operating an elementary and secondary school system than when operating an institution of higher learning. Cf. *Tilton* v. *Richardson*, 403 U. S. 672, 685–686 (1971) (opinion of BURGER, C. J.). With respect to the education of children in elementary and secondary schools, the school board may properly determine in many cases that a particular book, a particular course, or even a particular area of knowledge is not educationally suitable for inclusion within the body of knowledge which the school seeks to impart. Without more, this is not a condemnation of the book or the course; it is only a determination akin to that referred to by the Court in *Village of Euclid* v. *Ambler Realty Co.*, 272 U. S. 365, 388 (1926): "A nuisance may be merely a right thing in the wrong place,—like a pig in the parlor instead of the barnyard."

III

Accepting as true respondents' assertion that petitioners acted on the basis of their own "personal values, morals and tastes," App. 139, I find the actions taken in this case hard to distinguish from the myriad choices made by school boards in the routine supervision of elementary and secondary schools. "Courts do not and cannot intervene in the resolution of conflicts which arise in the daily operation of school systems and which do not directly and sharply implicate basic constitutional values." *Epperson* v. *Arkansas*, 393 U. S. 97, 104 (1968). In this case, respondents' rights of free speech and expression were not infringed, and by respondents' own admission no ideas were "suppressed." I would leave to another day the harder cases.

JUSTICE O'CONNOR, dissenting.

If the school board can set the curriculum, select teachers, and determine initially what books to purchase for the school library, it surely can decide which books to discontinue or remove from the school library so long as it does not also interfere with the right of students to read the material and to discuss it. As JUSTICE REHNQUIST persuasively argues, the plurality's analysis overlooks the fact that in this case, the government is acting in its special role as educator.

I do not personally agree with the Board's action with respect to some of the books in question here, but it is not the function of the courts to make the decisions that have been properly relegated to the elected members of school boards. It is the school board that must determine educational suitability, and it has done so in this case. I therefore join THE CHIEF JUSTICE's dissent.

Notes

1   Briefs of *amici curiae* urging reversal were filed by *Bruce A. Taylor* for Charles H. Keating, Jr., et al.; and by *David Crump* for the Legal Foundation of America.

   Briefs of *amici curiae* urging affirmance were filed by *J. Albert Woll, Marsha Berzon, Laurence Gold,* and *George Kaufmann* for the American Federation of Labor and Congress of Industrial Organizations et al.; by *Don H. Reuben* and *James A. Klenk* for the American Library Association et al.; by *Harold P. Weinberger, Justin J. Finger,* and *Jeffrey P. Sinensky* for the Anti-Defamation League of B'Nai B'Rith; by *R. Bruce Rich* for the Association of American Publishers, Inc., et al.; by *Irwin Karp* for the Authors League of America, Inc.; by *Robert M. Weinberg, Michael H. Gottesman,* and *David Rubin* for the National Education Association; by *James R. Sandner, Jeffrey S. Karp,* and *Elizabeth A. Truly* for New York State United Teachers; and by *Jerry Simon Chasen* and *Marcia B. Paul* for P. E. N. American Center.

   Briefs of *amici curiae* were filed by *Nathan Z. Dershowitz* and *Edward Labaton* for the American Jewish Congress et al.; and by *Whitney North Seymour, Jr.,* and *Martha L. Wolfe* for the Long Island Library Association Coalition.

2   The Amendment provides in pertinent part that "Congress shall make no law ... abridging the freedom of speech, or of the press." It applies to the States by virtue of the Fourteenth

Amendment. *Gitlow v. New York,* 268 U. S. 652, 666 (1925); *Grosjean v. American Press Co.,* 297 U. S. 233, 244 (1936).

3   The District Court noted, however, that petitioners "concede that the books are not obscene." 474 F. Supp. 387, 392 (EDNY 1979).

4   The nine books in the High School library were: Slaughter House Five, by Kurt Vonnegut, Jr.; The Naked Ape, by Desmond Morris; Down These Mean Streets, by Piri Thomas; Best Short Stories of Negro Writers, edited by Langston Hughes; Go Ask Alice, of anonymous authorship; Laughing Boy, by Oliver LaFarge; Black Boy, by Richard Wright; A Hero Ain't Nothin' But A Sandwich, by Alice Childress; and Soul On Ice, by Eldridge Cleaver. The book in the Junior High School library was A Reader for Writers, edited by Jerome Archer. Still another listed book, The Fixer, by Bernard Malamud, was found to be included in the curriculum of a 12th-grade literature course. 474 F. Supp., at 389, and nn. 2–4.

5   The Superintendent of Schools objected to the Board's informal directive, noting:

    "[W]e already have a policy … designed expressly to handle such problems. It calls for the Superintendent, upon receiving an objection to a book or books, to appoint a committee to study them and make recommendations. I feel it is a good policy—and it is Board policy—and that it should be followed in this instance. Furthermore, I think it can be followed quietly and in such a way as to reduce, perhaps avoid, the public furor which has always attended such issues in the past." App. 44.

    The Board responded to the Superintendent's objection by repeating its directive "that *all copies* of the library books in question be removed from the libraries to the Board's office." *Id.,* at 47 (emphasis in original).

6   The Fixer, Laughing Boy, Black Boy, Go Ask Alice, and Best Short Stories by Negro Writers. 474 F. Supp., at 391, nn. 6–7.

7   The Naked Ape and Down These Mean Streets. 474 F. Supp., at 391, n. 8.

8   Soul On Ice and A Hero Ain't Nothin' But A Sandwich. 474 F. Supp., at 391, n. 9.

9   A Reader for Writers. 474 F. Supp., at 391, n. 11. The reason given for this disposition was that all members of the Committee had not been able to read the book. *Id.,* at 391.

10   Slaughter House Five. 474 F. Supp., at 391, n. 10.

11   Laughing Boy. 474 F. Supp., at 391, n. 12.

12   Black Boy. 474 F. Supp., at 391, n. 13.

13   As a result, the nine removed books could not be assigned or suggested to students in connection with school work. *Id.,* at 391. However, teachers were not instructed to refrain from discussing the removed books or the ideas and positions expressed in them. App. 131.

14   474 F. Supp., at 396–397, citing *Presidents Council, District 25 v. Community School Board No. 25,* 457 F. 2d 289 (CA2 1972); *James v. Board of Education,* 461 F. 2d 566, 573 (CA2 1972); *East Hartford Educational Assn. v. Board of Education,* 562 F. 2d 838, 856 (CA2 1977) (en banc).

15   474 F. Supp., at 395, quoting *Presidents Council, District 25 v. Community School Board No. 25, supra,* at 291 (in turn quoting *Epperson v. Arkansas,* 393 U. S. 97, 104 (1968)).

16   After criticizing "the criteria for removal" employed by petitioners as "suffering] from excessive generality and overbreadth," and the procedures used by petitioners as "erratic, arbitrary and free-wheeling," Judge Sifton observed that "precision of regulation and sensitivity to First Amendment concerns" were "hardly established" by such procedures. 638 F. 2d, at 416.

17   Judge Sifton stated that it could be inferred from the record that petitioners' "political views and personal taste [were] being asserted not in the interests of the children's well-being, but rather for the purpose of establishing those views as the correct and orthodox ones for all purposes in the particular community." *Id.,* at 417.

18   Judge Mansfield dissented, *id.,* at 419–432, based upon a distinctly different reading of the record developed in the District Court. According to Judge Mansfield, "the undisputed evidence

of the motivation for the Board's action was the perfectly permissible ground that the books were indecent, in bad taste, and unsuitable for educational purposes." *Id.*, at 430. He also asserted that in reaching its decision "the Board [had] acted carefully, conscientiously and responsibly after according due process to all parties concerned." *Id.*, at 422. Judge Mansfield concluded that "the First Amendment entitles students to reasonable freedom of expression but not to freedom from what some may consider to be excessively moralistic or conservative selection by school authorities of library books to be used as educational tools." *Id.*, at 432.

19 Four of respondents' five causes of action complained of petitioners' "resolutions ordering the removal of certain books from the school libraries of the District and prohibiting the use of those books in the curriculum." App. 5. The District Court concluded that "respect for ... the school board's substantial control over educational content ... precluded] any finding of a first amendment violation arising out of removal of any of the books from use in the curriculum." 474 F. Supp., at 397. This holding is not at issue here. Respondents' fifth cause of action complained that petitioners' "resolutions prohibiting the use of certain books in the curriculum of schools in the District" had "imposed upon teachers in the District arbitrary and unreasonable restrictions upon their ability to function as teachers in violation of principles of academic freedom." App. 6. The District Court held that respondents had not proved this cause of action: "before such a claim may be sustained there must at least be a real, not an imagined controversy." 474 F. Supp., at 397. Respondents have not sought review of that holding in this Court.

20 Respondents also agree with these propositions. Tr. of Oral Arg. 28, 41.

21 For a modern version of this observation, see A. Meiklejohn, Free Speech and Its Relation to Self-Government 26 (1948):

"Just so far as ... the citizens who are to decide an issue are denied acquaintance with information or opinion or doubt or disbelief or criticism which is relevant to that issue, just so far the result must be ill-considered, ill-balanced planning, for the general good."

See also *Butler* v. *Michigan,* 352 U. S. 380, 383–384 (1957); *Procunier* v. *Martinez,* 416 U. S. 396, 408–409 (1974); *Houchins* v. *KQED, Inc.,* 438 U. S. 1, 30 (1978) (STEVENS, J., dissenting) ("[T]he First Amendment protects not only the dissemination but also the receipt of information and ideas"); *Saxbe* v. *Washington Post Co.,* 417 U. S. 843, 862–863 (1974) (POWELL, J., dissenting) ("[P]ublic debate must not only be unfettered; it must be informed. For that reason this Court has repeatedly stated that First Amendment concerns encompass the receipt of information and ideas as well as the right of free expression").

22 385 U. S., at 603, quoting *Sweezy* v. *New Hampshire,* 354 U. S. 234, 250 (1957) (opinion of Warren, C. J.).

23 By "decisive factor" we mean a "substantial factor" in the absence of which the opposite decision would have been reached. See *Mt. Healthy City Board of Ed.* v. *Doyle,* 429 U. S. 274, 287 (1977).

24 Petitioners acknowledged that their "evaluation of the suitability of the books was based on [their] personal values, morals, tastes and concepts of educational suitability." App. 142. But they did not accept, and thus apparently denied, respondents' assertion that some excerpts were objected to as "anti-American." *Ibid.*

25 For example, petitioner Ahrens stated:

"I am basically a conservative in my general philosophy and feel that the community I represent as a school board member shares that philosophy. ... I feel that it is my duty to apply my conservative principles to the decision making process in which I am involved as a board member and I have done so with regard to ... curriculum formation and content and other educational matters." *Id.*, at 21.

"We are representing the community which first elected us and re-elected us and our actions have reflected its intrinsic values and desires." *Id.*, at 27.

Petitioners Fasulo, Hughes, Melchers, Michaels, and Nessim made a similar statement that they had "represented the basic values of the community in [their] actions." *Id.*, at 120.

26 When asked to give an example of "anti-Americanism" in the removed books, petitioners Ahrens and Martin both adverted to A Hero Ain't Nothin' But A Sandwich, which notes at one point that George Washington was a slaveholder. See A. Childress, A Hero Ain't Nothin' But A Sandwich 43 (1973); Deposition of Petitioner Ahrens 89; Deposition of Petitioner Martin 20–22. Petitioner Martin stated: "I believe it is anti-American to present one of the nation's heroes, the first President, … in such a negative and obviously one-sided life. That is one example of what I would consider anti-American." Deposition of Petitioner Martin 22.

27 We have recognized in numerous precedents that when seeking to distinguish activities unprotected by the First Amendment from other, protected activities, the State must employ "sensitive tools" in order to achieve a precision of regulation that avoids the chilling of protected activities. See, *e. g., Speiser* v. *Randall,* 357 U. S. 513, 525–526 (1958); *NAACP* v. *Button,* 371 U. S. 415, 433 (1963); *Keyishian* v. *Board of Regents,* 385 U. S. 589, 603–604 (1967); *Blount* v. *Rizzi,* 400 U. S. 410, 417 (1971). In the case before us, the presence of such sensitive tools in petitioners' decisionmaking process would naturally indicate a concern on their part for the First Amendment rights of respondents; the absence of such tools might suggest a lack of such concern. See 638 F. 2d, at 416–417 (opinion of Sifton, J.).

28 As a practical matter, however, it is difficult to see the First Amendment right that I believe is at work here playing a role in a school's choice of curriculum. The school's finite resources— as well as the limited number of hours in the day—require that education officials make sensitive choices between subjects to be offered and competing areas of academic emphasis; subjects generally are excluded simply because school officials have chosen to devote their resources to one rather than to another subject. As is explained below, a choice of this nature does not run afoul of the First Amendment. In any event, the Court has recognized that students' First Amendment rights in most cases must give way if they interfere "with the schools' work or [with] the rights of other students to be secure and to be let alone," *Tinker* v. *Des Moines School Dist.,* 393 U. S. 503, 508 (1969), and such interference will rise to intolerable levels if public participation in the management of the curriculum becomes commonplace. In contrast, library books on a shelf intrude not at all on the daily operation of a school.

I also have some doubt that there is a theoretical distinction between removal of a book and failure to acquire a book. But as Judge Newman observed, there is a profound practical and evidentiary distinction between the two actions: "removal, more than failure to acquire, is likely to suggest that an impermissible political motivation may be present. There are many reasons why a book is not acquired, the most obvious being limited resources, but there are few legitimate reasons why a book, once acquired, should be removed from a library not filled to capacity." 638 F. 2d 404, 436 (CA2 1980) (Newman, J., concurring in result).

29 In effect, my view presents the obverse of the plurality's analysis: while the plurality focuses on the failure to provide information, I find crucial the State's decision to single out an idea for disapproval and then deny access to it.

30 At the outset, the plurality notes that certain school board members found the books in question "objectionable" and "improper" for junior and senior high school students. What the plurality apparently finds objectionable is that the inquiry as to the challenged books was initially stimulated by what is characterized as "a politically conservative organization of parents concerned about education," which had concluded that the books in question were "improper fare for school students." *Ante,* at 856. As noted by the District Court, however, and in the plurality opinion, *ante,* at 859, both parties substantially agreed about the motivation of the school board in removing the books:

"[T]he board acted not on religious principles but on its conservative educational philosophy, and on its belief that the nine books removed from the school library and curriculum were irrelevant, vulgar, immoral, and in bad taste, making them educationally unsuitable for the district's junior and senior high school students." 474 F. Supp. 387, 392 (1979).

31 In oral argument counsel advised the Court that of the original plaintiffs, only "[o]ne of them is still in school … until this June, and will assumedly graduate in June. *There is a potential question of mootness.*" Tr. of Oral Arg. 4–5 (emphasis added). The sole surviving plaintiff has therefore either recently been graduated from high school or is within days or even hours of graduation. Yet the plurality expresses views on a very important constitutional issue. Fortunately, there is no binding holding of the Court on the critical constitutional issue presented.

We do well to remember the admonition of Justice Frankfurter that "the most fundamental principle of constitutional adjudication is not to face constitutional questions but to avoid them, if at all possible." *United States* v. *Lovett,* 328 U. S. 303, 320 (1946) (concurring opinion). In the same vein, Justice Stone warned that "the only check upon our own exercise of power is our own sense of self-restraint." *United States* v. *Butler,* 297 U. S. 1, 79 (1936) (dissenting opinion).

32 Of course, it is perfectly clear that, unwise as it would be, the board could wholly dispense with the school library, so far as the First Amendment is concerned.

33 In *Rowan* a unanimous Court upheld the right of a homeowner to direct the local post office to stop delivery of unwanted materials that the householder viewed as "erotically arousing or sexually provocative."

34 Indeed, this case is illustrative of how essentially all decisions concerning the retention of school library books will become the responsibility of federal courts. As noted in n. 1, *supra,* the parties agreed that the school board in this case acted not on religious principles but "on its belief that the nine books removed from the school library and curriculum were irrelevant, vulgar, immoral, and in bad taste, making them educationally unsuitable for the district's junior and senior high school students." Despite this agreement as to motivation, the case is to be remanded for a determination of whether removal was in violation of the standard adopted by the plurality. The school board's error appears to be that it made its own determination rather than relying on experts. *Ante,* at 874–875.

35 *Epperson* v. *Arkansas,* 393 U. S. 97, 104 (1968). There are approximately 15,000 school districts in the country. U. S. Bureau of Census, Statistical Abstract of the United States 297 (102d ed. 1981) (Table 495: Number of Local Governments, by Taxing Power and Type, and Public School Systems—States: 1972 and 1977). See also Diamond, The First Amendment and Public Schools: The Case Against Judicial Intervention, 59 Texas L. Rev. 477, 506–507, n. 130 (1981).

36 Other provisions of the Constitution, such as the Establishment Clause, *Epperson* v. *Arkansas, supra,* and the Equal Protection Clause, also limit the discretion of the school board.

37 "The formless nature of the "right" found by the plurality in this case is exemplified by this purported distinction. Presumably a school board could, for any reason, choose not to purchase a book for its library. Once it purchases that book, however, it is "locked in" to retaining it on the school shelf until it can justify a reason for its removal. This anomalous result of "book tenure" was pointed out by the District Court in this case. 474 F. Supp., at 395–396. See also *Presidents Council, District 25* v. *Community School Board No. 25,* 457 F. 2d 289, 293 (CA2 1972). Under the plurality view, if a school board wants to be assured that it maintains control over the education of its students, every page of every book sought to be acquired must be read before a purchase decision is made.

38 The plurality speaks of the need for "sensitive" decisionmaking, pursuant to "regular" procedures. See *ante,* at 874, n. 26, and 875. One wonders what indeed does this mean. In this case, for example, the board did not act precipitously. It simply did not agree with

39 The plurality suggests that the books in a school library derive special protection under the Constitution because the school library is a place in which students exercise unlimited choice. See *ante*, at 868–869. This suggestion is without support in law or fact. It is contradicted by this very case. The school board in this case does not view the school library as a place in which students pick from an unlimited range of books—some of which may be inappropriate for young people. Rather, the school library is analogous to an assigned reading list within which students may exercise a degree of choice.

the recommendations of a committee it had appointed. Would the plurality require—as a constitutional matter—that the board delegate unreviewable authority to such a committee?

40 I also disagree with JUSTICE WHITE's conclusion that he need not decide the constitutional issue presented by this case. That view seems to me inconsistent with the "rule of four"—"that any case warranting consideration in the opinion of [four Justices] of the Court will be taken and disposed of" on the merits, *Ferguson* v. *Moore-McCormack Lines, Inc.*, 352 U. S. 521, 560 (1957) (opinion of Harlan, J.)—which we customarily follow in exercising our certiorari jurisdiction. His concurrence, although not couched in such language, is in effect a single vote to dismiss the writ of certiorari as improvidently granted. Justice Harlan debated this issue with Justice Frankfurter in *Ferguson* v. *Moore-McCormack Lines, supra,* and his view ultimately attracted the support of six out of the seven remaining Members of the Court. He stated:

"In my opinion due adherence to [the 'rule of four'] requires that once certiorari has been granted a case should be disposed of on the premise that it is properly here, in the absence of considerations appearing which were not manifest or fully apprehended at the time certiorari was granted. In [this case] I am unable to say that such considerations exist, even though I do think that the arguments on the merits underscored the views of those of us who originally felt that the cas[e] should not be taken because [it] involved only issues of fact, and presented nothing of sufficient general importance to warrant this substantial expenditure of the Court's time." *Id.*, at 559.

The case upon which JUSTICE WHITE relies, *Kennedy* v. *Silas Mason Co.*, 334 U. S. 249 (1948), was disposed of in an opinion which commanded the votes of seven of the nine Members of the Court. There could therefore be no question of an infringement of the "rule of four." Certainly any intimation from that case that this Court should not review questions of law in cases where the District Court has granted summary judgment is belied by subsequent decisions too numerous to catalogue. See, *e. g.*, *Ernst & Ernst* v. *Hochfelder*, 425 U. S. 185 (1976); *Cox Broadcasting Corp.* v. *Cohn*, 420 U. S. 469 (1975); *Mills* v. *Alabama*, 384 U. S. 214 (1966).

41 Rule 9(g) of the local rules of the United States District Court for the Eastern District of New York provides:

"Upon any motion for summary judgment pursuant to Rule 56 of the Rules of Civil Procedure, there shall be annexed to the notice of motion a separate, short and concise statement of the material facts as to which the moving party contends there is no genuine issue to be tried.

"The papers opposing a motion for summary judgment shall include a separate, short and concise statement of the material facts as to which it is contended that there exists a genuine issue to be tried.

[Footnote 2 is continued on p. 906]

"All material facts set forth in the statement required to be served by the moving party will be deemed to be admitted unless controverted by the statement required to be served by the opposing party."

42 Paragraph 4 of respondents' Rule 9(g) statement asserts that petitioners' "evaluation of the suitability of the books was based on [their] personal values, morals, and tastes." App. 139.

43 Paragraph 8 of respondents' Rule 9(g) statement reads:

"Defendants Ahrens and Martin objected to those excerpts because some contained profanities, some were sexually explicit, some were ungrammatical, some were anti-American, and some were offensive to racial, religious or ethnic groups." App. 140.

44 There are intimations in JUSTICE BRENNAN's opinion that if petitioners had only consulted literary experts, librarians, and teachers their decision might better withstand First Amendment attack. *Ante,* at 874, and n. 26. These observations seem to me wholly fatuous; surely ideas are no more accessible or no less suppressed if the school board merely ratifies the opinion of some other group rather than following its own opinion.

45 The right of corporations to make expenditures or contributions in order to influence ballot issues was the question presented in *First National Bank of Boston* v. *Bellotti,* 435 U. S. 765, 783 (1978), and the language which JUSTICE BRENNAN quotes from that decision, *ante,* at 866, was explicitly limited to "the Court's decisions involving corporations in the business of communications or entertainment." 435 U. S., at 783. In *Kleindienst* v. *Mandel,* 408 U. S. 753 (1972), the Court upheld the power of Congress and the Executive Branch to prevent the entry into this country of a Marxist theoretician who had been invited to lecture at an American university, despite the First Amendment rights of citizens who wished to hear him. *Stanley* v. *Georgia,* 394 U. S. 557 (1969), held that the First Amendment prohibits States from making the private possession of obscene material a crime, and *Griswold* v. *Connecticut,* 381 U. S. 479 (1965), held that the right of privacy prohibits States from forbidding the use of contraceptives. Finally, *Martin* v. *Struthers,* 319 U. S. 141 (1943), held that the First Amendment protects the door-to-door distribution of religious literature.

JUSTICE BRENNAN's concurring opinion appears in a case which considered the constitutionality of certain postal statutes. *Lamont* v. *Postmaster General,* 381 U. S. 301 (1965).

46 In *First National Bank of Boston* v. *Bellotti, supra,* public access to corporate viewpoints on ballot issues not directly affecting the corporations was foreclosed by the Massachusetts law prohibiting corporate expenditures to express such viewpoints. In *Kleindienst* v. *Mandel, supra,* the Court noted that the potential recipients of Mandel's ideas were completely deprived of the "particular qualities inherent in sustained, face-to-face debate, discussion and questioning." 408 U. S., at 765. The Georgia law in *Stanley* v. *Georgia, supra,* criminalized all private possession of obscene material, and the statute in *Griswold* v. *Connecticut, supra,* criminalized all use of contraceptive devices or actions encouraging the use of such devices. The ordinance at issue in *Martin* v. *Struthers, supra,* forbade all door-to-door distribution of religious literature, while the statute challenged in *Lamont* v. *Postmaster General, supra,* required persons receiving Communist propaganda in the mails affirmatively to state their desire to receive such mailings.

Index

About the Author

Anthony Aycock has written for *Slate, The Washington Post*, Literary Hub, *Reactor* (formerly Tor.com), *The Missouri Review, The Gettysburg Review, Ploughshares, Creative Nonfiction*, Information Today, and other venues. His first book, *The Accidental Law Librarian*, was released in 2013. He has spent 25 years working in government, academic, and private law libraries, as well as teaching academic and creative writing. He has an MLIS from the University of South Carolina and an MFA from Queens University in Charlotte. Check out his website at www.anthonyaycock.com.